The Henry Williamson S

NUMBER 31, SEPTEMBEF

A Special Issue

to

Commemorate

the Centenary of the birth of

Henry Williamson

1 December 1895

Portrait of Henry Williamson painted by Charles F. Tunnicliffe, January 1934.

We are grateful to the trustees of the Charles Tunnicliffe estate for permission to reproduce this portrait.

CONTENTS

Hut illustration on Title Page by Peter Rothwell

Cover illustration by Michael Loates, also illustrations on pp. 89 and 106

Illustrations by Doris Walker, pp. 44 and 101

Back cover design taken from poster designed for the Society by Anne Williamson

On Achieving Centenary

Richard Williamson, President of the Henry Williamson Society

'It is remarkable', said Thomas Hardy of *Tarka*, and as time placed Hardy as an everlasting, brilliant point of light in the constellations of human achievement, so now we begin to realise that Henry too is part of that starry group. Just as Orion and Perseus glittered to the ancients and now to us, undimmed, so for artists the orbit of fame will never set. It is one hundred years since Henry was born. He is not physically alive to achieve his centenary but because he was able to interpret the scenes and emotions of this world we all live through, he is immortal. Certainly to anyone who has read *Tarka* he is immortal. I first read *Tarka* when I was about eight years old, and I loved it then, as Hardy read and loved it aged eighty. It is the sound of life, like water rippling. No explanation is needed; it is not hard work to read if the words are bright and tumbling.

I never really thought of him as 'father' but as 'writer', a person ill-adapted for daily life. Where he touched, he discharged with sparks, so one learned at a very early age to insulate him as best one could. Yet it was exciting to see, like lightning coming close. This is the apparatus of the spirit, which is given brief earthly life. It cannot mix with normal, ordered existence, for it is designed to change and find new ways. The earthly body is very confused by this and thus is unable to find happiness, as Schubert shows us in *Der Wanderer*. But the spirit is the dominant partner and has to rule. Henry talked often of his Doppelganger, the wraith of the living body. In his extraordinary book *The Star-born*, the wraith tried hard to escape, to show itself to us, and to explain its birth and life unfixed as yet by its station in the soul's system.

In the Thirties, many people who themselves felt the tugging of the unseen Siamese found solace in its blueprint exposed by *The Pathway*. It was to many an explanation of what was going on within their own minds and lives, and as such brought the author considerable fame, particularly in America. Here was the earthly body of Eosphoros, striding upwards to the light of dawn over Exmoor, and almost for the first time describing the feeling of searching for light. The Aborigines and the Stone-Age cultures already knew and felt all this, long long ago, but did not record it except in stone and legend. Henry did record this Ancient Sunlight, what he felt was the Truth, and it was as shattering to some as the Gospels were to the early Christians.

After *Tarka*, my own favourite book is *The Phasian Bird*, for I was lucky to have seen and been part of almost the whole of that story before it was written. What I did not see, what no one saw except Henry and he only in his mind, was the death of the Phoenix-bird, Chee-kai, on that high jewelled throne at the point on earth where he had first arrived, in the egg, like the ancient Norse legend. In great splendour the allegorical bird awaited transformation to the stars, rather as Ancient Egyptians knew their Kings would transfer into the skies when Orion showed above the horizon. Again it was the dream of the artist trying to escape, after a dreadful life trying to avoid defeat, the humiliating destruction of the psyche before it had been able to accomplish what it had been ordered to do. Henry at this point was roughly the same age as Shakespeare was when he had the same longings after *The Tempest*.

Earlier death-wishes had been hauntingly played out in at least three other books, *Tarka*, *Salar*, and *The Gold Falcon* – like snakes sloughing off skins they have grown out of. In a way Henry was showing that there was nothing unnatural or frightening in death. The above scenes are not at all morbid, and do not depress. They do however release depths of emotion and also command a fine sense of occasion. In *Tarka* there is the hint that he does not die, but escapes perhaps to live an immortal life in a sunlit sea. Henry left it to us to use our own imaginations about what finally happened. He left us with hope.

But with the Norfolk Farm behind him Henry still had a long way to go, for he had not yet constructed the *Chronicle*, although the foundations had been laid over many years. How one can imagine his dread of having to climb this high altitude in the later years of his life. Being a farmer served a certain purpose but, although of course it gave some splendid material, it sapped too much vital energy. There are several precedents of artists being farmers, such as Malcolm Arnold the composer, and Middleton Murry, while others like Elgar found relaxation in prosaic hobbies that did not interfere with their work. But thank goodness Hardy did not go on to be an architect, or Beethoven an inventor of coffee-grinding machines! Henry wore himself out with his desires for perfection but knew at last that he had to quit some of his dreams to get the real job completed.

For some people the best of Henry's writings are his immediate transcriptions of what happened to be going on around him at the time, and into this category come the *Village* books, *Goodbye West Country*, and *The Story of a Norfolk Farm.* The childly wisom of Ernie playing with mud and apples in the village street will make generations chuckle in two hundred years from now. The honesty and charmingly cultured meanderings of the diarist in Goodbye will give hope to generations of puzzled people in years to come wondering whether anything they do in life has any point. The *Norfolk Farm* inspires us with the worth of a simple life and a job well done, and will grow good harvest in people's minds over and over again. Like Richard Jefferies' *Bevis*, it was the story of how the author longed for life to be, but wasn't. There is an underlying optimism, which was appreciated at that time of war but even here we return to the netherworld, when Henry shows us that the wild geese flying over at Christmas are the souls of all the dead on the battlefields, that the author has not joined.

Like meteors burning bright trails and vanishing, so much of Henry's life whether in reality or in the guise of otter, fish, or falcon, was spent in travelling. Arrival was final, a little death, but travelling was an adventure. As transport, his cars were the fleet of foot, the temperamental and the wayward, and his own journeys were as well chronicled as those of his creatures. In writing the effect of journeying is to show not only the landscape of travel, which Hemingway and Graham Greene did so well, but to describe the feelings of the subject as it decides where to go and the exterior influences that deflect it. Many will regard *A Chronicle of Ancient Sunlight* as one of the greatest journeys in modern literature, the entire life of a man, a wanderer through the century. Every facet of the landscape is carefully chronicled, from the humdrum to the terrifying. The whole of life – personal life and the life of the nation – is encapsulated there. Whatever one's own experience of life might be, there will be a parallel to be found in the pages of the *Chronicle.*

The inner landscape of the soul and the outer landscape of the eye are recreated for the millions who in industrialised Britain find their treadwheel is the journey to the centres of commerce, but who are let out into the open air for brief moments of ecstacy. Such is the lot of Richard Maddison. His son then becomes the traveller, and every event in puzzled, secret, ecstatic or frightened childhood is opened up as we stare with recognition into the mind of the child struggling to grow as roughly straight and upright as its upbringing will allow. Edwardian England, with its seaside and steam trains, birds' nesting and straw boaters, here has all the colour which the period monochrome photographs of the time lack, here has infinitely vaster descriptions than painters like Whistler could hope to portray.

But for many it is the First World War descriptions, drama and history in which they find Henry excels above all others. War and its paraphernalia must be the "mechanical particular" of half of all men. Henry misses very little in its apparatus, excels standard works in its effects, and adds a third dimension in its degradation. He read widely at the time of writing, thought continuously before starting, and experienced as much as most in the first instance. It is curious how writers benefit by witnessing war. Edward Thomas and R.H. Mottram come to mind, while the Scott Fitzgeralds of this world knew keenly what they had missed. What sort of writer would Henry have been if he had not gone down into the Underworld? Could the stars alone have sustained him – or do the greatest moments in *Tarka*, *Phasian Bird*, *Gold Falcon*, *Pathway*, as well as *Chronicle*, owe their creation to that ringside seat of flare and shell, and bomb and blast, which for those that survived was the closest that our century ever got to Gotterdamerung?

★ ★ ★ ★ ★

EDITORIAL NOTE

The planning of this important edition of the *Journal*, which celebrates the landmark of the centenary of Henry Williamson's birth in 1895, began over two years ago. The overall aim was to illuminate as far as possible all aspects of Henry's writing life. While that has not proved totally possible to achieve, it is hoped that you will find a great deal of interest within these pages, and that the new format will meet with your approval. There is an exciting mix of previously published, but possibly fugitive, items and new contributions shedding light on particular aspects that are central to Henry Williamson's total opus.

We are very grateful to everyone who has contributed and for all the various permissions to use work previously published elsewhere; and a special thankyou is due to Mick Loates for putting his talent at our disposal with the superb cover drawing.

AW

Roots: an examination of Henry Williamson's lineage

Anne Williamson

CERTIFIED COPY OF AN ENTRY OF BIRTH

The statutory fee for this certificate is 3s. 9d. Where a search is necessary to find the entry, a search fee is payable in addition.

GIVEN AT THE GENERAL REGISTER OFFICE, SOMERSET HOUSE, LONDON

Application Number 135099

REGISTRATION DISTRICT Lewisham

1896. BIRTH in the Sub-district of Lewisham in the County of London

Columns:— 1		2	3	4	5	6	7	8	9	10*
No.	When and where born	Name, if any	Sex	Name, and surname of father	Name, surname, and maiden surname of mother	Occupation of father	Signature, description, and residence of informant	When registered	Signature of registrar	Name entered after registration
36	First December 1895 66 Braxfield Road Brockley	Henry William	Boy	William Leopold Williamson	Gertrude Eliza Williamson formerly Leaver	Bank Clerk	W. L. Williamson Father 66 Braxfield Road Brockley Lewisham	Eighth January 1896	Thomas Allan Beleham Registrar	/

CERTIFIED to be a true copy of an entry in the certified copy of a Register of Births in the District above mentioned.

Given at the GENERAL REGISTER OFFICE, SOMERSET HOUSE, LONDON, under the Seal of the said Office, the 11th day of February 1966.

*See note overleaf

This certificate is issued in pursuance of the Births and Deaths Registration Act, 1953.

Section 34 provides that any certified copy of an entry purporting to be sealed or stamped with the seal of the General Register Office shall be received as evidence of the birth or death to which it relates without any further or other proof of the entry, and no certified copy purporting to be given in the said Office shall be of any force or effect unless it is sealed or stamped as aforesaid.

CAUTION.—Any person who (1) falsifies any of the particulars on this certificate, or (2) uses a falsified certificate as true, knowing it to be false, is liable to prosecution.

BX 243364

GENERAL REGISTER OFFICE ENGLAND

Photostat of Henry Williamson's Birth Certificate

IT is surely possible to state that the fictional writing of Henry Williamson mirrors more closely the real life of himself and his family and relations, friends and life generally in England, than the fictional writings of any other writer. So we are sure that we already know the story of his family tree and his life from the mirror of his writings. But like all mirrors with their flaws, cracks and worn patches, the mirror that reflects the ancient sunlight of Henry Williamson produces distortions and the picture reflected is not necessarily a true and exact copy of the original. Some of which may be due to the fact that while HW had quite a lot of personal experience and knowledge to draw on in particular areas, there were large areas of his family about which he knew very little, but also because to maintain a particular structure he preferred to use fictional elements threaded into his story line.

HW's immediate parentage is a known and well-recorded fact, for the characters of Richard and Hetty Maddison in *A Chronicle of Ancient Sunlight* are based on HW's actual parents, William Leopold Williamson and Gertrude Leaver. As far as can be ascertained, the lives and characters of Richard and Hetty in the novels are a reasonably faithful rendering of the lives and characters of William Leopold and 'Gertie'. We also know that the fictional life of Richard and Hetty's son, Phillip Maddison, reflects much of the real life of Henry Williamson himself (although with the poetic licence of diversions and embellishments) and that all, or nearly all, of the characters in his books have their counterpart in real life.

If the argument that nature and/or nurture (genes and/or environment) produces the child that is father to the man is a truism, then it is important to examine the nature and nurture roots of HW in order to help our understanding of the man and his writings, and this examination of the lineage of Henry Williamson is offered in that spirit. Particularly it will act as a basis for seeing how HW transformed reality with the act of creativity to produce a fictional family that we may truly believe in, and to provide clues as to the nature of his own personality and character.[1]

THE MATERNAL LINE – THE LEAVERS, TURNEYS AND SHAPCOTES

Some exploration of HW's maternal line and its roots in Bedfordshire has already taken place[2] which inevitably means some repetition here, but it is important to give the whole picture in one place to avoid confusion. The particular interest in this section being the detailed use HW made in his fictional work of both the lives of his relatives and the area they lived in.

HW's mother, Gertrude Eliza Leaver, was born on 26 July 1867 at 3 Arthur Terrace, Hornsey in north London. She married William Leopold Williamson on 10 May 1893. The circumstances of their marriage will be discussed in the second section, 'The Paternal Line'. Suffice it to say here that at the time of her marriage she was living with her parents, Thomas William and Henrietta Leaver at their home at 'Wespelaer', Cavendish Road, Sutton Surrey. The Leaver family had not lived here very long. Sutton Library records[3] show that they appear in the local directory for 1890 and in the 1892 rate book where Thomas Leaver is shown to own his own house; but that they do not appear in the 1882 rate book, so by deduction all that can be stated is that they went to live in Sutton some time before 1890. Diligent searching would no doubt produce a more exact date.

Thomas and Henrietta were married on 19 May 1863 in Hackney Parish Church and lived in Hornsey and later in Stoke Newington in north London. They had four other children beside Gertrude; Maude Henrietta born in 1865; Hugh Thomas born 25.4.1866; Percy, born 1869; and Ralph, born 1873. The graves in the Leaver family plot in Ladywell Cemetery, Lewisham provide evidence of their sojourn and deaths in that area. Maude married S. St. Paul Simpson. She died in 1920, aged 55, whilst S. St. Paul Simpson lived on until 1934, aged 71. There are photographs of Simpson children in the archive. Hugh, a traveller in his father's firm, is prominent in *A Chronicle of Ancient Sunlight* as 'Uncle Hughie' where he was sent down from Trinity College for placing a chamber pot on a statue, but there are no records for him in the archive lists for either Oxford or Cambridge Universities.[4] There is, however, a Horace George Turney who matriculated to Trinity College, Oxford, in 1880 and who later acquired several medical letters after his name. I have not been able to trace this person within the family tree – but HW may have known of his existence and transferred his university exploits onto 'Hughie'. One of the librarians at Oxford suggested that the 1880s was a little early for the joke of putting a 'po' on a spire (or similar escapade). But it was such a well-known undergraduate prank that HW no doubt used it to add 'local colour', not realising the discrepancy of dates. It is understood that Hugh contracted syphilis (but there are no details to substantiate this) and was to become an invalid, eventually dying a painful death in July 1920, aged 54. He too is buried in the Ladywell Cemetery. A document in the literary estate archive shows that both Ralph and Percy were alive in 1936 and that Ralph had a son also named Ralph, and Percy had a son named Tom. At this time there was acrimony over the terms of their father's will. Ralph had gone to live and work in South Africa, and felt that he had not had his proper dues. He objected to the fact that his father's house, 12 Eastern Road, was left entirely to Gertrude, when he was once promised a share of it and that a particular diamond ring which he also expected to receive had 'disappeared'.

Let us leave Thomas William Leaver for the moment and pursue the lineage of his wife, Henrietta, née Turney. Apart from the information already given by Tom and Joan Skipper in their 'Bedfordshire Roots' article, (op. cit.) in 1986 a letter arrived from Mrs. Peggy Turney, containing a copy of her research on the Turney family tree which was considerable. I duly thanked her and put the information on file. Very sadly, when I started my own research in earnest and tried to recontact Peggy, it was to learn that she had died in 1990. I am indebted to her work as the basis for this branch of the family tree. Married to Maurice Charles Turney, she was naturally more concerned with their immediate relations but she did cover the family overall, thus saving considerable ground work, and I was able to piece together the various items of information which results in a fairly comprehensive coverage.

The Turneys were a very large family and had lived in the triangle formed by Apsley Guise, Husborne Crawley, and Ridgmont, in Bedfordshire, near Woburn Abbey, the seat of the Dukes of Bedford, for several hundred years. The Skippers (op. cit.) tell us of their discovery of the row of Turney tombstones in the churchyard at St. James in Husborne Crawley, and Peggy Turney discovered that the family features largely in the census returns for the area.

The immediately direct traceable line goes back to a Thomas Turney who was baptised 8 January 1714, married Sarah Boughton in 1741 and had nine children, died in 1778, and was the son of George and Mary Turney. Before that there is a gap of about one hundred years with tabulated information available from 1584–1687. Peggy Turney had consulted the Wills of these early Turneys at Bedford County Record Office. Her notes state that 'these show them to be men of property rather than tenant farmers'. In 1783 Thomas Turney, farmer, son of the above, is recorded as having 178 acres of land in Husborne Crawley. His 'obstinacy and prevarication ... has been a plague to the parish for many years'. The reference is to the employment of 'roundsmen', wandering labourers. The roundsman system, whereby casual labour could be obtained cheaply was criticised in several entries in vestry minutes of the area as being demoralising to the farm labourers.[5] Thomas Turney was apparently not above availing himself of cheap labour at the expense of the local men. He married Mary Arnold in 1770 and they had five children.

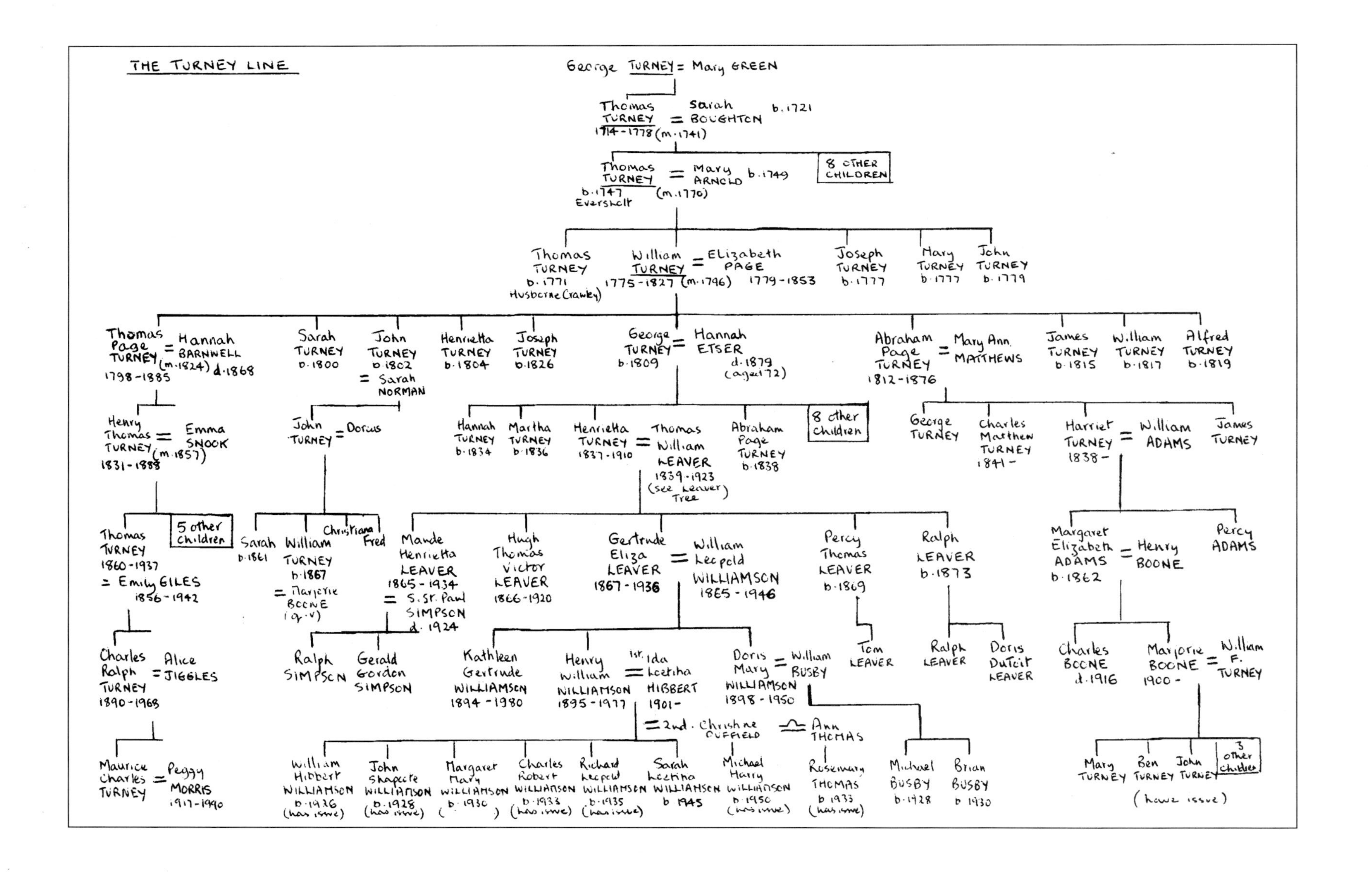
THE TURNEY LINE
George TURNEY = Mary GREEN
Thomas TURNEY 1714-1778 (m.1741) = Sarah BOUGHTON b.1721
Thomas TURNEY b.1747 Eversholt = Mary ARNOLD b.1749 (m.1770)
8 OTHER CHILDREN
Thomas TURNEY b.1771 Husborne Crawley
William TURNEY 1775-1827 (m.1796) = Elizabeth PAGE 1779-1853
Joseph TURNEY b.1777
Mary TURNEY b.1777
John TURNEY b.1779
Thomas Page TURNEY 1798-1885 = Hannah BARNWELL (m.1824) d.1868
Sarah TURNEY b.1800
John TURNEY b.1802 = Sarah NORMAN
Henrietta TURNEY b.1804
Joseph TURNEY b.1826
George TURNEY b.1809 = Hannah ETSER d.1879 (aged 72)
Abraham Page TURNEY 1812-1876 = Mary Ann MATTHEWS
James TURNEY b.1815
William TURNEY b.1817
Alfred TURNEY b.1819
Henry Thomas TURNEY 1831-1888 = Emma SNOOK (m.1857)
John TURNEY = Dorcas
Hannah TURNEY b.1834
Martha TURNEY b.1836
Henrietta TURNEY 1837-1910 = Thomas William LEAVER 1839-1923 (see Leaver Tree)
Abraham Page TURNEY b.1838
8 other children
George TURNEY
Charles Matthew TURNEY 1841-
Harriet TURNEY 1838- = William ADAMS
James TURNEY
Thomas TURNEY 1860-1937 = Emily GILES 1856-1942
5 other children
Sarah b.1861
William TURNEY b.1867 = Marjorie BOONE (q.v.)
Christiana
Fred
Maude Henrietta LEAVER 1865-1934 = S. St. Paul SIMPSON d.1924
Hugh Thomas Victor LEAVER 1866-1920
Gertrude Eliza LEAVER 1867-1936 = William Leopold WILLIAMSON 1865-1946
Percy Thomas LEAVER b.1869
Ralph LEAVER b.1873
Margaret Elizabeth ADAMS b.1862 = Henry BOONE
Percy ADAMS
Charles Ralph TURNEY 1890-1968 = Alice JIGGLES
Ralph SIMPSON
Gerald Gordon SIMPSON
Kathleen Gertrude WILLIAMSON 1894-1980
Henry William WILLIAMSON 1895-1977 = 1st. Ida Leetitia HIBBERT 1901-
= 2nd. Christine CUFFIELD
Doris Mary WILLIAMSON 1898-1950 = William BUSBY
Ann THOMAS
Tom LEAVER
Ralph LEAVER
Doris DuTeit LEAVER
Charles BOONE d.1916
Marjorie BOONE 1900- = William F. TURNEY
Maurice Charles TURNEY = Peggy MORRIS 1917-1990
William Hibbert WILLIAMSON b.1926 (has issue)
John Shakespeare WILLIAMSON b.1928 (has issue)
Margaret Mary WILLIAMSON b.1930 ( )
Charles Robert WILLIAMSON b.1933 (has issue)
Richard Leopold WILLIAMSON b.1935 (has issue)
Sarah Leetitia WILLIAMSON b 1945
Michael Harry WILLIAMSON b.1950 (has issue)
Rosemary THOMAS b 1933 (has issue)
Michael BUSBY b.1928
Brian BUSBY b 1930
Mary TURNEY
Ben TURNEY
John TURNEY
3 other children
(have issue)

Their second son William Turney was born in 1775 and married Elizabeth Page, 'a minor with parental consent' in 1796. They had a large family of ten children. The first, Thomas Page Turney, was born at Husborne Crawley in 1798. He married Hannah Barnwell in 1824 and is the great-great-grandfather of Peggy Turney's husband Maurice. They lived at Husborne Crawley Mill and on the 1881 census he was shown as at 134 Mount Pleasant, aged 83, retired miller, widower, his wife having died in 1868. The census also tells us that he had a housekeeper then, Mary A. Turney, aged 25. His son, Henry Thomas Turney, also worked the Husborne Crawley mill.

His brother, John Turney, born 1802, at the time of the 1881 census was also a widower, a retired baker, and had living with him a granddaughter, Christiana, aged 16, a lacemaker and born at Ridgmont. A family headed by John Turney aged 57, housepainter, can be found under the Ridgmont records with his wife and family, who are almost certainly the missing link in this branch, that is, these two 'Johns' are probably father and son.

Abraham Page Turney was born in 1812. He lived at 34 Mount Pleasant, Apsley Guise, a large double-fronted house built in the 1830s, and was a grocer by trade as his wife, Mary-Ann is recorded on the 1881 census as aged 72, 'grocer's widow'. Their son Charles Matthew, born 1841, took over the grocery business and was aged 40 and unmarried at the 1881 census. Their daughter, the eldest child, Harriet, born 1838, married William Adams, and was already a widow by the time of the 1881 census, her husband having been killed in a riding accident. They had two children, a son, Percy Adams, and a daughter Margaret Elizabeth, born in 1862, who married Henry Boone, secretary of the local gas company, and it was their son, Charles Boone, who was the cousin with whom HW was particularly friendly, and who was killed in action in 1916, and who features as Percy Pickering in the *Chronicle* novels. His sister Marjorie, born 1900, (Polly Pickering) was the cousin with whom HW experienced the first pangs of calf-love and the stirrings of sexual experience. In 1919 Marjorie married William F. Turney (possibly the great-grandson of John above, whose grandson William is mentioned on the 1881 Ridgmont census), and they had a large number of children, and eventually grandchildren. Henry and his mother were present at their wedding and Marjorie and HW remained friends and corresponded throughout his life. At least two letters from her in later years refer rather wistfully to the 'might have been'. Towards the very end of his life Marjorie went to see Henry several times on her annual holidays in Devon (see the biography *Dreamer of Devon*, op cit).

But the Turney brother from whom HW was directly descended was George, born in Husborne Crawley in 1809 and named in the 1881 census for Husborne Crawley as retired baker, aged 70. He married Hannah Etser (details not known) who died in 1879 aged 72. They appear on the 1841, '51, '61 Census returns at 3, Gloucester Place, Stoke Newington, in North London and had a large family of eleven children who were born there, of which there is only detailed information to hand about Henrietta, born in 1837 – HW's maternal grandmother, who married Thomas William Leaver as above. Henrietta died in December 1910, aged 73 years and is buried in the Leaver family plot (Plot G, grave No.82) in the Ladywell Cemetery. She is, of course, Sarah Turney in *A Chronicle of Ancient Sunlight.*

Her husband, Thomas William Leaver, born in 1839, was a partner with the manufacturing stationers, 'Drake, Driver, and Leaver', whose headquarters was 20-24 Rosebery Av., London, EC1, and which was a large and prestigious concern. As a partner he would have been a prosperous and well-to-do gentleman. The firm was wound up in 1953 and HW presumably still had some shares in it as he was informed of the final meeting, although he had sold a large block of shares in the 1940s. Diaries manufactured by them and some oddments of paper show some of the extent of their activities. As HW states for the firm 'Mallard, Carter and Turney' in the Chronicle, they were 'Law and Parliamentary Stationers, Printers and Lithographers ... to HM Stationery Office, Corpor tion of London - etc.'. Thomas William Leaver was 48 years old when he became a partner when the firm originated in 1887, and this may well have been the date that he went to live in Sutton. He is known to have travelled extensively, taking holidays abroad in Europe and Russia and Canada, and would seem to have been of quite an outgoing personality. For example there is a photograph of him in the Alhambra, Spain, in 1903, dressed up in costume and looking very foreign, which gives a quite different slant to his character than the one gained from the *Chronicle.*

Apart from that it would have been difficult to have found out anything personal about him but among the archive material was a book which had been presented to him at school and investigation of its history opened up a most interesting line of inquiry. In the front was a school book plate:

The Stratford-upon-Avon Royal Free Grammar School is also the school to which William Shakespeare went, and it still exists. It is a most impressive mediaeval building, part of a complex formed by the Guildhall, the Guild Chapel, the Old Vicarage and the Schoolhouse, which is the oldest surviving half-timbered building in the country.[6] Originally only Latin had been taught free, but in 1811 this was extended to include English grammar, reading and spelling. Handwriting and arithmetic and etc had to be paid for, and the boys were also expected to pay 2s.6d. for coal annually. Apparently the school wasn't open to just anybody so there had to be some connection between the Leaver family and Stratford-upon-Avon, and it was suggested that I contact the Shakespeare Birthplace Trust, whose Senior archivist, Dr. Robert Bearman, was most helpful. He did indeed have the name Leaver on the archive index – not Thomas William but his father, John Shapcote Leaver. But with evidence that Thomas William was of this area I was able to obtain a copy of his birth certificate. This stated that he was born in Tardebigg, Counties of Worcester and Warwick, on 25 November, 1839 and confirmed that his father was John Shapcote Leaver, and his mother Eliza, née Bartleet. John Shapcote Leaver's profession was given as Commercial Clerk, whilst on the birth certificate of a daughter, Eliza Sarah, in 1841, he put 'Railway Clerk'. This slightly misleading information disguises the fact that John Shapcote Leaver was quite a distinguished member of Stratford society. Some idea of his life can be gained from his obituary in *The Stratford-Upon-Avon Herald*, Friday April 16, 1886:

> *Death of Mr. J.S.Leaver – A gentleman well-known in this town and neighbourhood departed this life yesterday. For many years Mr. Leaver has filled a prominent place in Stratford affairs. He has occupied most of the principal offices of the town, being at the time of his death secretary to the Hospital, the Birthplace [i.e. the William Shakespeare Trust] the Savings Bank, Becher's Benefit Society and other institutions. Formerly he was the local representative of many newspapers and was quite 'a free lance' in this capacity.*[7] *Mr. Leaver's death was rather sudden. Yesterday week he was in his usual health, and was seen taking exercise on his tricycle, but early on Friday morning he was seized with an apoplectic fit. Mr. Lupton was instantly summoned, and although the case was considered a critical one, still hopes were entertained that Mr. Leaver's constitution was strong enough to enable him to survive the attack. On*

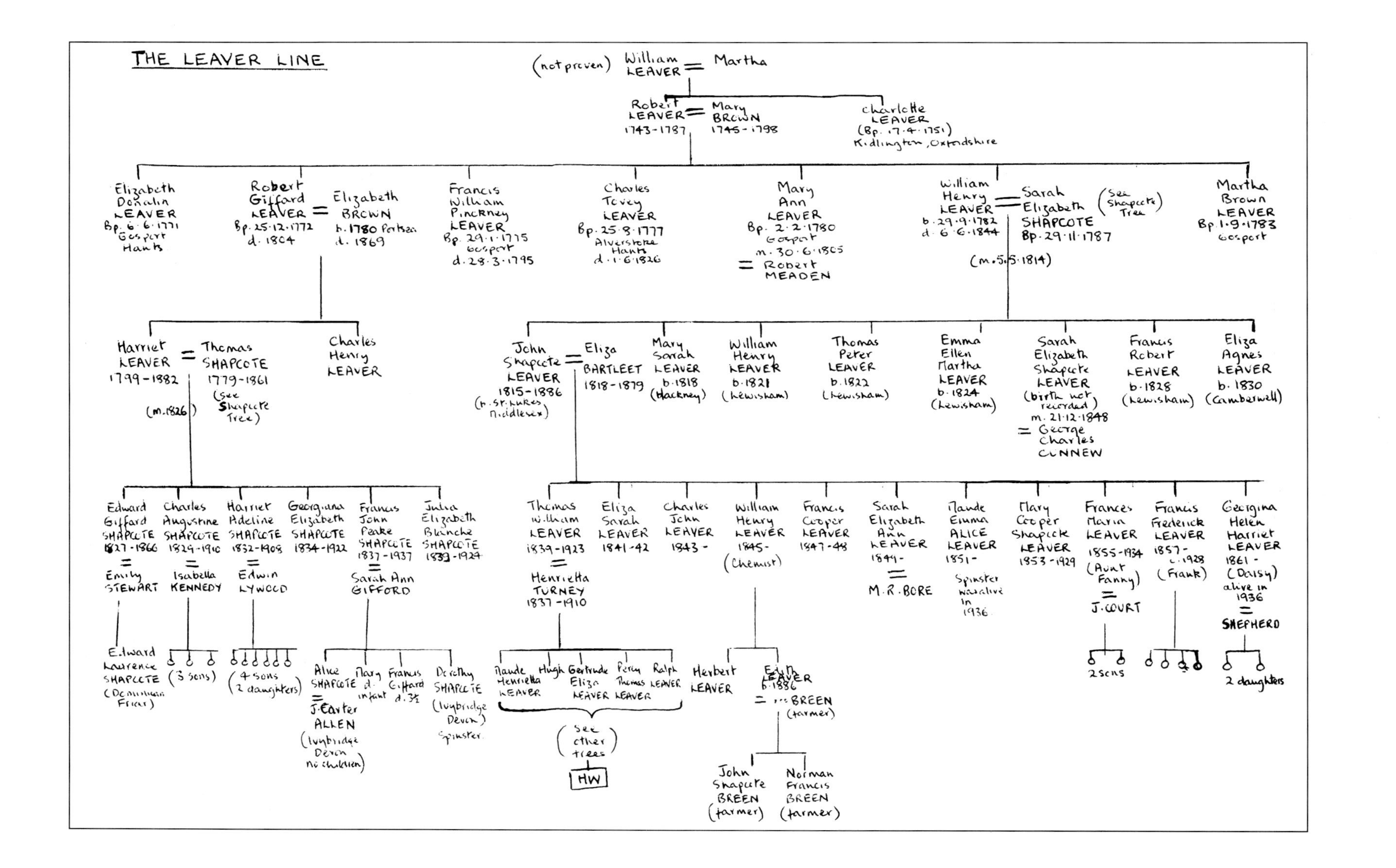
THE LEAVER LINE
(not proven) William LEAVER = Martha
Robert LEAVER 1743-1787 = Mary BROWN 1745-1798
Charlotte LEAVER (Bp. 17·4·1751) Kidlington, Oxfordshire
Elizabeth Donalin LEAVER Bp. 6·6·1771 Gosport Hants
Robert Gifford LEAVER Bp. 25·12·1772 d. 1804 = Elizabeth BROWN b. 1780 Portsea d. 1869
Francis William Pinckney LEAVER Bp. 29·1·1775 Gosport d. 28·3·1795
Charles Tovey LEAVER Bp. 25·8·1777 Alverstoke Hants d. 1·6·1826
Mary Ann LEAVER Bp. 2·2·1780 Gosport m. 30·6·1805 = Robert MEADEN
William Henry LEAVER b. 29·9·1782 d. 6·6·1844 = Sarah Elizabeth SHAPCOTE Bp. 29·11·1787 (See Shapcote Tree)
(m. 5·5·1814)
Martha Brown LEAVER Bp. 1·9·1783 Gosport
Harriet LEAVER 1799-1882 = Thomas SHAPCOTE 1779-1861 (See Shapcote Tree)
(m. 1826)
Charles Henry LEAVER
John Shapcote LEAVER 1815-1886 (b. St. Lukes Middlesex) = Eliza BARTLEET 1818-1879
Mary Sarah LEAVER b. 1818 (Hackney)
William Henry LEAVER b. 1821 (Lewisham)
Thomas Peter LEAVER b. 1822 (Lewisham)
Emma Ellen Martha LEAVER b. 1824 (Lewisham)
Sarah Elizabeth Shapcote LEAVER (birth not recorded) m. 21·12·1848 = George Charles CUNNEW
Francis Robert LEAVER b. 1828 (Lewisham)
Eliza Agnes LEAVER b. 1830 (Camberwell)
Edward Gifford SHAPCOTE 1827-1866 = Emily STEWART
Charles Augustine SHAPCOTE 1829-1910 = Isabella KENNEDY
Harriet Adeline SHAPCOTE 1832-1908 = Edwin LYWOOD
Georgiana Elizabeth SHAPCOTE 1834-1922
Francis John Peake SHAPCOTE 1837-1937 = Sarah Ann GIFFORD
Julia Elizabeth Blanche SHAPCOTE 1839-1924
Thomas William LEAVER 1839-1923 = Henrietta TURNEY 1837-1910
Eliza Sarah LEAVER 1841-42
Charles John LEAVER 1843-
William Henry LEAVER 1845- (Chemist)
Francis Cooper LEAVER 1847-48
Sarah Elizabeth Ann LEAVER 1849- = M.R. BORE
Maude Emma ALICE LEAVER 1851- Spinster was alive in 1936
Mary Cooper Shapcote LEAVER 1853-1929
Frances Maria LEAVER 1855-1934 (Aunt Fanny) = J. COURT
Francis Frederick LEAVER 1857- c. 1928 (Frank)
Georgina Helen Harriet LEAVER 1861- (Daisy) alive in 1936 = SHEPHERD
Edward Laurence SHAPCOTE (Dominican Friar)
(3 sons)
(4 sons 2 daughters)
Alice SHAPCOTE = J. Carter ALLEN (Ivybridge Devon no children)
Mary d. infant
Francis Gifford d. 3½
Dorothy SHAPCOTE (Ivybridge Devon) Spinster
Maude Henrietta LEAVER
Hugh
Gertrude Eliza LEAVER
Percy Thomas LEAVER
Ralph LEAVER
(See other trees)
HW
Herbert LEAVER
Edith LEAVER b. 1886 = ... BREEN (farmer)
2 sons
2 daughters
John Shapcote BREEN (farmer)
Norman Francis BREEN (farmer)

Wednesday, however, a change manifested itself, and his death took place yesterday morning from congestion of the lungs. The public positions he held brought the deceased into contact with a large number of people, all of whom could bear testimony to the assiduity and efficiency with which he discharged his onerous duties. His cheerful spirits and ready wit made him an agreeable companion, and his well-known figure will be much missed in the town. Mr. Leaver came to Stratford over forty years ago, and commenced life here in the work of education.

John Shapcote Leaver had married Eliza Bartleet on 7 January 1839, in the Parish church at Tardebigg. She was the daughter of William Bartleet, Needle Manufacturer, apparently an old Redditch family. His father was named as William Henry Leaver, Lieutenant in the Navy. William Henry Leaver was born 29.9.1782 in Gosport, Hants, one of seven children of which he was the second youngest, all of whom were born in Gosport. He had a career as Lieutenant in the Royal Navy, and died in what seems to have been a slightly bizarre accident from a blow to the chest in the Southampton Arms Public House in Lambeth in June 1844.[8]

The Shakespeare Birthday Trust has a family Bible[9] recording John Shapcote Leaver's birth in 1815, Eliza's birth as 18.8.1818 and death on 27.12.1879, and their eleven children of whom Thomas William is the eldest. Another document held by the Trust is a photograph of a portrait of an elderly gentleman of which there is an identical copy in the HWLEA, namely of John Shapcote Leaver.

Other documents pertain to his various duties as outlined in his obituary above. But what the Bible did not record was that John Shapcote was born in St. Luke's, Middlesex, and lived in Lewisham from aged five to fifteen and all his brothers and sisters were born in Lewisham or nearby. This is a most extraordinary coincidence and needs more investigation.

Another item in the HWLEA of interest is a postcard addressed to Mrs. T.W. Leaver at 12 Eastern Rd., Brockley, and dated 28 November 1922, postmark 'Stratford-on-Avon'. It is from 'Alice' at 7 Wellesbourne Grove. The handwriting has many flourishes and although not easy to read, is decipherable:

A very happy birthday to you. I suppose you will soon be going to Brighton. Let me hear from you when there. I hope Mary is better. I know how kind Percy and Flo are as she tells me so. Love to all. Alice.

Alice is the sister of Thomas William Leaver; christened Maude Emma Alice, she was born in July 1851, and was a spinster. There is also a photograph which is marked 'Alice taken with the Prince of Wales at Shakespeare's House, S-on-Avon – June 1923.' Edith Breen (see below) referred to her as being 84 in 1937.

The Leavers flourished and there must be many 'Leaver' relatives around today. Particularly of interest is a letter HW received from Edith Breen in 1937. Edith, hitherto unknown to HW, was the daughter of William Henry Leaver, brother of Thomas William. She wrote to say (possibly she had just read HW's most recent book *Goodbye West Country* published that year) that her son was named John Shapcote Breen after his great grandfather, and she mentioned the family nose, 'we all have it'. Edith Breen herself worked in the Shakespeare Museum in the 1930s as one of several 'Birthplace Assistants'.

But what really excites our interest is that the name 'Shapcote' has appeared in the 'tree', for we know that HW set great store by his Shapcote roots and through them claimed Exmoor as his spiritual home. At this point however, they are established in the Midlands and it is necessary to delve further.

John Shapcote Leaver's mother was Sarah Elizabeth Shapcote. Born on 29 November 1787, she married William Henry Leaver in 1814 in Southwark. Her brother Thomas Shapcote, born 27.12.1779 at Stepney, married her husband's niece Harriet Leaver in 1826 in Stoke Damerel, Devon, so they were a closely knit family. Thomas was also a Lieutenant in the Navy and retired with the courtesy title of Captain.[10] As both families came from a naval background, they no doubt all knew each other.

Interestingly, there is quite a lot of information about this generation which was given to HW by a relation, Miss Dorothy Shapcote of South Devon, who was the granddaughter of Thomas and Harriet Shapcote. She wrote to HW in 1957 after reading an article in the *Western Morning News* – 'Note in the West' which mentioned HW's son, John Shapcote Williamson, who had achieved a gliding record at that time. She was wondering if there was a family connection and stated that she was the last member of the family to bear the name by right of birth and not marriage. (Looking at the family tree, she would appear incorrect in her assumption as her uncle, Charles Augustine Shapcote, had three sons, who would have been her cousins, unless they had all died in the First World War, or similar tragedy.) In due course she handed over to HW the Shapcote family papers in her possession and these are in the Literary Archive. They include the will of Elizabeth Leaver, mother of Harriet. Elizabeth (née Brown) was the wife of Robert Giffard Leaver, born in Gosport 25.12.1772, older brother of William Henry Leaver, and who died in 1804. The 1851 census record shows Thomas Shapcote and his wife Harriet and her mother Elizabeth all living at 4, St. Jean D'Acre Terrace, Stoke Damerel, Devon. Thomas died in 1861, Elizabeth in 1869, and Harriet in 1882.

Miss Shapcote stated in her letter:

My father's people for some generations were naval and descend as far as we can now ascertain from Philip Shapcote of Knowestone, North Devon, whose monument is in the vestry of that church.

Thus it can be seen how HW was able to assert in *A Clearwater Stream* the information which has previously been a little puzzling:

My mother's family of Shapcote had lived only a few miles away on the edge of Dartmoor at Knowestone, at least ten generations before the heraldic visitations of 1610. A century after that date the place was sold, the family moved to Exeter and Sarah Shapcote married an Irish post-captain in the Navy at Plymouth called Thomas William Leaver, my great-great-grandfather. (Clearwater Stream)

The only outstanding problem is Henry's claim for the 'Irish' background of Thomas William Leaver – perhaps that will be clarified in due course. HW has mistakenly transposed his grandfather's name, for Sarah Shapcote's husband was Captain William Henry Leaver. Dorothy Shapcote stated that apart from Sarah and Thomas there was another brother, Peter, born 1770, who died at sea sometime after 1790. Official records do not corroborate this but show five others in the family (see Shapcote line of the family tree). Their father was John Shapcote who died at sea about 1790 (another source gives 1782 as the date). The probate of his Will is supposedly in the Sydney Museum, NSW, Australia, but despite letters to that institute and others, no record has been found to date. A personal search is necessary.

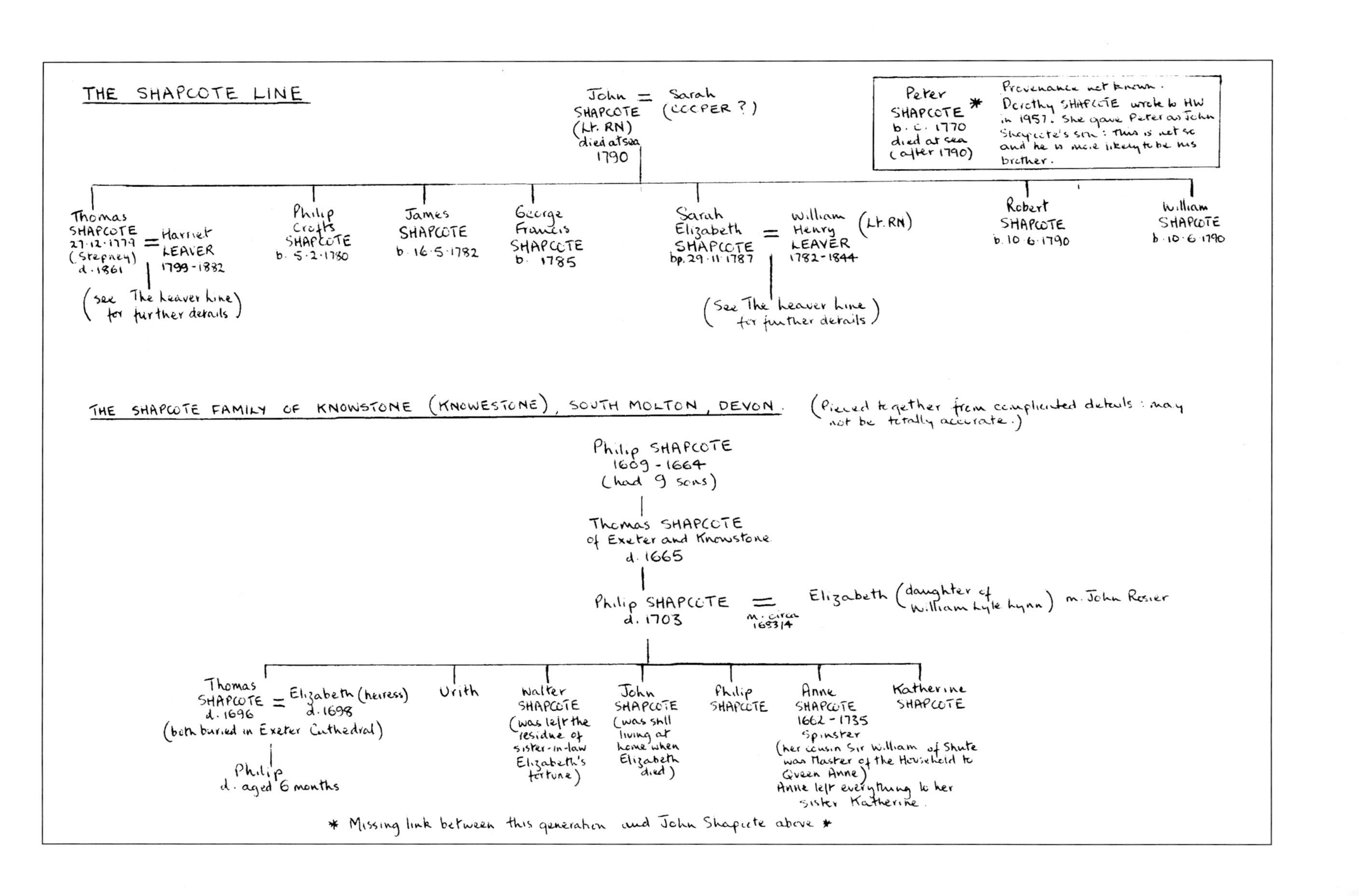

THE SHAPCOTE LINE
John SHAPCOTE (Lt. RN) died at sea 1790 = Sarah (COOPER ?)
Peter SHAPCOTE * b. c. 1770 died at sea (after 1790)
Provenance not known. Dorothy SHAPCOTE wrote to HW in 1957. She gave Peter as John Shapcote's son: this is not so and he is more likely to be his brother.
Thomas SHAPCOTE 27.12.1779 (Stepney) d. 1861 = Harriet LEAVER 1799-1882
(see The Leaver Line for further details)
Philip Crofts SHAPCOTE b. 5.2.1780
James SHAPCOTE b. 16.5.1782
George Francis SHAPCOTE b. 1785
Sarah Elizabeth SHAPCOTE bp. 29.11.1787 = William Henry LEAVER (Lt. RN) 1782-1844
(See The Leaver Line for further details)
Robert SHAPCOTE b. 10.6.1790
William SHAPCOTE b. 10.6.1790
THE SHAPCOTE FAMILY OF KNOWSTONE (KNOWESTONE), SOUTH MOLTON, DEVON.
(Pieced together from complicated details: may not be totally accurate.)
Philip SHAPCOTE 1609-1664 (had 9 sons)
Thomas SHAPCOTE of Exeter and Knowstone d. 1665
Philip SHAPCOTE d. 1703 = m. circa 1653/4 Elizabeth (daughter of William Lyle Lynn) m. John Rosier
Thomas SHAPCOTE d. 1696 = Elizabeth (heiress) d. 1698
(both buried in Exeter Cathedral)
Philip d. aged 6 months
Urith
Walter SHAPCOTE (was left the residue of sister-in-law Elizabeth's fortune)
John SHAPCOTE (was still living at home when Elizabeth died)
Philip SHAPCOTE
Anne SHAPCOTE 1662-1735 Spinster (her cousin Sir William of Shute was Master of the Household to Queen Anne) Anne left everything to her sister Katherine.
Katherine SHAPCOTE
* Missing link between this generation and John Shapcote above *

Recourse to the reference books in the HWLEA quickly revealed the Knowestone connection. A Philip Shapcote of Knowestone, near South Molton, was born in 1609, died 1664 and had nine sons – one of whom, Thomas Shapcote of Exeter and Knowestone, died in 1665 and his son, Philip Shapcote (died 1703) had seven offspring. The resolution of Wills and property was very complex, his eldest son dying before him in 1696 and his wife, an heiress in her own right, in 1698 – both are buried in Exeter Cathedral. Their son Philip died in infancy, aged six months. Another of Philip's sons was named John. He was still living at home when his sister-in-law died in 1698. Although it has not been possible at the moment to make a direct connection it could be his son who was the John Shapcote who died at sea in 1790. The Shapcote family certainly lived at Shapcote, Knowestone, until 1770, when it was sold. Research in the local reference libraries of Plymouth and/or Exeter would perhaps resolve the connection but a letter of inquiry as to whether records are held received no reply. Again a personal search is necessary.

What can be said with certainty is that these Shapcote/Leaver forebears were mainly naval, with well-to-do landed gentry connections and that roots on the maternal side were certainly firmly planted in the rich red soil of Devon, and Henry could justifiably claim Exmoor as his spiritual roots.

THE PATERNAL LINE – THE WILLIAMSONS AND THE LUHNS

HW portrayed fairly faithfully the life of the relatives on his mother's side in the *Chronicle.* We could/would therefore expect him to portray equally carefully the life of the relatives on his father's side. But it is this area of HW's actual lineage which proved the most difficult to establish. There were very few recorded facts to be found in his literary archive, and it was soon obvious that HW did not use reality quite so firmly as the basis for the fictionalised episodes concerning his paternal relations. Thus clues in the novels which lead fairly easily to the Leavers and Turneys often lead to a total dead end on the actual Williamson side, or to such a misleading conclusion that the truth is completely obscured. Although once the reality is known, then it is sometimes possible to see the connections, and often impossible to see why it was previously so baffling!

HW was very reticent about his own family. When I referred some queries at an early stage of this inquiry to his first wife, Mrs. Ida Loetitia Williamson, who had known his parents, William Leopold and Gertrude, well, she said that he never talked about his own family, and she was unable to answer any queries, her knowledge really only covering the information that is obvious. Some of Henry's reticence may well stem from the fact that he knew very little himself anyway. For instance in April and again in May 1954 he had applied to Somerset House for a birth certificate for his grandfather – with no result for he had given them the wrong dates to search in. Their official forms of reply are in the archive. This is odd because his grandfather's death certificate was in his possession, with his age on it, and he could have deduced the information by a simple sum, as I myself did. (He wouldn't, of course, have been able to obtain the information from Somerset House anyway, as this pre-dates the keeping of official records which is from 1837 onwards.)

So, to work; the starting point for this line of search, naturally, was to look at documents held in the HWLEA, where there are some (but not all that many) useful items. For example, a photograph of a very stern elderly lady, with a note in HW's writing on the back 'Adela Williamson (née Lühn) HW's Bavarian grandmother'; the Will of 'William Williamson' dated March 25th 1872; and other items which only began to make sense as the research progressed and bit by bit pieces of the jigsaw puzzle began to fit together. Richard Maddison is the first character that we meet in *A Chronicle of Ancient Sunlight* and as we know that he is based on William Leopold Williamson, let us begin with William Leopold and work out and back from there.

William Leopold Williamson was born on 7 May 1865 at Wood St., Ryde, on the Isle of Wight. His birth certificate states that his father was Henry William Williamson and his mother Adela Leopoldina Williamson, formerly Lühn. His father's occupation is given as Architect and Surveyor. His mother registered the birth on 14 June. The deduction would be that the family were living on the Isle of Wight in 1865 – but were they? This did not really fit in with other known facts, and very soon I came to the conclusion that this was not actually so, or if they were it was certainly for a very short time, a visitation rather than a domicile. I think it is possible that Adela went to the Isle of Wight for the sole purpose of her confinement. Perhaps she was in poor health and it was considered that the bracing and warmer island air would be beneficial. After all, if the Isle of Wight was good enough for Queen Victoria (and her German husband) it would thus have been considered a fashionable and sensible place to go to. That this is mainly correct will become apparent in due course. But let us for the moment trace William Leopold's development as it is shown by the little documentary evidence there is.

William Leopold's main education was at the Thanet Collegiate School in Margate, deduced from the fact that in the archive there is a school bill relating to him for the Summer of 1877. This education appears to have been paid for under a clause in his grandfather's will (see later paragraph). Although his name does not appear on the few school records that are available in Margate Records Office, it has been suggested that if he was good at sports his name might be in the local newspapers of the era, and this is a task that needs to be undertaken at some point. More importantly from the research point of view there is also in the Literary Archive a photograph of him as a young boy at Grove Park School, Sutton, Surrey, in 1872. This proved a puzzling item until further research revealed its import.

Grove Park School, Sutton, Surrey, in 1872. William Leopold Williamson – second from left, sitting down front row, and looking remarkably like Henry did at the same age.

William Leopold became a bank clerk by profession and worked all his working life for the National Bank Ltd., Old Broad St., London, hence – 'over the flagstones of London Bridge [and up towards Liverpool St.] fourteen thousand and five hundred occasions'.

The somewhat extraordinary circumstances surrounding the marriage of Richard and Hetty in the *Chronicle* appears to have happened in real life. Their marriage certificate shows that William Leopold Williamson married Gertrude Eliza Leaver on the 10th. May 1893 at the Register Office at Greenwich. William was twenty-seven years old, Gertrude was twenty-five. William's profession is given as 'Banker's Clerk'. His father's name is given with profession of 'Surveyor', whilst Thomas William Leaver is a 'Manufacturing Stationer' (as previously detailed). Neither father was present at the wedding, which was witnessed by Henrietta Leaver, the bride's mother, and W.C.Cornish. It does seem a rather daring enterprise to have undertaken within the strictures of the Victorian regime that pertained at that time. The family were obviously more progressive than the impression gained from the novelised version. It is not at all clear why the young couple should have gone to such lengths to hide the fact of their marriage. They were both well beyond the legal age of twenty-one, and Thomas William Leaver does not appear really in general to have been such a difficult man.

William Leopold's address at the time of his marriage was 19, Cranfield Rd., Brockley (lodgings, as we learn from his fictional counterpart, Richard, in the *Chronicle*); whilst Gertrude's address is, as stated in part one, the parental home – Wespelaer, Cavendish Rd., Sutton, Surrey.

At some point in this early stage of the research I jotted down what few facts I knew on a piece of paper to try and make some sense of them and to see what my next move could be. The above information was included. Also, one of the items in the archive is the death certificate for Henry William Williamson, William Leopold's father. I will return to that in a moment, but on it was, of course, his address at the time of his death, viz., Hildersheim, Cavendish Rd., Sutton, Surrey. The significance being that William Leopold's father and Gertrude's parents both lived in the same road in Sutton. They were neighbours. William Leopold, allowing for the fact that he was living in lodgings away from home, had in effect married the girl next door. This gives an entirely new viewpoint on Richard's journeys to 'visit some friends of Dora's who lived in a village in the midst of the herb fields to the west of Croydon'. Thus William Leopold must have known Gertrude right from the start, not being introduced to her by his sister as happens to Richard in the novels.

The records held at Sutton Library confirmed this: in the Local Directory for 1890 there is indeed a Henry William Williamson and a T.W.Leaver living next door to each other in Cavendish Road. Henry William appears in the 1882 rate book and they are both in the 1892 rate book. Unlike Thomas Leaver, the house lived in by Henry William was not his own but owned by a C.E.de Lacy who owned most of the property in that road (surprisingly, for I had presumed that Henry William would have owned his own house, for reasons to be stated in due course). Henry William died in 1894, and so disappears off these local records. T.W.Leaver was still there in 1896 but was not listed in the 1898 volume. (This was too early for him to have moved to Eastern Road, so there may be an interim dwelling somewhere in the area.)

In the *Chronicle* Richard and Hetty have a brief honeymoon in the nearby Kent countryside at the 'Seven Fields of Shroften' (Shroffield) and Hetty then returned to the parental home in Sutton and the couple lived separately for several months, until Hetty becomes pregnant, and her father had finally to be told the truth, in a very difficult scene. Without any factual evidence either for or against, I think it is fairly reasonable to presume that this is probably how it all happened in real life. It has not been possible to establish whether bank clerks were really banned from marrying until a particular stage of income was reached. It seems a rather draconian measure. Certainly, in real life, William Leopold did not lose his job on this account, for he continued at the Bank throughout his working life. The fact that he was the son of a man whom we are led to believe from the *Chronicle* was dissolute, and whom we now know was his next-door neighbour, may well have given Thomas William Leaver an extreme prejudice against him. He very probably had higher hopes for his daughter than that. Shortly before this Thomas William Leaver had taken his daughter on a visit to Canada (see the biography for further details of this trip), where she was quite possibly introduced to a young man he particularly wanted her to marry. HW would appear to have translated this in the *Chronicle* into the recuperative holiday taken by Hetty and her mother in the South of France.

We must presume that it was at this point, as in the novels, i.e. following the revelation of the marriage and subsequent pregnancy, that William Leopold and Gertrude set up home together, at first in lodgings. Establishing information about the births of HW and his sisters was reasonably easy. A copy of HW's birth certificate is in the Literary Archive and the extremely helpful Registrar at Lewisham very kindly searched the years either side of his birthdate for the two sisters. The first child was Kathleen Gertrude, born on 13 June 1894 at 66 Braxfield Road, Brockley, just over a year after the wedding, which gives the right sort of time to encompass a real-life scenario similar to the fictional one. Henry William was, as already stated, born on 1 December 1895, also at 66, Braxfield Rd., whilst Doris Mary was born on 5 August 1898 at 165, Ladywell Road. Her birth wasn't actually registered until 24 October. This latter birth record presented a minor query, because this daughter was called 'Biddy' by everyone without fail, from birth, and I had therefore presumed the birth name would be 'Bridget'. The Registrar kindly looked for evidence of another birth under Bridget in case Doris Mary had been a fourth child who died, but this does not appear to have been the case. It is unusual that HW should have used her real name of Doris in the novels, although as she was always called Biddy, it would not have made a problem, and I think that if there had been a child-death in the family, then HW would have written it into his novels.

HW found Biddy very irritating in childhood although he seemed to have held her in some affection later in life, but he thoroughly disliked his elder sister, Kathy. There was obviously the usual childhood rivalry but it was far deeper than that. He spoke of her and her attitudes and deeds with anger and irritation. Letters between them showed hostility throughout their lives. They were, I think, too alike in temperament and neither could understand or make allowances for the other. HW frequently told a story of childhood squabbling in which Kathy is supposed to have pushed him onto the fire. In her old age, after his death,[11] Kathy related that it was in fact HW who pushed her onto the fire and that he got one of his frequent beatings for the deed.

Kathy was educated at the Ursuline Convent in Thildonck (or Tildonck, depending on which of Belgium's political factions is followed), whilst the younger sister was at a local 'Ladies' College'. Their school fees would appear to have been paid for by their maternal grandfather, Thomas Leaver. The scene in *Young Phillip Maddison* where Hetty takes Phillip over to Belgium to see his sister at school near Antwerp really happened. There is a school bill for Kathy for the Convent signed by the Mother Superior – Mère Ambroisine! Much searching of a good map with a magnifying glass for many hours eventually produced the name. Not near Antwerp as described in the novel, but just north-east of Brussels. The nearest village is Wespalaer! As Wespelaer (sic) was the name of the Leaver dwelling at least as early as 1890, it appears that Gertrude (and even her mother) were educated at this Ursuline community. This is borne out by the fact that Gertrude refers in a 'Log-book' recording her trip to Canada to the fact that the french speaking Canadians reminded her of Belgium, and also Henry shows in the *Chronicle* that Mère Ambroisine obviously knew 'Hetty'. However, letters of enquiry to the Convent (in French as well as English!), which still exists as a teaching unit, have not been answered.

Biddy (Doris Mary) married William Busby and they had two sons, Michael, born 1928 and Brian born in 1930. This marriage did not work out and Biddy was left to cope with the two boys on her own, working as a teacher to earn their living. She died at a comparatively early age. Kathy followed in her father's footsteps with a career in banking. She did not marry and died aged 88 in 1982 in Bournemouth where she had gone to live with her father in his retirement, and was quite a well-known breeder of pekinese dogs.

To conclude the lineage facts about William Leopold: he died in Parkstone, Bournemouth, Dorset, on 31 October 1946 (stated age 83, but May 1865 to October 1946 actually makes him 81+). Having retired, he had moved to Parkstone soon after his wife's death in 1936, probably at the outbreak of the Second World War, where other members of his family were living (see later). This gives us the source of the often repeated false information seen in some reference books, that HW was born in Parkstone. Incidentally, William Leopold went on a three month cruise to South America and through the Panama Canal to San Francisco at the beginning of 1937, which he thoroughly enjoyed. Henry then records several times that his father became very friendly with a young girl (and refers to them being alike in this respect).

Let us now return our attention to his father, Henry William Williamson. He died on the 10th March 1894 in Newcastle-upon-Tyne from 'Injuries accidentally received'. The *Newcastle Evening Chronicle* recorded both the accident and the subsequent inquest:

A serious accident occurred today at the Prudential Buildings, Dean St., Newcastle. It seems that Mr. Williamson, connected with Mr. Rickman's firm, London, carrying on business as quantity surveyors, was engaged in what is known as adjusting the quantities and measurement of work done in the new building, and whilst so employed, he accidentally fell through an open trapdoor, a distance of about a dozen feet.

On Tuesday 13 March 1894 the same paper reported the Inquest:

THE FATALITY IN DEAN STREET

An inquest was held on Monday night .... on the body of Henry William Williamson who was killed on Saturday by falling down a trapdoor in the new premises of the Prudential Ins. Co. at the head of Dean St., Newcastle. Leopold Williamson, bank clerk of Broxfield [sic] Kent identified the body as that of his father, who was in his 61st. year ... He was a house and quantity surveyor employed by Mr. Thos. Miller Rickman for about 30 years.

Apparently whilst Henry William was going about his business in the building someone had opened a trapdoor to gain entrance to the strong-room below. As the building wasn't finished, no safety rail was in place. Henry William retraced his steps, not noticing the gaping hole before him, down which he plunged, sustaining enough injury to render him unconscious. A doctor was called and he recovered a little and was taken away in an ambulance, but died later. The Prudential representative argued that he shouldn't have been in this particular place which was private, but William Leopold riposted that there was nothing to denote that it was private. (He surely could also have argued that if his father was making an official inspection, then he no doubt had to pass through the area in question.)

The magistrate in summing up reminded the jury that it was not their job to decide if negligence had occurred on anyone's part although they could add a rider to their verdict if they wished; but their verdict was merely 'that the deceased died from injuries accidentally received'.

The baby born to William Leopold and Gertrude three months later was, as we have seen, a girl, but when the next child, born eighteen months later, was a boy, he was named Henry William, after this paternal grandfather. William Leopold must have held his father in much respect and affection to have wished to do so, despite the stories of 'dissolution' that are associated with his counterpart in the novels, and which are no doubt to some extent based on the truth. For William Leopold apparently told HW that there had been no compensation for the accidental death of his father because he was proved to have been 'inebriated' at the time. HW's version of Capt. Maddison's death in the *Chronicle* as 'run over by a brewer's drey' is now seen as an extremely clever piece of irony.

After the funeral of Capt. Maddison in the *Chronicle*, we learn that Richard is left £2000, with which money he thinks to buy one of the houses being built next to the 'Hill'. In real life Henry William appears to have left very little. I use the word 'appears' advisedly, because there would seem to be discrepancies among the information I have obtained. Henry William would have inherited his share of his father's will (see later), although there is no guarantee that he kept it, and if he was really dissolute or even just a spendthrift, it may easily all have disappeared. William Leopold was granted 'Letters of Administration' of his father's estate on the 25th May 1894, wherein it states that the gross value of the said estate amounted to '£116.9.10d and no more': shared between the five offspring – just over twenty-three pounds each, which even translated to the value of money at that time, cannot have been considered very much.

But William Leopold did buy, fairly soon after his father's death 'one of the houses being built next to Hilly Fields', namely 11 (as it was then) Eastern Road, Brockley (Lewisham) for which he paid a deposit of ten per cent, £48, of the Purchase money of £480 on November 15th. 1898 – somewhat less than that paid by Richard in the *Chronicle*. However, there is a letter from a solicitor to William Leopold, some time after his father's death, which would appear to refer to the sale of a property (owned by Henry William as it mentions a copy of the Letters of Administration being provided as proof of legality) which would thus possibly have provided the capital with which to buy 11 Eastern Road, for William Leopold was not himself at all to be considered 'wealthy'.

It is appropriate at this point to move sideways and consider William Leopold's brothers and sisters, HW's aunts and uncles. We learn from the *Chronicle* that Richard had several, and their lives are well tabulated there, as they thread in and out of the verbal tapestry. I expected to find seven real life brothers and sisters with a real life history that would more or less tally with the *Chronicle* characters, but to find a starting point to work on was not easy.

Luckily I had access to the Will of Mary Leopoldina Williamson, sister of William Leopold and HW's aunt. Mary Leopoldina is the basis for Theodora Maddison. Without any archive evidence as backup, I am sure that the picture that HW draws of 'Dora' in the *Chronicle* would appear to be a reasonably accurate portrayal of Mary Leopoldina in real life. She did indeed publish, as J. Quiddington West, *The Incalculable Hour* in 1910.[12] Privately printed, and only forty pages long, this strange allegorical tale has deep mystical undertones, rather like a female version of some of William Blake's work, very visionary. This Aunt was obviously a great influence on HW. Apart from anything else it was she who introduced him to Devon, and also sent him a volume of the work of Francis Thompson in the First World War. There are several letters from her in the Literary Archive which are quite acerbic in tone, and which show her grasp of HW's innate character. As known, HW used phrases from *The Incalculable Hour* to obtain the title for his early work, the tetralogy *The Flax of Dream*, and to provide his original structure of working titles. Mary Leopoldina died in 1945 and the Devon address in her Will gave access to her death certificate. On this she is described as seventy-five years old and 'spinster of no occupation'.

More importantly her Will enumerates bequests to various family members including two sisters, which is the first real evidence of their existence, Isabelle Adela Williamson, spinster, and Mrs. Maude Helen Gregg (widow) and her son Hubert Theodore Gregg. Addresses for the sisters were given; Isabelle in Essex, and Maude Helen in Parkstone, Dorset, the house being called 'Quiddington' which immediately alerted the thought processes.

Another family Will which is in the archive is that of another brother, Henry Joseph Williamson. This Will and its accompanying Accounts show him to have died in December 1934 in Parkstone, Dorset. By profession Henry Joseph had been a Purser in the Mercantile Navy, retired by the time of his death. (He was supposedly married and divorced, but I have not traced these details.) Henry Joseph was comparatively well-off. Apart from specific bequests he left everything to be shared among his three sisters, but also in particular his house, 'Quiddington', specifically to Maude Helen, who had lived with him, presumably since the death of her own husband, Theodore Gregg, architect. Obtaining Henry Joseph's death certificate, I found him to have been sixty-two years of age, the cause of death arising from complications setting in after an operation (the word is in latin but it was seemingly prostate).

The money left by Mary Leopoldina, although not a lot by modern standards, was a considerable sum for 1945 and although she had been left some money from her brother's bequest ten years previously, the fact that she had always led an independent life suggests that she had always had money of her own. As she only inherited a one-fifth share of her father's £116.9.10d, it must have been from elsewhere. Perhaps she inherited a share of her grandfather's wealth via a secondary source, e.g. a maiden aunt.

William Williamson's Will which as stated earlier is in the HWLEA is a crucial document. It is both surprising and puzzling. The surprise was that William Williamson was a very wealthy man. A note among the archive papers in HW's handwriting states that his father (William Leopold) had told him that *his* grandfather (HW's great-grandfather) was worth £140,000 at his death, although the official record at Somerset House states the 'value of personal estate less than £16,000' (but there is no indication what is included in 'personal estate'). HW does not seem to have mentioned this wealth to his family nor really to have used such information within the novels of the *Chronicle*, which does seem strangely reticent. He was always very scathing of the Hibberts (his first wife's family) who had, in his opinion, frittered away their family fortunes (by default rather than intent). Can we assume that he vented his anger and frustration about his own family's fall from fortune onto the Hibberts, but was too ashamed to admit to exactly the same situation in his own family?

Dated 1872, William Williamson's Will is so explicit in detail, and apparently a key factor with lots of information contained in it, but it is actually a most frustrating document. It starts; 'I, William Williamson, of Lower Norwood, Surrey, gentleman' – so delightfully vague for research purposes. But at least it establishes him in South London at that time, interesting in itself. Lower Norwood no longer exists but by buying some reprint copies of Victorian maps of South London and checking them against the definitive modern 'A to Z' London Street maps, I placed this area at what is known today as West Norwood. We learn from this Will the names of his wife and family. His wife, Isabella, was named as a beneficiary in his Will, along with his children, Henry William, Christiana, Isabella, Martha, and Mary. His wife was to have the household effects, listed in some detail and including books, prints, and musical instruments, wines, liqours, etc. Of his 'ready money', including a life policy, Isabella was to receive a third, the remaining two thirds to be shared equally between his five children. Much property is listed, viz;

i) Freehold messuage at 14 Holywell St., Strand.
ii) Leasehold houses in Manor St. and Little Manor St., Clapham,
iii) Buildings and 3 cottages in Park Place, Clapham.
iv) 12 houses at Upper Tooting
v) 2 leasehold cottages in Salvador, Lower Tooting.
vi) 6 houses and land, Lower Mitcham

Various shares are listed, and of the income generated his wife was to receive an annual sum of £300 (£75 each quarter day) whilst the remainder was to be divided amongst his five children.

There was a particular bequest, a Trust via his son, Henry William, which involved the income from a particular property, his 'freehold estate at Lower Tooting, Surrey' for the education, maintenance and benefit of his grandson, William Leopold and his heirs for ever. And also another grandson, Charles William Cakebread, the son of his daughter Isabella and her husband, was treated in a similar manner.

However, a codicil of 1879 (showing that William was then living at St. Nicholas Road, Upper Tooting, Surrey) adds a further dimension. The wording of this seems to revoke the two latter Trusts and to strike these two boys out 'as if they did not exist'. This seemed rather extreme and I made a note: 'What on earth had happened in these five years to provoke such action?'. If it was just concerning William Leopold then his father's supposed 'wild ways' may have accounted for it but how did the other grandson fit into this? And even so, surely it was even more important to safeguard William Leopold's education and well being etc. And on reflection and rereading, over the time lapse of this research, I have decided that the Codicil is actually a tidying up of the original wording, making it more secure. It is this bequest of course, that lead me to state that William Leopold's fees at the Thanet Collegiate School were paid for by his grandfather William. And it is fairly certain that it was this property that was sold after Henry William's death, and that this enabled William Leopold to buy 11 Eastern Road.

Trying to establish any proof for William's domicile in Lower Norwood has proved negative so far.

Records for anywhere in South London are very difficult to track down. Boundaries have changed and sometimes it is not really known where records now reside. Many were lost through bomb damage in the Second World War. And the rules have been so tightened recently that unless one can make a personal search, it is highly unlikely that the very stretched staff can help. So it was very difficult to see how to progress.

But Clapham crops up in that list of properties belonging to William Williamson. On the back of one of the photographs in the HWLEA, Henry had written at some point a note to the effect that an early forebear, a Robert Williamson, had had a house next to Clapham Common and that he had been a church warden. I decided to try and pursue this route.

At this point I was guided (by my local Record Office to whom I turned for advice) in the direction of the Mormon IGI records.[13] This proved excitingly fruitful; finding a library that held copies of these records, I went through the alphabetical microfiche for Williamson for the Clapham area, and name after name appeared, and with much jotting down of notes, I was afterwards able to piece together a whole new generation with dates of birth and location.

Firstly, the names of William and Isabella's children, known from the Will, appeared as if by magic. They were all 'christening' dates and they all came under Tooting Graveney: Martha – 31 March 1833; Henry William, 13 Sept. 1835; Isabella, 25 March 1838; no dates for Christiana and Mary Ann – possibly William and Isabella moved and so the names would appear on the list for another district.

Also from this register I further discovered that William married Isabella West (note surname) on 28 August 1826 at Camberwell St. Giles;[14] that he was born on 1 January 1800 under a heading 'Clapham Baptist' and had siblings thus: Christiana, b. 12 Jan. 1797; Robert, b.19 June 1798; William himself, b. 01 Jan 1800; Martha Ann, b.19 Oct, 1801; Daniel, b.4 March, 1803; Caleb, b.13 Aug. 1804; Benjamin B., b.7 Sept. 1808. All come under the same heading of Clapham Baptist. Unfortunately the old Clapham Baptist Church, and its records, has long since gone from its original site, found on an old map on the south-east corner of the Common, where, as I discovered from a visit, schools, light industry and flats now abound. Other names were also established from the IGI Register which are plotted on the Family Tree. Caleb married a Sarah West, who was very possibly the sister of Isabella. The Williamson parents were Robert and Judith, née Judith Quiddington, daughter of George and Anne Quiddington, baptised on 25.9.1768 at Coulsdon. Robert was a builder and was in business with his sons Robert and William. In the course of their building work they must have gradually and systematically acquired property – which would have enabled William the status to refer to himself as 'Gentleman'. Robert died in 1829. Judith's death was recorded on 22.10.1844, widow, at 158 Manor St., Clapham, where she had been living with her son Robert, as was shown on the 1841 census returns.

So we find in two generations of Williamson wives the names, Quiddington and West, that combine to make up Mary Leopold Williamson's pseudonym 'J. Quiddington-West' and the source of the name of Henry Joseph's dwelling in Parkstone. But how one longs to know more of these long-ago people.

There is a further piece of this jigsaw, or rather several small pieces which fill in quite a large area of our total picture. An area which is possibly the most exciting and is almost certainly the crux of our quest in searching out HW's roots and in applying the knowledge gained in understanding the man and his writings. For of all the factors that are part of the total, a major clue to our understanding must surely lie in his German connection, the woman his grandfather married, Adela Leopoldina Lühn, HW's 'Bavarian grandmother'. The photograph of her in the archive shows a woman of most striking appearance, with very strong features and a very stern look. (Reproduced in the biography, op cit.)

Up until now that is all that has been known about her. It is the central mystery in the story of HW's background, for if nothing else, from her must arise his attitude to Germans and Germany, and his readiness to see only the good that Hitler was achieving with his agrarian reforms, his youth movement, his building of good roads, the emphasis on industry, and the general clearing and cleaning up of litter and filth, without seeing the evil shadow that the man's flawed personality was creating. But even above that, it is obvious that when examining HW's lineage that there is a very real possibility that in Adela Leopoldina lies the main clue to our understanding of HW's nature, and that investigation of her life would prove of great interest. But there is very little information in the HWLEA from which to start.

Not long after HW died in 1977 I wrote to the German Embassy asking if they could give any help with where to begin to track her down. Their reply was very dampening: according to them Lühn is apparently equivalent to Smith in England. They really did not want to be bothered (and why should they?) with such a minor, irrelevant matter. I had been somewhat naive. I looked at old maps showing Bavaria – vainly – for what was I looking? Then the thought that William Leopold named at least two houses that we know about 'Hildersheim' must surely provide a clue. Again checking the atlas shows that there is a town called Hildesheim in Germany, just south of Hannover (and the irrelevant and irreverent thought crossed my mind that this explained everything – HW was a reincarnation of the Pied Piper from nearby Hamelyn!) and although well north of the area once known as Bavaria, it is near enough for there to be a connection, even if tenuous. There really does not seem to be any other good reason why a staid Victorian family should call its house by a fairly obscure German name. HW's fictional 'Lindenbaum' would have been the more normal choice, if one just wanted a German word. (I did spend some time with a German dictionary trying to find out if Hilde/heim were German words which could be translated in the same way that Linden/baum can, but without result.)

The only facts known was that she was Henry William's wife and the date of birth of William Leopold. From the ages at date of death of the other offspring from their death certificates I could calculate their likely date of birth, so logically I could guesstimate the date of the marriage of Henry William and Adela. But where would that have taken place? I knew that when Henry William had died he had been living at Sutton, and there was the further clue of the photograph of William Leopold at school in Sutton, which seemed to fix the family in Sutton at an early stage of the marriage. In default of any other lead I felt there was nothing to lose in trying the Sutton Registry Records for that era. By a lengthy process of elimination (I have mentioned previously that boundaries have changed and records have not necessarily moved with them) via a very roundabout route I was put onto Lambeth Registry Office as the repository for these particular records. My letter of inquiry there was answered by Roger Lewis, Superintendent Registrar. My information was at fault, his office did not have the records I was seeking, but (over and above the call of his duty) he offered to do a check at St. Catherine's House, the National Repository for the records of Births, Deaths, and Marriages, as he had occasion to go there that week on other business. Very shortly a further letter arrived; he had tracked down the information I was seeking.[15] He had very kindly noted the addresses from whence I could obtain this, and informed me of its gist. He had discovered the dates and place of birth of Leopold's brothers and sisters, Henry and Adela's offspring, and most extraordinarily the date and place of marriage of Henry William and Adela. I wrote immediately to the Registry Offices concerned with the covering cheques, and a few days later the certificates arrived.

My instinct had been correct: the children of Henry William and Adela had mainly been born in Sutton, apart from the first, Isabelle Adela, born 25.11.1863 in Pimlico; then William Leopold, already annotated; then Mary Leopoldina, b. 2 Dec. 1867 in Sutton (no road given); Henry Joseph, b. 24 June 1872, at Alfred Road, Sutton; and Maude Helen, b. 25 March 1876, at 5, Victoria Road, Sutton. These roads still exist. There was a further daughter, Ethel Margaret, born 1878. In one paper in the archive, Henry refers to a photograph he once saw in his Aunt Maude's house of the children with their mother Adela, in which there were four girls, one of which was 'Effie', and further Maude herself refers in a letter (in the HWLEA) to 'my two brothers and three sisters' being so happy as a family. Ethel Margaret appeared on the 1891 Census, aged thirteen but there is no further information about her, so presumably she died young.

The circumstances of the marriage of Henry William Williamson and Adela Leopoldina Lühn was a total surprise, and I don't think a stranger coincidence can possibly have occurred. They were married on 7 April 1863, by special licence at St. Mary's Church, Lewisham. They had no apparent connection with Lewisham whatsoever. Adela's address is given as 'Parish of St. George, Hannover Square'. She was apparently born in 1838 in Frankfurt-am-Main, Bavaria, and her father's name was Joseph Lühn – (deceased) – Captain. Henry William's address is given as 'Elliot Place', occupation 'Solicitor's Clerk'; father, William Williamson (deceased) – Surveyor. (This fact was, of course, untrue, William was alive until at least 1879 as the Codicil to his will showed. Henry William apparently did not want to have to produce his father at this marriage.)

How they met and why they should marry at Lewisham Parish Church has really to remain a mystery. The birth of Isabelle only seven months later most probably explains the need for a Special Licence – remember William Henry was considered to be 'dissolute' and also he did not want his father present at his wedding, so he probably did not want anyone to be doing sums when the baby was born (although equally the babe may have been two months premature). A difficult first birth then may have been the reason for Adela's sojourn on the Isle of Wight for the duration of William Leopold's birth.

Now it was possible to cross check with Sutton for other records of their presence. The 1881 Census Index for Sutton gives: Adela L. Williamson, aged 41, and Henry William Williamson, aged 46, living at Victoria Road, Sutton. And of course it is now obvious how William Leopold attended Grove Park School, Sutton.

THE WILLIAMSON LINE

Robert WILLIAMSON d. June 1829 = Judith QUIDDINGTON 1768 - 1844 d. of George and Anne QUIDDINGTON

Christiana WILLIAMSON bp. 12 Jan. 1797 (Clapham Baptist) = John SHERRIN m. 25.1.1818

Robert WILLIAMSON bp. 19.1.1798 (Clapham Baptist) = Ann

William WILLIAMSON b. 1.1.1800 d. 5.1.1881 (Clapham Baptist) = Isabella WEST 1801 - 1884

Martha Ann WILLIAMSON bp. 19.10.1801 (Clapham Baptist)

Daniel WILLIAMSON bp 4.3.1803 (Clapham Baptist)

Caleb WILLIAMSON bp. 13.8.1804 (Clapham Baptist) = Sarah WEST

Mary WILLIAMSON bp. 19.7.1806

Benjamin WILLIAMSON bp. 7.9.1808 = Jane —

Martha WILLIAMSON Bp. 31.3.1833 = CRUMP

Henry William WILLIAMSON 1834 - 1894 = Adela Leopoldina LÜHN 1838 - 1892

Isabella WILLIAMSON 1837 - = CAKEBREAD

Helen

Christiana WILLIAMSON 1841 - = Abraham WALTON

Mary Ann WILLIAMSON 1847 -

Caleb WILLIAMSON Bp. 15.2.1829 (Clapham Holy Trinity)

Mary 2.4.1832

Robert WILLIAMSON Bp. 2.3.1834 (Lambeth Stockwell Newington)

Isabella WILLIAMSON Bp. 25.10.1846 (Newington)

Harriet Kate WILLIAMSON Bp. 24.4.1849 (Clapham)

Benjamin Harold WILLIAMSON Bp. 6.11.1835

Isabelle Adela WILLIAMSON 1863 - (1944) Spinster (Governess)

William Leopold WILLIAMSON 1865 - 1946 = Gertrude LEAVER 1867 - 1936

Mary Leopoldina WILLIAMSON 1867 - 1945 Spinster

Henry Joseph WILLIAMSON 1872 - 1934 (married + divorced) no details

Maude Helen WILLIAMSON 1876 - 1958 = Theodore GREGG

Ethel Margaret WILLIAMSON 1878 -

Charles William CAKEBREAD

Kathleen Gertrude WILLIAMSON 1894 - 1980 Spinster

Henry William WILLIAMSON 1895 - 1977 = 1st. 1925 Ida Loetitia HIBBERT 1901 - = 2nd 1949 Christine DUFFIELD; Ω liaison Ann THOMAS

Doris Mary WILLIAMSON 1898 - 1950 = William BUSBY

Hugh Theodore GREGG d. 1958 = Phyllis

William Hibbert WILLIAMSON 1926 - (has issue)

John Shaplok WILLIAMSON 1928 - (has issue)

Margaret Mary WILLIAMSON 1930 - (adopted issue)

Charles Robert WILLIAMSON 1933 - (has issue)

Richard Leopold Calvert WILLIAMSON 1935 - (has issue)

Sarah Loetitia WILLIAMSON 1945 -

Michael Harry WILLIAMSON 1950 - (has issue)

Rosemary THOMAS 1933 - (has issue)

Michael BUSBY 1928 -

Brian BUSBY 1930 -

At this point, it was time to visit St. Catherine's House, London, to consult the central registry for some outstanding items, mainly the dates of death for William and his wife, Isabella, and also for Adela. The codicil to William's Will was dated 1879, and knowing that he was already seventy-nine years old at that time and thus fairly likely not to have lived for very long after, I started there, working through the very large heavy bound indexes, quarter by quarter. William's death appeared in the March quarter for 1881. Isabella's followed in May 1884. Adela's death is recorded for 1 March 1892. Her age was given as fifty-two (but she must have been fifty-four) and she died of diabetes complications, from which she may well have suffered for years.

But there was a further problem to solve for HW refers in the *Chronicle* to Richard's mother, 'my grandfather's wife' (Adela von Fohre) as being buried in the churchyard at Rookhurst. One would presume from the information now collated that her counterpart in real life, Adela Leopoldina, having lived in Sutton all her married life (William Henry was still there after her death) would be buried in the churchyard at Sutton, and that one could deduce from that that Sutton and 'Rookhurst' would have a connection.[16]

The Archivist at Sutton Library checked the burial records for the Parish Church, St. Nicholas, but this proved negative. A second church (which is now the church for the immediate area we are concerned with) built just before the date we are looking at, does not have a burial ground, but a Cemetery also came into being at this time and on enquiry to the Superintendent I was sent full details in answer. Adela Leopoldina Williamson is interred in a family plot, Grave No. 139 T, inscribed to 'Our dear parents', which includes a memorial to her husband, who was buried at Newcastle where he died. This was all organised by William Leopold. Also there was the surprising information that Doris Mary Busby, HW's sister, is also buried in this plot.

I am still engaged in trying to find out about Adela's origins – a very difficult task, and so far without any definite result. I have written to various archive repositories in Germany in the hope that the names may be on record somewhere. Most replies have merely indicated negative results to searches or that not enough information is available to instigate a search. But again one archivist was interested 'above and beyond' the call of duty. Dr. Rauchs from the State Archive of Munich (Bavaria-Bayerisches), also could find no record but put together the little information I had provided and offered a 'hypothesis' which fits historically and with the little known family history.

For in the course of writing the biography I had eventually found hidden in the HWLEA some notes by HW reciting information supposedly told him by his Aunt Maude, stating that Adela did have a connection with Hildesheim, and also Bavaria and Württemburg (these are the sources of the 'negative' results mentioned above), and that she was 'hochgeboren' (my dictionary translates that as 'highborn') and her mother was 'baronin'. That her father and brothers had been killed in the Bismarck wars and their 'schloss' burned to the ground and that she had then fled to England. My immediate research of Bismarck and the complicated wars instigated throughout that era, showed this to be unlikely, for the real wars did not occur until after we know Adela was already in England and married to William Henry Williamson. However I had stated this information in my origiinal letters to the German Archive Repositories.

Dr. Rauchs had digested all this conflicting information and most kindly offered the following suggestion which does give an explanation that covers the circumstances. Dr. Rauchs stated that the locality of Hildesheim remained Catholic at the time of the German Reformation due to the 'Hochstifts' (the dictionary translation is 'extremely proud, haughty') character of the people of the territory. (Adela certainly looks Hochstifts! See photograph in the biography, op cit.) Since 1813 Hildesheim had come under the jurisdiction of the Kingdom of Hannover. Dr. Rauchs further postulated that Adela's father, Captain Josef Lühn, could have been a Catholic Hannoverian, who was part of the British Army which came into being in the British Hannover Union of 1827 and that he could have served in a war of 1853–56 (which was eventually ended with an Italian civil agreement to maintain honour and dignity) in which he was killed. Dr. Rauchs made a further suggestion about Adela's mother, explaining that the name 'Leopold' is a typical name for the House of Saxe-Coburg and Gotha, especially for the Belgian branch. Dr. Rauchs particularly hypothesised that Adela's mother may thus stem from a branch of the Dukedom of Saxe-Coburg.

I personally would not have placed too much faith in the import of HW's note without some burden of proof, as it may well have been romanticising on his part, and it is not possible to know if his Aunt Maude really stated these things. But as Dr. Rauchs, a historical scientist with no doubt impeccable qualifications, can offer such a plausible rationale for the events and clues related, without even querying their veracity, I feel that this would all bear further investigation in the future. In the meantime, it is not possible to do more than to offer the hypothesis for what it is, and to thank Dr. Rauchs for opening up a possible way forward.

There is one further area that needs consideration and clarification. HW makes reference in the *Chronicle* to his Scottish and aristocratic forebears, and to farming activities in the north. On the surface there would appear to be no justification for this in real life, but I do know how this (fictional) claim arose and although to date I have not been able to prove a definite real life connection, I can show its origin.

In the Literary Archive there is a small book. In the front are written a few words, with the signature of one Augustus Williamson and the date 1856. Attached to it is a note written by HW:

> *Augustus Williamson (note how the signature resembles that of H.W.Williamson, my grandfather, W.L.Williamson, my father, and even my own signature) was in the 30th Regiment of Foot. He was the son of Henry William Williamson, son of Sir Hedworth Williamson, Bart., of Durham.*
>
> *HWW 12.11.1958*

I think HW is being a little self-delusive about the handwriting here – from the few examples of William Leopold's writing that I have seen, mainly his signature, he has a large cursive script very different to HW's small cramped style. Augustus Williamson appears to have merely written in the front, in the manner that one would in an autograph book – a note for a friend. HW uses his words (which may in themselves be a quotation but I have been unable to find them) in *A Test To Destruction*, Part Four, 'The Lost Kingdom' (p.313):

> *A man may bear a World's contempt when he bears that within that says he is Worthy. When he contemns himself – there burns the Hell. Augustus Williamson.*

There is no way of telling how this little notebook came to be in HW's possession. It may be that it really was handed down from previous generations and thus that the family of Augustus Williamson actually were forebears, but I suspect that actually HW was browsing through an antique emporium and on seeing the inscription, found the coincidence to his liking, and a fitting source for his fictional forebears and a detail for his novel sequence. As HW had obviously done, to produce his note above, I looked Augustus Williamson's family up in the peerage reference books in his archive. They did exist as he states, and for interest I append a copy of the family tree as far as I have been able to establish it. The family seat is Monkwearmouth, Co. Durham, which gives us the 'farming area in the north'. The further coincidence of the names Henry William appearing is an almost irresistible trap to fall into but I could have believed in HW's (fictional) acquisition of this family if the over-riding name of 'Hedworth' had cropped up in his own traceable family tree.

Augustus Henry Williamson was born in 1831 and died in 1900. He was a Captain in the 30th Foot Regiment. His actual dates are too late for him to be a forebear of HW. I think that my research on HW's immediate lineage shows that any supposed connection can only be before the birth of Robert Williamson, HW's great-great-grandfather in what would have been about 1760/70. However, Augustus's grandfather, The Revd Thomas Williamson was Rector of Stoke Damerel, Devon. I have stated that Miss Dorothy Shapcote wrote to HW in 1957 from South Devon and that information HW gained at that time showed the Shapcotes to have lived in Stoke Damerel. He would I think have visited her in order to collect the family papers which are in a large wooden box, which he would presumably have collected in person. He would also quite possibly have visited the various places that appear as family residences, including nearby Stoke Damerel. Thus he could have found the booklet in a local antique shop (his note about the handwriting is dated Nov. 1958. which would fit into the timescale for such a supposed visit to South Devon) – or there may be a real family connection which I have not discovered. There are certainly some 'further issue' of this family – younger sons of younger sons within the Baronetcy, and before it was established, which I have not tracked down, which indeed could have some connection with our first known Robert Williamson. It needs some time spent in order to prove yea or nay.

But whether there is a real-life connection or not, this is almost certainly the source of the fictional forebears of Phillip Maddison. HW may well have driven to look at their family seat at Monkwearmouth to satisfy himself of its suitability and to fix the location in his mind, to provide local colour for his novels.

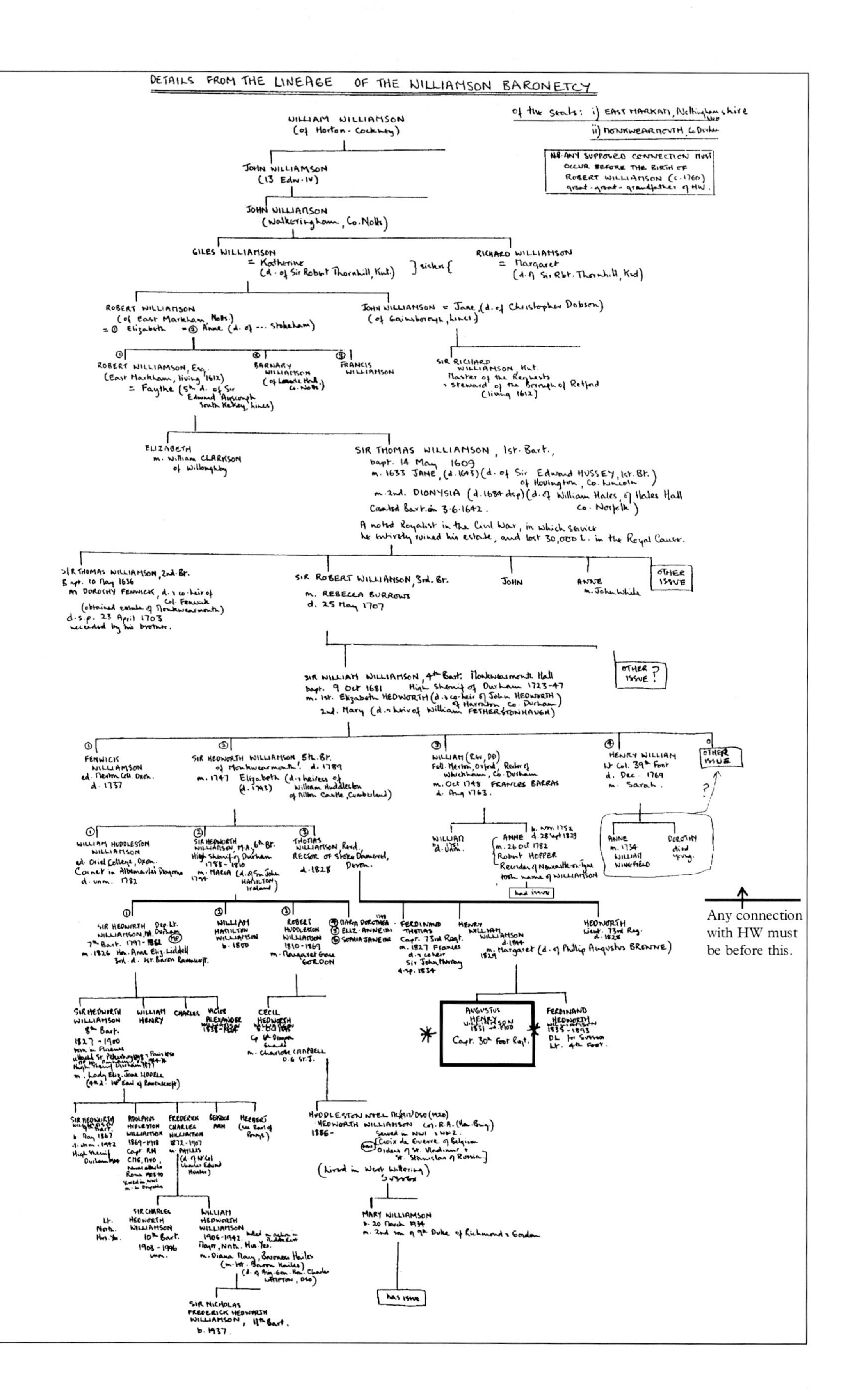

DETAILS FROM THE LINEAGE OF THE WILLIAMSON BARONETCY
of the Seats: i) EAST MARKAM, Nottinghamshire
ii) MONKWEARMOUTH, Co Durham
NB ANY SUPPOSED CONNECTION MUST OCCUR BEFORE THE BIRTH OF ROBERT WILLIAMSON (c.1760) great-great-grandfather of HW.
WILLIAM WILLIAMSON (of Horton-Cockney)
JOHN WILLIAMSON (13 Edw. IV)
JOHN WILLIAMSON (Walkeringham, Co. Notts)
GILES WILLIAMSON = Katherine (d. of Sir Robert Thornhill, Knt.)
sisters
RICHARD WILLIAMSON = Margaret (d. of Sir Robt. Thornhill, Knt)
ROBERT WILLIAMSON (of East Markham, Notts.) = ① Elizabeth = ② Anne (d. of ... Stokeham)
JOHN WILLIAMSON = Jane (d. of Christopher Dobson) (of Gainsborough, Lincs.)
ROBERT WILLIAMSON, Esq. (East Markham, living 1612) = Faythe (5th d. of Sir Edward Ayscough, South Kelsey, Lincs)
BARNABY WILLIAMSON
FRANCIS WILLIAMSON
SIR RICHARD WILLIAMSON, Knt. Master of the Requests, Steward of the Borough of Retford (living 1612)
ELIZABETH m. William CLARKSON of Willoughby
SIR THOMAS WILLIAMSON, 1st Bart., bapt. 14 May 1609
m. 1633 JANE (d. of Sir Edward HUSSEY, 1st Bt.) of Honington, Co. Lincoln
m. 2nd. DIONYSIA (d. of William Hales, of Hales Hall Co. Norfolk)
Created Bart. on 3.6.1642.
A noted Royalist in the Civil War, in which service he entirely ruined his estate, and lost 30,000 l. in the Royal Cause.
SIR THOMAS WILLIAMSON, 2nd Bt. Bapt. 10 May 1636 m. DOROTHY FENWICK, d. & co-heir of Col. Fenwick (obtained estate of Monkwearmouth) d.s.p. 23 April 1703 succeeded by his brother.
SIR ROBERT WILLIAMSON, 3rd Bt. m. REBECCA BURROWS d. 25 May 1707
JOHN
ANNE m. John White
OTHER ISSUE
OTHER ISSUE ?
SIR WILLIAM WILLIAMSON, 4th Bart. Monkwearmouth Hall bapt. 9 Oct 1681 High Sheriff of Durham 1723-47
m. 1st. Elizabeth HEDWORTH (d. & co-heir of John HEDWORTH of Harraton, Co. Durham)
2nd. Mary (d. & heir of William FETHERSTONHAUGH)
① FENWICK WILLIAMSON ed. Merton Coll. Oxon. d. 1737
② SIR HEDWORTH WILLIAMSON, 5th Bt. of Monkwearmouth. d. 1789 m. 1747 Elizabeth (d. & heiress of William Huddleston of Millom Castle, Cumberland)
③ WILLIAM (Rev, DD) Fell. Merton, Oxford, Rector of Whickham, Co. Durham m. Oct 1748 FRANCES BARRAS d. Aug 1763.
④ HENRY WILLIAM Lt Col. 39th Foot d. Dec. 1769 m. Sarah.
OTHER ISSUE
ANNE m. 1734 WILLIAM WINGFIELD
DOROTHY died young.
① WILLIAM HUDDLESTON WILLIAMSON ed. Oriel College, Oxon. Cornet in Albemarle's Dragoons d. unm. 1782
② SIR HEDWORTH WILLIAMSON, M.A., 6th Bt. High Sheriff of Durham
③ THOMAS WILLIAMSON, Revd. RECTOR OF STOKE DAMEREL, Devon. d. 1828
WILLIAM d. unm.
ANNE m. 26 Oct 1782 Robert HOPPER Recorder of Newcastle-on-Tyne took name of WILLIAMSON
had issue
① SIR HEDWORTH WILLIAMSON, 7th Bart. m. 1826 Hon. Anne Eliz. Liddell 3rd d. 1st Baron Ravensworth.
② WILLIAM HAMILTON WILLIAMSON b. 1800
③ ROBERT HUDDLESTON WILLIAMSON 1810-1869 m. Margaret Grace GORDON
FERDINAND THOMAS Capt. 73rd Regt.
HENRY WILLIAM WILLIAMSON m. Margaret (d. of Phillip Augustus BROWNE)
HEDWORTH Lieut. 73rd Reg.
SIR HEDWORTH WILLIAMSON 8th Bart. 1827-1900
WILLIAM HENRY
CHARLES
VICTOR ALEXANDER
CECIL HEDWORTH
AUGUSTUS HENRY WILLIAMSON Capt. 30th Foot Regt.
FERDINAND HEDWORTH
HUDDLESTON NOEL HEDWORTH WILLIAMSON 1886- (lived in West Wittering, Sussex)
SIR CHARLES HEDWORTH WILLIAMSON 10th Bart.
WILLIAM HEDWORTH WILLIAMSON
MARY WILLIAMSON
has issue
SIR NICHOLAS FREDERICK HEDWORTH WILLIAMSON, 11th Bart. b. 1937.
Any connection with HW must be before this.

That completes the investigation into HW's roots to date. The information is not complete; there are many questions that remain unanswered. Possibly some never will be answered. Some can perhaps be answered by deduction from sequences in *A Chronicle of Ancient Sunlight*, and I hope that there will be some contribution on this in due course. Some can be answered by further research, by following up open ended points within this present inquiry. With the main roots now firmly planted, perhaps some further fruit will ripen and be harvested. I recently discovered that another member of the Henry Williamson Society, Brian Dolan, has also researched the family tree in great detail, and in a far more scientific manner than myself, which would have saved me a lot of trouble if I had known – except that we agree with each other that the excitement of the chase was worth the effort involved. Our findings agree in the main, but I know that Brian is already working on some of the gaps, particularly the early naval records, and that he does have some extra information already, and hopefully he will send in his findings to be published in a future issue of the HWSJ. He has already supplied me with the answers to some details I had been unable to discover. There are also a certain number of small details in my research file which do not appear in this article (there is a limit as to just how much information can be crammed in!), but none which have any direct bearing on thc story of the roots of Henry Williamson.

NOTES

Throughout the notes The Henry Williamson Society *Journal* is abbreviated to HWSJ.

1. The biography: Anne Williamson, *Henry Williamson: Dreamer of Devon*, (Alan Sutton, Autumn 1995) complements this article especially with regard to photographic illustration. There is necessarily a certain amount of overlap of information between the two. However, the amount of detailed information contained here far outweighs what was possible in the biography itself, in which only outline information could be given.
2. See John Gillis, 'The Maddisons and the Turneys, HWSJ, No.2, (Oct 1980), p.7 and also Tom and Joan Skipper, 'Henry Williamson's Bedfordshire Roots', HWSJ, No. 6, (Oct. 1982).
3. I am grateful to the Librarian at Sutton Library for providing information from the library records.
4. Archive Lists for the Nineteenth Century are available for both Oxford and Cambridge Universities. Hugh Leaver does not appear on them although for both Cambridge and Oxford there are other Leavers who do not appear to be part of the immediate family.
5. See *A History of our District* (The Apsley Guise School Historical Society, 1931).
6. See the pamphlet *Shakespeare's School*, A brief history of the Grammar School, Stratford-Upon-Avon. (The Guild School Ass., 1987.)
7. This interesting reference to the journalistic activities of John Shapcote Leaver shows a family trait in that direction. I am fairly cetain that HW would not have known about this. It would be most interesting to discover examples of JSL's work.
8. I am indebted to Brian Dolan who discovered the circumstances of WHL's death from Naval records.
9. The Shakespeare Birthplace Trust. Documents for Leaver, John Shapcote. I am indebted to the generous help given by Dr. Robert Bearman, the Senior Archivist, in obtaining copies of documents held in the archives.
10. Research into the Naval records of various members of the family is being undertaken by Brian Dolan. It is proving of great interest and it is hoped that these findings will be published at a later date.
11. An instance illustrating HW's attitude to Kathy is that members of his family were not encouraged to have contact with her and Richard and I were not even aware of her existence until after his death.
12. For further details see, J.W. Blench, 'The Incalculable Hour', HWSJ, No. 8,(Oct. 1983), pp 18-20. The full text of J. Quiddington West, *The Incalculable Hour* can be found printed elsewhere in this Journal.
13. The Mormons have made an Index of Births and Marriages (and some deaths) from Parish records to cover the time previous to the official registers starting in 1837. These are available on microfiche at certain libraries.
14. You will note that in the *Chronicle* HW arranged the marriage between Richard and Hetty at Camberwell Register Office and that Hetty had been born in Camberwell Green where her parents had lived in the early days of their marriage, thus transferring the facts to the fictional maternal line.
15. I am very grateful to Roger Lewis for the trouble he took over this query.
16. Certainly it is worthwhile looking at Sutton as a source for 'Rookhurst'. Sutton is near the North Downs, an area of chalk-based hills, and HW's own schooldays at Colfe's Grammar School are more easily transposed. Thus, looking at old maps it would be possible to more or less trace the walk taken by Mr. Rore in *Dandelion Days* from Colham School to his own house in Rookhurst, that is in real life – from Colfe's to Sutton. it was then a simple matter for HW to 'lift' the whole area and place it at first vaguely in the West Country for *The Flax of Dream* and then more definitely somewhat west of The Great Plain – Salisbury Plain – for *A Chronicle of Ancient Sunlight.* In my biography of HW (op. cit.) I suggest 'Trefusis', the house in Falmouth, Cornwall, in which HW spent a long convalescence in 1917, as a possible source for the actual Maddison family residence.

The Incalculable Hour

by J. Quiddington West[1]

Earth's crammed with Heaven,
And every common bush afire with God.
E. B. BROWNING

Gardens where a place is found for
Rosemary and rue.
MICHAEL FAIRLESS

THE other day, looking from my window, I saw a beautiful thing. It was a morning of tempestuous weather, and heavy showers of sleet and rain alternated with brief gleams of sun along the vapour-laden hills. Overhead, great masses of cloud, leaden-coloured and burdened with rain, swept westwards, with here and there a momentary glint of serene blue between their torn and rolling edges. A wild wind blew from the snow-covered slopes of Mount Aenos, and harried the waters of the bay to an anger of leaping, foam-crested waves. Opposite my window the mountains rise abruptly from the water's edge, their lower slopes an almost precipitous face of grey rock, where only the scantiest vegetation finds precarious roothold; but higher up their great, rounded sides are dotted with olive woods and vineyards, or little fields of springing corn, for every yard of mountain soil is cultivated by the industrious peasant, who wrests, by patient labour, a frugal subsistence from the unwilling earth. Often he will build a little wall, and, gathering behind it a few spadefuls of soil, will cultivate with infinite care two or three vines or a patch of scanty corn, making a tiny oasis of bright verdure amid the prevailing grey. To-day, as I looked in an idle moment across the bay, my eyes rested on one of the hill villages nestled among its olive groves and vineyards. It is ordinary enough: just a cluster of lowly habitations set between two flanking spurs upon a rising steep—the homes of a cheerful, poverty-stricken race of mountaineers, who live on the produce of their olive woods and vines, content, as were their forefathers, if the harvest yield them sustenance enough for the year. But as I looked, a gleam of sunshine came through a rift in the clouds, and shone into the misty valley, and, behold! a miracle. The sullen, rain-charged vapour was changed on the instant to a shining sea of glory, iris-dyed with radiant colour; rich purple and tender blue, chrsyoprase and gold and pure rose, melting and changing, fading and flushing as the colours in an opal, the encircling mists gathering a faint reflection of its splendour in paling tints of amethyst and amber and green and the soft yellow of early dawn. It was as though the Angel of the Covenant hovered above the village, and, lo! it was even as a City of Heaven, builded of precious jewels.

It was a strange contrast: above, the hurrying storm-wrack; far below, the restless, troubled sea; but in the valley the peace of an ineffable beauty—the sign of God's covenant with man. Many times my eyes had. rested upon the familiar scene, but suddenly it, was invested with a new significance.

Life, I thought, as I watched the rainbow splendour, is like that. About it lies the glory of a spiritual beauty, no less real than the sweet and intimate beauty of the world about us, though it is fashioned only of the hopes and dreams, the aspirations and desires and prayers that are born of the soul's continual longing; but it needs the light from Heaven to reveal the hidden prism to our startled vision.

Of old the poets and song-makers, the painters and hewers of stone knew it, and wove their knowledge into all to which they put their hand, so that there is not any romance, or song, or picture, or statue which has survived the ruin of its time, that is not instinct with the wonder of spiritual longing. And as their work is the expression, so it is the inspiration of all noble and beautiful life everywhere. It is out of their light that we see; it is by their wisdom that we may learn to cull an immortal beauty from the mortal dream. Yet, when we would traverse the paths they trod, know the same wonder, behold the same vision, we seek in vain. The wind has stirred among the grasses their eager footsteps brushed aside, and there is no sign that any, save ourself, has passed that way. We had deemed as we journeyed that we were one of a great company and, behold! there is none with us. Looking back, we see only the solitary track of our own feet. The bitterness, that is born of Disillusion, brims slowly up as we realise that the way of the spirit is even the way of the wind, which comes and goes, leaving no trace. There is no open road to the Land of Dream; none may journey thither through the obscure tracks of another's mind. The path which leads me straight to my kingdom of Heart's Desire is no more than a maze leading nowhither to another, even to him who dwells within my love.

Yet it is in the Hour of Disillusion that we first set our feet upon the way. As we gaze, perplexed and weary-hearted, across the desolate waste that lies before us, a thought takes shape from the silence and the loneliness. The wind blows suddenly about us, and in the wind is an unvoiced cry, the echo of a multitude of calling voices. Vague, elusive, faint as the sea-murmur within the shell, beautiful as a remembered voice, the cry comes to the inward ear. To one it may be a meaningless abstraction, to another a beautiful unreality, but to the third it is as a light shining and an open road. For he who passes through the earth by quiet ways, along shadowed paths, whose breath is upon the heart of the world, has come and laid tender hand upon our tired eyes, and his touch is as the sun illumining the mist. Thus it is that the Master of Dream comes to us in the Incalculable Hour; a swift weaving of shadows about our feet, a whisper against the ear, a strange leaping of thought. to wed with thought; and the Portals of Dream are flung wide. We have come, not to the kingdom of those others, but to our own; and the beauty of their land, which we knew only by reflection, is as nothing to the new beauty. Slowly there dawns, upon us a vision of wide spaces, sun-flushed through radiant depths of air; of white palaces gleaming upon a far horizon; of shining waters, rainbow-spanned; and beyond, the dim blue hills of dream, whither we are bound. In the light of the thought conceived of despair, the way lies clear before us: we stand upon the threshold, and the heart leaps to greet the beloved unknown. So it has ever been. Our Land of Heart's Desire is woven of our own thoughts and longings and aspirations, and no two weave alike. And it is well if, returning thence, we bring with us gifts worthy of acceptance. For many, to whom the Weaver gives the flax of Dream, weave hurriedly, and the web is spoilt. It needs time to gather the joy and sorrow, the love and suffering, the wisdom that go to make the perfect design; and through all the weft of it must run the thread of self-sacrifice like a scarlet flame, touching it to inconceivable beauty.

But upon those who have once wandered through the Land of Heart's Desire, whether they have gathered of its treasure or not, there is a weariness of longing until they may return again to them the light that dwells upon its wide solitude is the light of home ; in the silence that sleeps upon its quiet hills is peace; the dews that fall from its tranquil skies at evening are to the healing of all sorrow. It is rather the shadow of that land they would have in their hearts than all the gold of the world.

Yet I think there are few now to whom its beauty is familiar, fewer, to whom it is a living reality. Who, amid the press and thronging tumult of our busy life, has time to seek the hidden iris within the cloud? or to listen to the myriad-voiced murmur of the wind? We have little leisure for weaving, even if we have the flax.

The Land of Dream would seem to belong to the past rather than the present. To the uncomprehending eyes of the multitude it enshrines only the vanished ideals and outworn beliefs of peoples, whose destiny is fulfilled; who are remembered only because they *dreamed.* And the land their dreams inhabit is a land of illusion, rainbow-lit with vain longings, where the splendour of a tradition that has outlived the passionate fire of the hearts that kindled it, fades slowly upon a grey horizon. Upon it is the shadow of a despairing love.

The old ideals are gone; the old, visionary spirit, which could conceive of the elemental forces as continual presences of more than mortal beauty, is no more; the Phrygian music, beloved of the gods, dies upon a long silence. And with the passing of the old order have passed also the old ways of thought, the simple wisdom, the occult, gracious influence, which more than any other fashioned to noble manhood and womanhood the races which believed on them.

And yet, strange though it may seem in face of what I have just written, I believe there has never been a time when the traditions of the past have been richer in significance, in arrestive and compelling power, more instinct with all the influences that shape the spiritual history of nations, than they are now.

We are beginning at last to acknowledge the poverty of our genius, to realise the incredibly narrow and selfish outlook, engendered by a persistent endeavour to attain material success; and instinctively we are turning again to the ancient founts of wisdom, the ancient, forgotten beauty that our fathers knew and loved with a passionate love.

To the watchful eyes, signs are not wanting that a new spiritual world is coming to the birth—that we are on the eve of a great spiritual change. Already the longing is in many hearts; the seed has been sown, which shall spring up and bear fruit an hundredfold. It may be that we who wait, shall yet see the dawn of a divine redemption, when He, who redeemed the world once as Man, shall come again, but this time as a Spirit, whose coming shall be peace, and whose Breath upon the souls of men shall be as healing dews upon a parched and fainting ground. In that day the broken dreams and faiths of ancient, forgotten races shall be informed with new and immortal meaning; their passionate yearning shall merge into a no less passionate and beautiful reality. Meanwhile, until that time shall come, we cannot cease to hope, to believe, to be uplifted on the continual wings of new and more beautiful dreams—to remember.

But our dreaming must be beautiful and wide and deep if it is to become again a significant factor in the world's progress. The vision of old was instinct with the beauty of mystery and longing unrealised; but to the new must be added the splendour of purpose fulfilled.

Erringly, perhaps, yet because I find no other word so apt to convey my meaning, I have called this faculty of inward vision dreaming; but in truth it is more than that. I should, with more wisdom, affirm that it is the outcome of the spiritual history of the whole human race, the heritage which the countless lives of unremembered generations have patiently builded up for those who should come after them. Memory and dream, dream and memory, what are they but the immortal treasure gathered by a multitude of hearts as they journeyed through the land of Heart's Desire? Is it not of these that the imagination is woven that shall reveal the imperishable beauty? Is it not for this that the perpetual incense of longing rises to-day from your heart and from mine, as it rose from the hearts of those who loved and suffered and dreamed a thousand years ago? All the story of life is in that immutable desire. It is the gift that the dead have bequeathed to us, the living; and by reason of it we are one with them and they with us. The outcome of their joys and sorrows, their experiences and memories are ours; they toiled in bondage, that we might be freer than they were; they sorrowed, that we might the more perfectly understand the heritage of their love; their heart-hunger is to our fulfilling. It is, in truth, a magnificent trust that has come down to us, only awaiting the awakening touch to blossom into splendid reality whether of dream or action—the one is not less than the other.

This faculty of inward vision is the possession of one whom I have known long and intimately, though, like all moments of supreme passion or intense emotion, it recurs only at rare and uncertain intervals. It mysteriously comes and as mysteriously goes, one knows not whence or whither; but for beauty its brief passing is like the light, flashing upon the white wings of a bird flying through the gloom of storm.

What I would write here is the memory of such an hour, wherein the spiritual was so strangely interwoven with the material that at first it may well seem that I am writing only of the habitual: so bewilderingly real, so confusedly like, is the land of Dream to the actuality of which it is, in part, the presentiment. But even so there are mysteries of which I cannot speak; for what God says to the heart in the incalculable hour neither I nor any may find words. But those who have themselves journeyed through the land of Heart's Desire will understand.

That I have written it is at least a testimony to my belief in the prescience of the Soul's vision.

The dove-grey vapours of the rain brooded in a solemn stillness, low upon the horizon, their long folds lying quietly above the darkening hills. Before sundown the rain had ceased, and the wandering breaths of air, moving idly hither and thither, were penetrated with the fresh pungency of rain-wet earth.

A great quietude lay upon the earth; everywhere the shadows were gathering in their multitudes, and the rich colouring of the summer world withdrew momentarily into a deepening mystery of purple. In the late twilight little was visible save a wide expanse of field and meadow, sloping gently to the hills, and the darker gloom of the storm-worn pines lifted upon their sides.

A cottage standing a little back from the long road, that stretched shadowless into the dusk, was the only dwelling visible; in the half light it had a strangely forlorn look, as though it lacked the care of kindly hands, the cheerfulness of human life within its walls. The garden was forlorn in its neglect; all distinction of flower border and vegetable plot had long since disappeared before the invasion of a host of weeds and gay wayside vagrants, that flourished in profusion everywhere; rank grasses and thistles, nettles and dandelions, and a multitude of lesser growths made a tangle of wild disorder, among which some bushes of southernwood and fragrant rosemary, and a few clusters of white cloves still throve.

A rose-bush, loosed from its fastenings on the wall, swung loosely forward across the red-tiled path, its arching stem a mass of sweet blossoms. Beside the doorway some lavender bushes already thrust a few spikes of purple fragrance above the grey-green leafage.

Within the garden a woman stood motionless, her hands clasped loosely before her. She was so sombrely clothed that her form was scarcely distinguishable in the gathering dusk, but her face, slightly raised, stood out palely clear against the dark background. Here and there the earth, roughly turned, showed an attempt to reduce the wilderness to some sort of order, and testified to a spirit which outran a strength unskilled to such labour; and indeed her hands, though vigorous, were delicate and finely formed. She held herself very still; but the eyes, lifted to the quiet hills, were dark with the burning of unshed tears; a line of troubled thought showed between the intent brows.

Once and again she drew a long breath, and perhaps the good, sweet smell of new-turned earth and the scent of rain in the air penetrated the tumult within, for she found herself thinking in this wise:

"I am even as this garden is; my life has brought forth no fruit. Where I sowed good seed and waited its growth with patience, there sprang up tares, and my labour was for nought. I looked for much, and, lo! it came to little. Each harvest-time, when I would gather in, there was no ripeness in fruit or grain, and it sufficed not for my need. And this happened, not once nor twice, but many times. Wherefore my weariness waxed with failure, until at length I said in my secret thought: 'I will plant no more, for this my garden is worthless and barren, and the soil incapable of bringing forth. Rather will I let the wild poppy spring up, that it may fling a garment of oblivion upon the garden. Briars and thorns shall come up to hide its desolation, and the hemlock shall seed upon the pleasant ways, and encroach upon its secret beauty. It shall become as a garden without water, and there shall be no more pleasure in it. Only in this corner will I set cypresses, that their straight gloom may shadow the unprofitable earth, and hide that my lilies have not stirred the dry soil, nor my roses bloomed though the slimmer be hot upon the land.'

"But while these thoughts were upon me, God planted a small seed in my garden beneath the cypress boughs, and chancing to pass, I beheld the first tender growth piercing the earth like a green flame. At first I heeded not, for I esteemed it a vagrant growth, brought thither by chance. But the sun shone and the south wind blew upon it, and into its green life was woven the beauty of earth and heaven, of sunshine and shadow, until in fairness it surpassed the lilies for which I had grieved. Only the gloom of the cypress, beneath whose sheltering boughs it grew, mingled strangely with its radiant purity, as the shadow in the white heart of a rose. The whole garden was beautiful because of it: upon the rough and unlovely places its shadow lay and covered their unsightliness; about the weeds of evil growth its fragrance lingered, until even they caught of its beauty and grew fairer. When, tired, I stole away to my garden, I found within its closed doors a prevailing peace, a still delight as of old forgotten days, a beauty which fulfilled all longing.

"But one, envying, laid axe to the root, and the tree withered ere ever it came to the fruiting.

"Surely the blind bittemess has come upon me, now that I have seen the failure of that which God Himself had sowed. Hope failed me, love has failed ; and now I must rise up and put from me even the desire that I had, believing it would surely come to pass."

A faint wind arose and sighed to silence through the garden; it was as if withdrawing airs from a vast height passed swiftly about her, and the shadows fell away on every side. Yet no leaf stirred. The rhythmic rush of the blood tides was suddenly in her ears, as when one listens intently for a sound from the world without; a pulse leaped in her throat, and she drew breath sharply. Slowly, as one in fear, she lifted her face to the night.

In the air was a pale shining, seeming from a great

way off, as of dawn when first its white flame burns through the film of night. With each slow moment it waxed in strength, until the garden was lit with a radiance, fair and serene as the clear sun of noon upon a windless day, yet exceeding in beauty all light that she had ever seen.

And she was abashed and bowed her head, though her spirit was moved to sudden exaltation.

For an incalculable space she stood, holding herself in awe of that which should come.

There was no word that the ear heard, yet through the silence came a voice from within the unrevealed light, speaking through measureless space.

"Why dost thou grieve, oh Soul?" it said: "Wherefore shouldst thou think that Love hath failed thee? Because that the axe was laid to the root of the tree which God had planted, and thou sawest the branch wither, thou sayest, 'Behold, it is dead, and my garden is waste.' When at any time hath God failed, or that which He hath decreed fallen short of its fulfilling? Hast thou weighed Love in the balance and found it wanting, that thou sayest, 'I have no more hope'? And against what didst thou measure it?—the pride of thy heart or the wisdom of thy knowledge? Nay, but verify these are as a small dust in the balance compared with Love. Who hath taught thee to judge of Love and place a bound on that which is boundless? Canst thou compass the heavens with a rule, and say, 'Thus and so much are the length and the breadth thereof'; or measure with a flaxline the distance between one star and another, and say, 'So far are they apart'? Even so canst thou not search out the foundations of Love, neither the height nor the breadth, for Love excelleth all."

While she listened to the voice shame came slowly upon her, because she knew that faith, rather than love, had failed; and she stood with her face bowed upon her hands.

"Is not the holy seed in the midst of thy garden?" continued the voice, that was as her own thought. "Yet hast thou deemed it barren and incapable, because it hath borne no harvest that thou couldst pluck, and say, 'This is the fruit brought forth of my labour.' Surely thou hast not done well in this thing; yet, because thy endeavour was honest, and thou hast striven painfully through the winter of thy desire, though thy hands were wearied and thy heart heavy with distress, thou shalt see there is a fruit that cometh to perfection only through the travail of the spirit. Cast fear behind thee, and look upon the work that God doeth in the lowly places of the earth, when He causeth the tender herbs to spring forth in the desolate and waste ground, and see the love that compasseth all the creatures of His hand, and accounteth even the things of the dust worthy."

Though fear constrained her, she raised her head. At first a mist swam before her sight, and her eyes were dazzled and felt dry between the lids, as one waking suddenly from deep sleep. But after it might be a moment's span, the veil drew from before her eyes, and she saw clearly; yet rather, as it seemed, with the spiritual than with the mortal vision. For now the material was become as the immaterial; within each living herb and tree she saw the life revealed as a throbbing radiance, white and pure, of indescribable beauty; in each weed burned the living flame; upon each branch and leaf was set the seal of its divinity. But within each she saw also the obscure suffering, as the inmost darkness lies within the flame.

A great wonder drew upon her, and a great awe, so that she sank upon her knees, but the loneliness of the still flames of life still held her gaze. And as she knelt it seemed as if one unseen laid gentle hands upon her, and, leaning, kissed her on the brow. And with the passing of the unseen presence she understood suddenly the meaning of that upon which she looked.

"I have been as one blind," she thought in sudden contrition. "Have I not said within myself that their sufficiency is of God, and they know not those things whereby we go in misery: neither love nor sorrow, nor envy, nor malice, nor despair? Yet they, even as we, suffer tribulation, each in his capacity; distress comes upon them also, for all their sustenance is sure."

Shame and remorse welled up in her heart as she realised the beauty of the lowly life about her: the meek acceptance of adversity; the patient endurance of trial, the persistent endeavour to bring the gifts, bestowed by God, to the uttermost perfection of which they are capable.

Again the voice of the Unseen Presence spoke, saying:

"Even so it is as thou hast seen. Every life must be proven, if it be good or evil—whether there be in it the fibre that shall endure for ever, or whether for a season it shall suffer destruction ere it be renewed. There is no end to the thing God taketh in hand. By trial and suffering is the life strengthened to further endeavour. Thus must it ever be: the fans of God cease not to winnow the good grain from the bad; and the wind blows upon all.

"Yet art thou blind, oh Soul! Though thou seest indeed the living fires that God hath sown about thee, thou hast not discerned that from the inner darkness issues the light that purifies and annuls the evil, which else would destroy. But now shalt thou pass within the shadow of the circle of life and behold the glory thereof, which is the glory of perfect service."

Wondering, she raised her eyes, and looked again, and saw that which before she had not seen. . . .

Suddenly she wept, and the tears ran down upon her lips, and her soul tasted their bitterness. Yet with her shame mingled a joy so great that it partook of fear. As she wept the silence thrilled again with the sweetness of unheard speech.

"Behold, this thing that I have shown thee is an image of thine own Soul. The life whereon thou hast looked is even as thine own—the difference is of degree only. Within all burns the flame of sacrifice; upon all rests the seal of a continual love. Wherefore go no more unhoping nor without peace. Follow the light that is within thyself: what thy Soul certifieth thee is good, that do thou, heeding not that failure will sometimes be where thou hast looked for success. Of that whereof thou seest but a small part thou canst not judge. See to it that thou tend heedfully the seed of the living fire, that the weeds overrun it not, and it perish for lack of care. Much labour and many tears must go to the making of thy garden, for there is naught accomplished, save with tribulation. The fruit that cometh of the travail of the spirit accounteth much in the sight of God and shall be in no wise cast away.

"Do faithfully that which God will put into thine hand to do, suffering no thought that the fame of thy doing shall be noised abroad. Seek counsel only of thine own Soul that it is well done. Take no heed that the harvest seem scanty, and thou hast little reward of thy long toil. Canst thou quicken by one hour the swelling of the fruit to ripeness with all thy care? Even so in the garden of the Soul God proceedeth slowly. Work only from thine own heart, and leave the judgment with Him who knows that which, He does, and sees the end in the beginning."

The light waned and was gone, as a flame outblown by the wind. The silent night was about her where she knelt; the cool air, fragrant with the green life of wood and meadow, passed by her and stirred her hair; but she did not move. A great weariness had come upon her, as of one who has travelled far in a strange country; but in her eyes was the knowledge of peace, though the tears were yet wet upon her cheek.

At last she rose and walked slowly, not feeling the ground beneath her feet, but going as though the burthen of thought lay heavy upon her. In her heart was a desire infinite as the sea. As she moved, dreaming, onward through the darkness there came slowly to her the knowledge that she was no longer alone. For a space she stood listening; but no sound broke the stillness; no footfall save her own stirred within the garden. She would have put the thought from her, but the sense of a near presence drew more strongly upon her and compelled her to turn again whither she had come. At first the gloom was impenetrable and she could see nothing. Then it was as a mist of moonlight shining upon that place, and she saw distinctly. Slowly against the brooding shadows a vision took form—a vision that made her pulses quicken their throbbing, her breath catch in her throat with the wonder of it. Scarce a stone's throw distant, she saw a dim figure standing; of so divine a beauty that her heart stood still as she gazed upon it, yet so forsaken in its human loneliness that her soul died within her at the revelation. Her very life was stayed as she looked upon the quiet figure: the hands folded in prayer; the head bowed with the weight of its sorrow; mortal anguish upon the suffering brow; yet about that patient form there breathed a solemn atmosphere of peace, enduring beyond all conflict; in the supplicating pose was an immortal dignity, a strength beyond all human comprehension.

Near her she saw other figures among the shadows, drooped in wearied attitudes of repose, asleep upon the ground. And He who prayed, turned and gazed upon them; she saw the divine tenderness of the quiet lips, the redeeming love shining in the sorrowful eyes. A supreme fear shook her, yet she did not move.

Impotent, dumb, as one in a trance, she stood and watched the Sacrifice of Love.

Suddenly she could no longer bear the mystery of this immeasurable love; bowing her head, she turned away, but when she would have wept, the grief that laboured in her heart dried up her tears. And He, coming, stood before her and spoke; though the silence was not broken there was speech between them. Like the living freshness of rain upon a thirsty land, the unspoken words brought to her soul an exceeding peace; the anguish of failure, of humiliation and despair, changed beneath the healing touch of that infinite compassion to an unspeakable glory.

As she looked into His eyes, the pain that bound her heart was loosened, and she bowed her head and wept. But in her weeping there was no bitterness, only a supreme joy. In that moment of silent commune she stood face to face with the splendour of God's Love, and upon her soul was the stillness of its understanding.

NOTES

1. Mary Leopoldina Williamson, Henry Williamson's aunt; she is Theodora Maddison in the *Chronicle* novels. Mary Leopoldina was a great influence on Henry Williamson; see Dr J.W. Blench 'The Incalculable Hour', HWSJ, No. 8 (Oct. 1983) pp. 18-21; and also Anne Williamson's biography *Henry Williamson, Dreamer of Devon* (Alan Sutton, 1995).

Thought to be Mary Leopoldina Williamson.

The Lewisham of Henry Williamson

Brian Fullagar

On what proved to be a significant day in March 1921 Henry Williamson wheeled out his beloved Norton racing motorcycle and, vaulting into the saddle, drove off noisily down Eastern Road. He was leaving Brockley bound for a remote village in North Devon where it was his intention to embark on a free-lance career as a writer. Despite the recent exciting news that his first novel had been accepted by a publisher he was turning his back on a restrictive home life and a short and frustrating spell as a Fleet Street journalist.

Readers of *Sun in the Sands* could be excused for thinking that this event marked the end of Henry's 'London Period' as a 'prentice writer, and that from this moment on all of his creative work was to be inspired by the fresh beauty of the North Devon coastal landscape. However, it is clear that this was not yet to be the case. In his essay 'Some notes on *The Flax of Dream* and *A Chronicle of Ancient Sunlight*',[1] Henry Williamson describes how and where the first part of *The Pathway* came to be written:

> *As I have said,* The Pathway, *ultimate volume of the* Flax, *was written between 1924 and 1928, and published in October of that year. Twenty years were to pass before the first sentence of the new series of novels was written. And during those twenty years the proverb of Blake was chronically before my mind, 'He who desires but acts not breeds pestilence'.*
>
> *The reason for the chronic putting-off lay, I told myself, in the changed circumstances of my living since 1924. Part One of* The Pathway *had been written during the last few weeks of that year, easily, with clear imaginative excitement, and devotion. The book was broken off just before Christmas, which was to be spent in the home of the girl I was going to marry. She was the 'original' of Mary Ogilvie, and her father was Sufford Chychester in the story, Mary's great-uncle. With what joy did I think of the West Country, from the empty house near London in which I had been writing my novel, at night, in the flame of a single candle set in a Cromwellian brass stick! The bare walls and floor boards, the flickering shadows, the coal fire, the garden room where my uncle had died in pain and torment—many years later to arise in Phillip's story as Hugh Turney. At last the third week of December came, and I set off to Devon.*

Thus we can establish Henry's return to the 'Gardenfeste', the garden room in his late grandfather's empty house where *The Beautiful Yers* had been completed. Up until his marriage and the arrival of a family it would seem that Lewisham still drew Henry Williamson back to his roots!

That vast output of writing based on or inspired by the Devon countryside and in particular the continued universal popular and timeless appeal of *Tarka the Otter*, tends to categorize the author solely as a West Country writer. Indeed, even the splendid trio of 'London Novels' that begin the *Chronicle* saga were written in the small hilltop Writing Hut at Ox's Cross which overlooks the silver ribbon of water which is the Estuary of the Two Rivers, glistening far below.

Nevertheless, as it was with Richard Jefferies who, despite having left his homeland years before, retained throughout his lifetime constant recollections of his boyhood at Coate Farm and the countryside around Swindon, so Henry Williamson returned time and again to memories of the South London of his youth and the green woods and pastures of Kent. These were the formative years seminal to the development of character and vital to his future progression as a country writer in the rural tradition. We read of an unhappy Brockley childhood, the difficult relationship with his father and the daily torment of school life. Throughout his writing run the recurring themes of bitter-sweet yearning for lost loves and fled springtimes which owe their origins to the early impressionable years of youthful awakening. But there must also have been happier and brighter times during this period. Surely it could not have remained totally loveless and without laughter? For how else could his books retain such a delightful sense of fun and good humour even during the grimmest of occurrences, such as in the trenches of the Western Front.

At the time of Henry Williamson's birth in 1895 Brockley was still part of rural Kent. Although the widening tentacles of suburban London were even then reaching ever outward, farmland and green meadows extended to the southern slopes of what is now Hilly Fields. Up until that time the Hill had been used for market gardening and the production of bricks made from the local clay, baked in the two kilns at the Hill's base. Down in the village of Ladywell, Joy Farm and Slagrove were still being worked and along the course of the Ravensbourne river a number of water mills operated. Wildlife could be found in the woodland, and thickets and hedgerows that bordered the fields were home to a variety of birds.

This was the town and country environment in which Henry grew up, roaming free whenever released from school regime or home tensions. Within minutes from his front door on a bicycle, Henry could be searching the hedgerows for birds' nests, or fishing in one of the many cattle-drinking ponds or flooded marl pits in the fields close by. With his Boy Scout patrol he camped in the woods and explored the countryside. Using a book on etiquette borrowed from the public library, he sought permission by letter to the owners of nearby country estates to study bird life on their property. In every case he received a gracious response.

Permission having been granted, this enabled the young Henry to visit many of the great country houses in Kent such as Holwood Park, Keston, home of Lady Constance Derby, and High Elms, the estate of Lord Avebury. The sylvan beauty of these spectacular parklands were a poetic inspiration for a young boy soon to leave school and already displaying signs of a developing talent as a writer, in the journal he kept to record his country expeditions.

Holidays spent with his favourite country cousins at Apsley Guise in Bedfordshire further heightened the boy's powers of observation and an appreciation of the natural world. But it was not only a love of nature that commanded the young Henry's attention. From an early age he developed a strong sense of 'Spirit of Place', a remarkable awareness of the social and historic milieu of a locality. This gift is brilliantly characterised in the 'London novels' where descriptions of late Victorian and Edwardian Lewisham and its environs evoke a vivid picture of the distant past. In his book *On Foot in Devon*, Henry Williamson observes:

> *Some of his disciples, having read* The Pathway, *have journeyed to see me; leaving with the conviction of having interviewed a false prophet.*[2]

Ever since *The Pathway* was published in 1928, eager literary pilgrims have set off in search of the author and locations in the novels that comprise *The Flax of Dream* trilogy. This is also the case with fans of *Tarka the Otter*. Thanks to the success of the Tarka Trail Project it is now possible for enthusiasts to walk a trail of some 53 miles that follows Tarka's water journey from Lynmouth to Bideford along the South West Peninsula Coast Path (including sections on the tracks of disused railways). Henry Williamson's Lewisham holds a similar attraction for followers on the trail of 'Ancient Sunlight'. The pages of the *Chronicle* are full of carefully observed scenes of local colour which depict a South London suburb at the turn of the century. Streets, shops, and houses of Lewisham stand out from the page and have an authenticity and character all of their own. These same locations are readily identifiable today from the author's faithful word-painting.

As the photographs and text that accompany this introduction will show, much of the old Lewisham district that Henry Williamson knew still exists despite the ravages of wartime bombing and recent modern redevelopment. The renumbered house at 22 Eastern Road is perhaps the most evocative in its association with Henry and his fictional family saga. But the Leaver family grave in nearby Brockley and Ladywell cemetery provides, in microcosm, a remarkable chapter in the Williamson story. That simple headstone illustrates how skilfully the writer wove real-life incidents and people into the fabric of his fictionalised narrative in order to intensify the dramatic impact of the story. In this small plot of ground are buried Henry's maternal grandparents, Henrietta and Thomas Leaver (the Turneys of the *Chronicle*), his Aunt Maude and her husband, together with the unfortunate Hugh Leaver (Phillip's tragic Uncle Hugh in the novel).

Unlike the mythical sites of 'Rookwood' and 'Malandine', 'Wakenham' and 'Randiswell', the original Brockley and Ladywell landscape and place names are but thinly disguised in the *Chronicle* narrative. Not every reader feels the need to know the real name of 'Twistleton Road' of the novels, or verify the accuracy of Richard Maddison's route to Randiswell railway station. But for many, the unravelling of such lexicons is an absorbing recreation. Apart from the challenge posed by these puzzles it does demonstrate how faithfully the author recorded details of known and familiar places.

With the formation of the Henry Williamson Society in 1980 the band of Lewisham literary researchers delving into the landscapes of the *Chronicle* has grown steadily in number. John Gillis was perhaps the first of these to publish an account of his hours of 'HW sleuthing' (HWS *Journal* No. 2).[3] The first London meeting of the Society held in May 1982 produced a wealth of information on the 'Lewisham connection'. John Glanfield's fascinating account of his tour of 'No. 11 Hillside Road'[4] and

Joan Read's splendid illustrated talk on 'Edwardian Lewisham' contributed greatly to our knowledge. David Hoyle produced an informative pamphlet entitled 'The Ladywell of Henry Williamson'. This was the first Society guide to the area. In 1987 Robert Tierney introduced his excellent article, 'Places and Association in *Young Phillip Maddison*' (HWS *Journal* No. 15).[5] Then in 1988 Joan Read collaborated with Robert Tierney to produce her first-class definitive guides, 'Henry Williamson Walks 1 and 2'.[6] Thus there is now in existence a comprehensive archive of reference information on Henry's Lewisham available to the would-be literary explorer in that area, which I am sure will continue to be added to.

It will be seen that the Lewisham area has had a significant influence on the establishment of Henry Williamson as a major writer in the rural tradition: his early awakening to the world of nature, in woods and fields which by now have largely vanished under housing estates and roads; his education, under a system that the author strongly condemned as being inhibiting and restrictive to a child's natural growth. (In spite of those views it has to be said that his masters at Brockley Primary and Colfe's School must be credited for setting his feet on his chosen craft as a writer.) Then there is the town itself, with its unique history and local chracter to which Williamson's exceptional 'Spirit of Place' responded. From his parents' home in Eastern Road in August 1914 Henry set out to join his Territorial battalion at the outbreak of the Great War. That terrible conflict was to be the major obsessional experience that was to influence his whole life and work. At the end of the War he returned to Brockley, resolved to one day write the story of his family and all that he had personally endured.

So it is that readers of his books follow in his footsteps, visiting the scenes and locations of the novels, reliving the experiences and tribulations of Henry Williamson and his *alter ago*, Phillip Maddison. One day, perhaps, when this celebrated writer's true literary merit is at last recognised, we shall see an official waymarked 'Williamson Trail' to guide the faithful round those familiar streets of Lewisham.

Those fortunate enough to have made a 'pilgrimage' around Ladywell, Lewisham or Brockley, will, I am sure, have been much impressed by how little the area has changed since the early years of this century when Henry Williamson lived there and subsequently used it as the basis of the opening volumes of *A Chronicle of Ancient Sunlight.* The town has encroached on the countryside since that time, of course, and the evocative 'Seven Fields' lost long ago beneath brick and concrete, along with many of the ponds, hedgerows and woods beloved of the young Henry. But even in his youth, their death-knell had sounded (we read in *The Lone Swallows* the bitter-sweet regret at the rape of the Kent countryside by the London County Council and property development).

Despite these more obvious ravages, Ladywell and Brockley retain numerous fine reminders of how the place must have looked before the Great War, so let us set off on that absorbing trail of 'Ancient Sunlight', as we pinpoint those places which have a particular association with Henry Williamson.

★ ★ ★ ★ ★

NOTES

1. 'Some Notes on *The Flax of Dream* and *A Chronicle of Ancient Sunlight*, Henry Williamson. From *Henry Williamson, The Man, the Writings: A Symposium*, ed. Brocard Sewell (Tabb House 1980) p. 149.
2. *On Foot in Devon*, Henry Williamson (Alexander Maclehose & Co. 1933) p. 27.
3. See John Gillis, 'The Maddisons and the Turneys', HWSJ No. 2 (October 1980) pp. 7-9; 'To the Fishponds and Back', HWSJ No. 4 (November 1981) pp. 27-30.
4. See John Glanfield, 'Lindenheim', HWSJ No. 5 (May 1982) pp. 5-13.
5. See Robert Tierney, 'Places and Associations in *Young Phillip Maddison*', HWSJ No. 15 (March 1987) pp. 8-17.
6. Joan Read, 'Henry Williamson Walks 1 and 2' (available from Brian Fullagar, Mailing Circulation Manager).

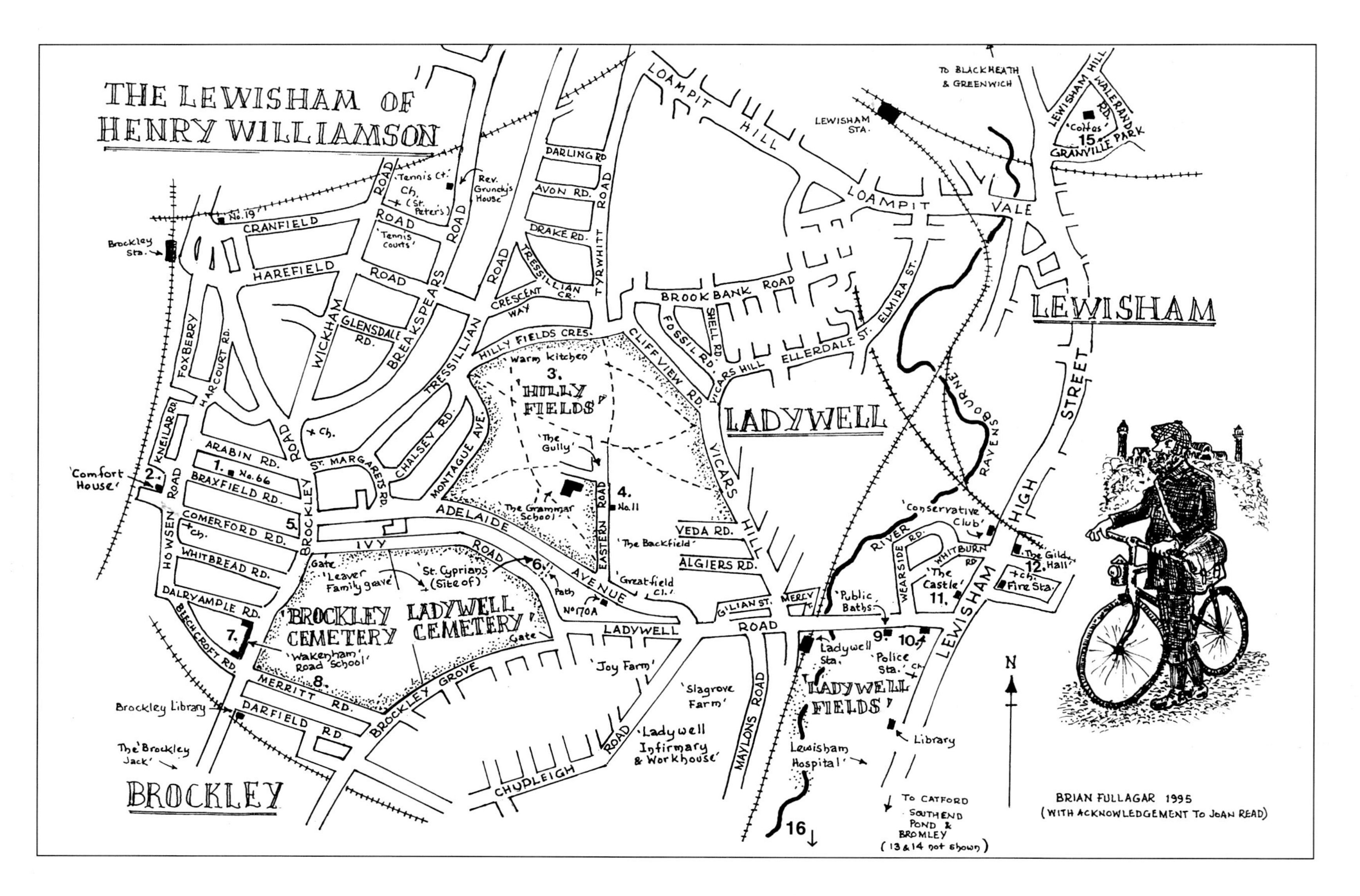
THE LEWISHAM OF HENRY WILLIAMSON
LEWISHAM
LADYWELL
BROCKLEY
BRIAN FULLAGAR 1995
(WITH ACKNOWLEDGEMENT TO JOAN READ)
N
TO BLACKHEATH & GREENWICH
LEWISHAM HILL
WALERAND RD.
GRANVILLE PARK
'Coltas'
15.
LEWISHAM STA.
LOAMPIT VALE
LOAMPIT HILL
LEWISHAM HIGH STREET
RAVENSBOURNE
ELMIRA ST.
ELLERDALE ST.
BROOKBANK ROAD
SHELL RD.
FOSSIL RD.
VICARS HILL
CLIFFVIEW RD.
VICARS HILL
'Conservative Club'
The Gild. Hall
12.
+ch.
Fire Sta.
WHITBURN RD.
'The Castle'
11.
WEARSIDE
RIVER RD.
'Public Baths'
9.
10.
Ladywell Sta.
'Police Sta.'
ch.
LADYWELL FIELDS
Library
TO CATFORD SOUTHEND POND & BROMLEY (13 & 14 not shown)
Lewisham Hospital
16
MERCY
GILIAN ST.
VEDA RD.
ALGIERS RD.
'The Backfield'
'Greatfield Cl.'
LADYWELL ROAD
MAYLONS ROAD
'Slagrove Farm'
'Ladywell Infirmary & Workhouse'
'Joy Farm'
CHUDLEIGH ROAD
TYRWHITT ROAD
DARLING RD
AVON RD.
DRAKE RD.
TRESSILLIAN CR.
CRESCENT WAY
HILLY FIELDS CRES.
'Warm kitchen'
3.
HILLY FIELDS
'The Gully'
4.
Hall
EASTERN ROAD
'The Grammar School'
No 170A
Path
6.
ADELAIDE AVENUE
TRESSILLIAN ROAD
MONTAGUE AVE.
CHALSEY RD.
ST. MARGARETS RD.
IVY ROAD
Gate
'St. Cyprians' (Site of)
BROCKLEY CEMETERY
LADYWELL CEMETERY
Gate
'Leaver Family grave'
'Wakenham Road School'
8.
BROCKLEY GROVE
MERRITT RD.
DARFIELD RD
Rev. Grundy's House
'Tennis Ct.'
Ch. (St. Peter's)
'Tennis courts'
BREAKSPEARS ROAD
GLENSDALE RD.
WICKHAM ROAD
Ch.
CRANFIELD ROAD
HAREFIELD ROAD
No. 19
BROCKLEY ROAD
5.
ARABIN RD.
No. 66
1.
BRAXFIELD RD.
COMERFORD RD.
+ch.
WHITBREAD RD.
DALRYAMPLE RD.
7.
BEECHCROFT RD.
HARCOURT RD.
FOXBERRY ROAD
KNEILAR RD.
2.
HOWSEN ROAD
'Comfort House'
Brockley Sta.
Brockley Library
The 'Brockley Jack'

1. 66, Braxfield Road

Where better place to begin that at the very house in Brockley where, on the 1st December 1895 Henry Williamson was born. In the past his actual place of birth has been variously ascribed to a number of sites from Bedford to Dorset. However, the record of his birth proves it to be Brockley beyond further doubt! This modest terraced artisan's cottage is in excellent repair and, despite some modernisation, still retains many of its original features.

2. 'Comfort House', Comerford Road

Just around the corner from Braxfield Road in a small cul-de-sac at the far end of Comerford Road, close up to the railway embankment (just as the 'London' novels of the *Chronicle* portray), solid 'Comfort House' (Richard and Hetty Maddison's first home, and where Phillip Maddison was born). David Hoyle in his early 'Guide' pamphlet pondered the interesting question as to why Henry '. . . adapted a reality' rather than make use of the Braxfield Road location. (Could it have been that 'Comfort House', which he must have played beside as a boy, provided a more romantic setting which also enabled a colourful historic development of the narrative?) Research shows that within living memory people recall donkeys being grazed on the embankment and an allotment being worked there.

3a

3b

3c

3d

3e

3f

3. 'Hilly Fields' and Eastern ('Hillside') Road

Over the years the parkland of the Hill has been slowly whittled away. The tall elms on its crown are gone, as are the bandstand and wooden shelter, along with the stunted Socialist Oak. But replacement trees are rapidly growing once more on top of the Hill and they will soon give the same visual effect as is obtained by the mature trees close by in Adelaide Road (which were planted after the 1939-45 war). Wooden shelters come and go, due to vandalism and lack of finance. The Gully which leads up over the Hill from Eastern ('Hillside') Road is almost unchanged. In Photograph 3b you see a view looking down Eastern Road from the Gully towards Adelaide Road at the bottom. The new housing development marks the site of Mrs Tetley's (Neville) flat at 170a Adelaide Road, which was only recently demolished to make way for new housing. In the far distance can be seen the water tower of the old Workhouse and Infirmary where Lily Cornford worked (*The Golden Virgin* ch. 20).

Below the crest of the Hill still over all broods the dark solid facade of the old West Kent Grammar School (3c). 'True love was there too... love in sweet silence listening to the bleat of lambs in the field beside the dark building of the grammar school.' (*The Dark Lantern* ch. 1).

On windy days gaily coloured kites still soar above the summit. In winter when snow blankets the steep slopes of the Hill and toboggans race down into the 'Warm Kitchen' to the accompaniment of children's happy cries, we may conjure up thoughts of a tall, bearded figure in a deerstalker hat, climbing with his new sledge up the north slope of the Hill! This rare postcard (3d) of the period appears to have been taken straight out of the *Chronicle*. Note the bandstand in the background. During the 1939-45 war some of the houses at the Adelaide ('Charlotte') Road end of Eastern Road were destroyed by bombing. A block of flats was subsequently built on the site and, following a recommendation by Joan Read, the Borough Council named the block 'Greatfield', thus preserving HW's use of the old name for the area: '... Dick Turpin had hung out in the wood at the southern base of the Hill near the Great Field which was now the cemetery.' (*The Dark Lantern* ch. 1).

Fortunately, most of the houses in Eastern Road, homes of all those fascinating characters so familiar to us through the pages of the *Chronicle*, have survived the passage of time. The Bigges, Groats, Jenkins, etc., can all be identified here from the novel's description. But fair Helena Rolls' bower, the turret house at the top of the row, can now only been seen in early photographs. Some years ago whilst the turret house stood empty, it was set on fire by vandals and had to be demolished. A new house has been built on this site, its bright, white brickwork contrasting with the drab grey of the older houses. (Perhaps in years to come it may be mistaken for Helena's home?)

4. 11, now 21, Eastern Road ('Lindenheim')

For devotees of the *Chronicle*, possibly the most evocative of all HW locations is the family home of the Maddisons and, next door, that of Richard's in-laws, the Turneys. As the photographs show, what delights this old house contains! The handsome tesselated pavement, fine cast-iron and glass canopy, together with the balcony joining the two houses. Inside No. 21 the layout of the rooms match exactly Henry's detailed description, which proves how remarkable was the author's memory and power of recall. It was from this house that Henry left one summer morning, 5 August 1914, on his way to join his Territorial battalion of the London Rifle Brigade. To this house he returned at the end of that terrible conflict. From here also he completed his first novel, *The Beautiful Years*. Most appropriate therefore that the Henry Williamson Society chose this house as the location of the first memorial plaque dedicated to the great author's memory. The plaque was installed by Lewisham Borough Council and unveiled on Saturday 19 May 1984 at a special commemorative ceremony. The unveiling was carried out by Mrs Loetitia Williamson and Joan Read, whose enthusiasm originated the plaque project and saw the plan through to completion.

5. Brockley Road (c. 1900 and c. 1995)

John Chappell & Sons, Funeral Directors, had the corner shop (estab. 1840). The ornate shield below the roof remains today as the modern photograph shows, but the shop is now a turf accountant's! Edward Sprunt had the shop next door. The horse and cart stand at the corner of Comerford Road. On the opposite side of Brockley Road, the man on the bicycle (could it be a 'Starley Rover'?) is approaching the junction with Adelaide Road. Cranfield ('Harefield') Road is also on the right beyond the church. Back over on the left hand side at the foot of the church tower, a break in the row of shop fronts shows the entrance to Braxfield Road.

6. St Cyprian's Path

The church of St Cyprian was destroyed by a bomb in the winter of 1940/41 but the short pathway with its iron railings, which links Adelaide Road with Ivy Road and the gates of the cemetery, remains as a nostalgic reminder of the past. It was here that Phillip and the lads of the Bulldog Patrol met the ill-fated Hugh Turney. 'Waving a stick at his nephew, Hugh Turney stopped by the iron cannon embedded in the asphalt of the footpath.' (*Young Phillip Maddison* ch. 9) The iron cannons have gone but the location is a fascinating reminder of the literary use HW made of familiar local landmarks.

7 Brockley ('Wakenham') Road School
The site of Henry/Phillip's school, Colfe's Grammar School. A V1 'flying bomb' destroyed the original building, so graphically described by Henry in *Young Phillip Maddison*. The 'Boys' and 'Girls' original gateways still exist.

8. Merritt ('Skerritt') Road
In this road, adjoining Brockley High Road, lived Phillip's great friend Horace Cranmer. Henry describes this as a poor district but today the twin rows of elderly, neat and well kept villas show a different picture.

9 Ladywell ('Randiswell') Baths
The original building still stands in Ladywell Road, although not now used as public baths since the 1960s. A circle of ancient stone slabs in the forecourt of the building are reputed to be coping stones from the old holy well, from which Ladywell takes its name. In far off times no doubt some miraculous cures were said to have taken place at this spot, which would be connected with Our Lady by the faithful, and so the name has been handed down. The site of the well is recorded as being near two old cottages close by Ladywell Cemetery.

10. Lewisham Police Station
Situated near the junction of Ladywell Road with Lewisham High Street, this fine old red-brick building retains its original exterior facade. It was here that the evil Detective-Sergeant Keechey took Phillip to hear of his recall to the Front. Richard Maddison set out from here on his nightly war-time patrols as a Special Constable (*The Golden Virgin* ch. 12)

11. The Castle ('Freddies') Public House
In Lewisham High Street, the famous 'Freddies Bar' of the *Chronicle*. Alas, little now remains of the original building's fabric, so faithfully described by HW. This existed up until a few years ago, when the stained glass and handsome varnished wooden screens were all swept away and with them the special atmosphere that still lingered there from when the pub was owned by William Frederick ('Freddie') Coates.

12. *The Gild Hill*

Known as the Temperance Billiard Hill, this splendid structure has now become a Mecca Bingo Hall and the sumptuous gilding replaced with a paint of ghastly mauve hue! Happily, this is a listed building and any alteration to the exterior is strictly controlled.

'Over the porch was fixed the legend: "THE GILD HALL, Billiards, Refreshments"; the letters gleamed but dully on a raw Saturday night in the late autumn of 1915.' (*The Golden Virgin* ch. 1.)

13. *Whitefoot Lane*

How well this early postcard captures the spirit and feeling of the old Whitefoot Lane at the turn of the century. Ancient oak trees stand in the hedgerows which flank the dusty lane. Wild flowers star the grassy banks that slope to ditches bordering the roadside. On the right of the picture a wooden stile gives access to lush meadows beyond. Not a single wheeled vehicle is in sight, just a group of young men out for a stroll on a golden day before the outbreak of the First World War.

What a contrast to the dense traffic that fills the dual carriageway of the 'Lane' today! Hetty and Richard would have walked that way while spending their honeymoon at the nearby keeper's cottage and Henry, too, wandered along this lane. 'Spring came again with the larks battling over the Seven Fields and the wind anemones raising like stars above the dead leaves.' (*The Lone Swallows* p. 184)

Originally this road, running from Grove Park to South End, Catford, was known as Shroffield Lane and it was the meadows and pastureland of Shroffield Farm that Henry identified as the mythical 'Seven Fields of Shrofften', all now lost beneath several large housing estates. One road in Bellingham retains a ghostly memory in its name, 'Shroffold Road'.

14. Southend ('Cutler's') Pond

Southend Pond and its old mill were once popular places to go on Sunday afternoons and high holidays. Later, between the wars, there were added the delights of Peter Pan's Playground with its little pleasure boats on the pool. In the late '30s it fell into decline and the pond became much polluted, but in recent years a large 'Homebase' store has been built on the site, and the pond has been cleared and restocked with fish so that today swans and wild fowl prosper there, unperturbed by the traffic's roar. All of which would have delighted Henry as it realised the hopes for the future he expressed in 1920 when he wrote his essay 'The Old Pond'. Part of the old mill still survives, much dilapidated. The old engine house is in use as a second-hand furniture and fireplace store.

15. Colfe's School

The original site of the school in Walerand Road until its destruction by wartime bombing. This was the 'Colham School' of *Dandelion Days* and the 'Heath School' of the *Chronicle*. The modern school is now located at Horn Park Lane, SE12.

16. The Ravensbourne River

The photograph shows a section of the 'Randisbourne' river at a point where it flows under the road into 'Cutler's' Pond. Phillip and Tom Ching passed this way on their disastrous walk beside 'a dying stream' to its source at Caesar's Well (*A Test to Destruction* ch. 22.)

Scarecrow Cottage – Four articles from 1921-22

Henry Williamson

(Originally printed in the *Sunday Express* 18 December 1921 to January 1922)

A House of No Morals

We think our readers will agree that this brilliant and remarkable narrative stamps its young writer as a coming author of distinction. Mr. Williamson (in spite of his beard) is still in his twenties. If he keeps his poise he should travel far.

For me London was dead. It lay like a corpse by my side at night and kept me from sleep. It was killing me, the vile thing, with its breath of river fog, its Piccadilly death-grin, its limbs crawling with those maggots of civilisation—smoking trains, grinding buses and cabs blowing blue filth into the air. My doctor said, "You have not recovered from an adolescence in the war."

I replied, "Possibly. But three girls in succession have jilted me, I cannot get work, I have no money; and in spirit I am for ever roaming my Devon hills, with the ravens and the wild hawks."

CHARMING KLEPTOMANIAC

My literary friends said: "You haven't grown up yet: all these ideas of yours are but youthful vapours." My suburban neighbours said: "He is potty, y'know."

So I left the filthy rat-run that is called London and walked, without money and unfriended and with a sprouting beard, to Devon.

I have discovered the art of living: my life has the simplicity of the Greek ideal. My bed is made of sweetest bracken laid on springy poles of fir. I rent a cottage for £1 a year. And I have many dear companions dwelling with me in my limewashed hermitage. They love me and I love them.

They have no manners, and they snatch food from one another's mouths, but I don't care. Some of them eat uncooked mice; the favourite dish of a young lady is a live, slimy eel from the near brook; two other females have been seen to rake over a neighbouring dustheap. One young man is, I fear, a confirmed kleptomaniac, but so charming is he that when people from whom he has stolen come and tell me of it they invariably laugh and stroke his little head.

HIDING FROM JUSTICE

My home is sanctuary for the crippled and those hiding from justice. I have four friends who dare not venture out in the daytime. Were they to do so they would be mobbed and followed by jeering crowds. So they leave at evelight. They are barn owls, foam-white of breast, and on their soft backs is laid a mantle of tarnished gold-cloth. They are my brothers.

The young lady whose favourite dish consists of live eels is an otter cub. How I tamed her is another story. There are, indeed, a score of stories that I could tell. But who would print them? Editors' ideas are usually as dull as the river-water by the Embankment—where for many nights I sat and made moan at that terrible thing—peace after war.

MY COMRADES

Perhaps the "Sunday Express" can appreciate a new writer. If the Editor cares to give his readers the opportunity of hearing a new voice, I will speak. He can please himself whether he hears of the Christmas preparations I am making for my comrades, who are:

4 Beautiful Owls,
1 Wilful Otter cub,
1 Cunning Carrion Crow (shot by a farmer, left for dead, and nursed back to life by myself—two outcasts together),
3 Lovely Spaniels,
2 Gentle Kittens,
1 Naughty Herring Gull (broken-winged; caught presumably by a wave crest),
1 Kleptomaniacal Jackdaw,
2 Scrounging Magpies,
1 Enormous Buzzard Hawk

—all living in harmony, with myself as the supreme adjudicator of any quarrel or argument.

"What a curious fellow he must be," I hear some one in London saying, "to live in a dirty house."

"ODDMEDODD"

Oh, I am a curious fellow. "He'm be mazed like an oddmedodd," as the Devon dialect would render it. "Praper slaverer, he'm be, aiy, aiy!"

I *am* mazed, and the London fellow is sane. He likes sulphurous soot; I like the pure air of the sea. He likes dirty cow milk or chemical whisky; I milk my own goats, and drink my own berry wine. He likes a fumous atmosphere of music halls; I prefer to watch the stars, especially that winter giant below Orion, Sirius the Dogstar, shaking with crimson fire, then flashing a ray of blue. Perhaps he is an artist, and loves to paint lily-pale women, classic beauties; let him paint them; and leave me my dear birds and animals, yea, even the merry rats who gallop in the yard-thick cob wall all night, the black-eyed graceful mice, the beetles, who creep from their cracks in the dark, the moths, the spiders, even an occasional flea.

Mad? Perhaps, but if this article finds its way into print I can promise you that on Christmas Day my cottage will be one of the happiest and merriest spots in all England.

But if the "Sunday Express" refuses this then I shall have to content myself with a pipe and watch the wisps of smoke steal upwards through the chimney and on, I suppose, until they reach the understanding moon.

"Scarecrow Cottage"

In last week's "Sunday Express" we introduced this new writer with his story, "A House of No Morals". We feel sure that our readers will agree that Mr. Williamson has a remarkable career ahead of him.

Myself and ghosts of Scarecrow Cottage were surprised when a cheque and a letter came from the Editor of the "Sunday Express".

No one in the village had seen a cheque before, and the only way to cash it was to go to London. I must confess that I felt a small enjoyment at the prospect of seeing London. I had left it an out-of-work, a poor starving devil, without hope in life, unfriended, and nearly insane.

"London at Christmas time will be at its best," I thought.

A foul mist hung over Clapham and Vauxhall. At Waterloo there was hurry, and people were pale and tired. The ghastly scream of engines and the honk of cabs bewildered me. I wanted to return immediately.

WAITING

But I persisted, and walked to the Strand. There huge coppery arc-lamps threw harsh shadows, there were the same grinding atoms of humanity, pushing and jostling, out-of-work men hawking Christmas toys and no one buying. An omnibus nearly killed me; I apologised. And a taxicab-driver bawled at me as I dodged his beastly vehicle.

Then I saw a happy sight. A small group of men were playing Carols. "The waits," I thought . . . here was a link with my happy childhood.

"Yes, they waits," tonelessly replied an ex-soldier to my inquiry, "they waits for work. Like I waits for someone to buy my toys. Like my nippers waits for grub. Like the toffs' kiddies waits for Santy Claus."

At dinner I saw fat old men with their over-dressed wives swigging champagne, or ancient bucks, with young and slender girls, whose company they had purchased. The new-rich. Outside the new-poor, and the old-poor, the out-of-works, and the maimed beggars unheeded. Grind of brakes, a repulsive floating dust, inane giggle and whisky-bulged eyes, a tawny stain hung in the sky.

BACK TO DEVON

A child tried to pick my pocket. I caught him. He whined. I gave him sixpence and he ran away jeering. Still, I pitied him, the peaky-faced, tattered mite, and I cursed London, the hothouse that had withered that frail blossom of childhood.

And so, with a mournful fatigue, I went back to Devon. The sight of green and red fields filled me with ecstasy. I was a coward but to remain in London meant a broken heart and a throbbing head.

A bottle-green dusk brimmed the valley as I alighted from the train. Here was peace and tranquility, the sweet smile of a winter's eve. I paused in the lane to hear the rustle of the rufous mice as they searched the hedge-bottoms. Afar the tide droned around the headland, and Hartland Point lighthouse flared with sudden crimson.

As I neared Scarecrow Cottage my spirit rushed up to the stars and fled along their golden trackways. Sirius burst into a molten flame of scarlet, then lanced a blue ray at me. I saw Aldebaran, the dull red Bull's Eye, and Capella, like a sulphur jewel in the zenith. I hooted for my owls, and a mellow plaint answered.

OUR PRICELESS GIFTS

Yak-yak-urik the beautiful phantoms called, fluttering like enormous moths round my head. I heard a sudden clangour of barking; my faithful spaniels giving tongue! Then they rushed round the corner, leapt up at me, spattered me with mud—the dear, ruddle Devon mud—whined and yowled, telling me they loved me, how they had missed me; but never reproaching me for my treachery.

I lit a roaring fire of logs, and cooked the supper. They ate it out of one big basin, revelling in stew of rabbits, fish, and potatoes.

Afterwards we all mused. The hours sank away, and the time of Santa Claus' visitation drew on. I had no presents for them. I had none for myself—no one comes to Scarecrow Cottage. Perhaps . . . but that belongs to the dead past, and howsoever one is ravaged or heart-broken, there is always remaining the will-to-be-brave.

I pondered what present my old birds and animals would have preferred, and then I knew: I was their lord returned, and in me was their happiness: and my happiness was in serving and caring for my dependants. Those were our priceless gifts to each other.

The Woman of Scarecrow Cottage

Readers of the "Sunday Express" will remember that Mr. Williamson retired to his country cottage in an endeavour to escape from the world. Even here in his hermitage he is not left undisturbed; and to-day Mr. Williamson tells how his placid existence was ruffled by an unexpected visitor.

To most men come at different times in their lives visions and exaltations of the spirit. There have been many dreams in Scarecrow Cottage, where I live alone in harmony with my owls, my crow and seagull, and my animals. The spaniels are a comfort to my loneliness; they come and lay their loving heads on my knee, and their eyes tell me their worship.

My otter likes me, so does Mewliboy, the buzzard. I love them—and I try to make them fill my heart. All my plans for a happy, primitive life, alone with the sun and the wind, the wild flower and the star, are broken, for an angel has visited Scarecrow Cottage, has filled it with radiance, and departed, leaving me miserable and brooding.

BY MY FIRESIDE

Last night I had a jolly fire, because there has been a wreck recently, and much good wood has been left by the tide. The pot, slung on its chain, was boiling. The kittens purred on my lap, the dogs sprawled on the hearthrug—two corn sacks sewn together. Jackdaw on the bookshelf asleep, magpies outside somewhere, herring gull, as usual, on the cask of berry wine (guarding it from the carrion crow, who is inclined towards drunkenness, I fear). Roar of flames up the wide chimney.

A white beam swung through the window and swept the wall. I went to the door and saw a motor-car at the borrom of my "tater-patch". Some one got out, opened the gate, and came slowly through the cabbages. The wind was chilling, and a flurry of snow was in the air.

She was nervous when she saw me. Perhaps my manner rebuffed her, for I said formally that it was kind of her to come to pay me a visit; kinder still to have brought a basket of bones for the spaniels.

I asked her to come in and sit down. In the flame-light I could see that she had a sweet face, and her cheeks were like bramble-blossom. She told me timidly that she had determined to pay me a swift visit in her father's car. "I read your things in the 'Sunday Express'," she said. "I understand so well, really I do. I know your circumstances. . . . How you left London, I mean, and I thought . . . I thought . . . it is so brave of you."

She spoke like an eager schoolgirl. I watched her face as she sat by the fire. She did not look at me, but I could see her bright eyes and her smiling lips; she hugged the kittens and called them "sweet little things"; she stroked the long soft ears of my dogs, who tried to steal her gloves; she said that the place was untidy, and that the cobwebs should come down. She was quite firm about the cobwebs.

Dully I watched her and could say no word. I felt the desolation of the past years returned, and I resented her presence.

MEMORIES OF THE PAST

She gave the dogs the bones, and soon there was a merry cracking and gnawing, growling and spitting, wing-flapping and general rough-and-tumble. Moodily I stared in the red shell of fire, while purple and gold and blue flames licked the black pot.

She asked me questions about the owls, and I replied that each one caught thirty mice a night. I tried to think of something else to say, but could not. We sat a short time in silence. I could see that she was disappointed.

"Once I knew a girl who was like my visitor," thought I, regarding her, "one who was so true to an ideal that she kept away from me in order that I might be a nobler man. Her vision of nobility was probably strongest when I was huddled on the stone seats of Waterloo Bridge at night."

DEAD DAYS

I have known good and bad, serious and frivolous girls. I have centred all my dreams on them (when I was younger), and once I nearly died. I'm not ashamed to tell you this. It is quite true, so why should I fear to tell it? I wrote a letter of farewell, and held my old service revolver to my head. Dully I hoped that my death would make the girl a better woman. But I was afraid. Poor little fool of an immature poet and dreamer I must have been!

As I mused by the fire everything returned—the accumulated effect of an adolescence spent at war, and its hideous aftermath of "peace" (O irony!), the loneliness, the desolation, the broken hopes, the tragedies of others that I could not help; add to these things a hateful existence in the ant-heap of London. As I mused my spirit cried out against the girl's visit. What right had she to come and be so kind, so tender, to look at me with her sweet maiden eyes of brown.

THE WOUNDED ROOK

I am like a rook that Farmer Civilisation has shot and hung up by its neck, left for dead, and then rescued by some little boy with a soft heart and a naturalist's eye, who wonders if it would be nicer to have it cooked, stuffed, or kept as a pet. I am shot, and I have crawled away to die in the remote country—to die as far as civilisation is concerned.

Leave me to hang by the neck; don't take me down and stroke my head, and mutter with wet eyes, "Poor thing." Leave me. I shall soon die, and be a hideous warning to other young men who feel they must break away from the hypocrisy, the sordidness, the spirit-crushing sameness of life. My brothers are in the tumuli on the old hills, ancient Britons interred there because they wanted to be with the wind and the harebells; and my other brothers are interred on the hills of Picardy.

My visitor, who came with joyous heart, left subduedly, disillusioned. She will not come again to Scarecrow Cottage. If she reads this, I hope she will understand, and leave the shot rook to hang.

The Day's Round at Scarecrow Cottage

Town dwellers may wonder how the voluntary exile in the country fills up his days. Mr. Williamson in the following article shows that he has not many wasted moments in the twenty-four hours.

Every moment in Scarecrow Cottage is valuable. So joyful is existence now the chains of convention, routine, and London are knocked off, that life is intensive and its enjoyment a thing of spontaneity. The moment that passes without consciousness of time is happiness. In the cities clocks tick off tame hours of wasted sunshine and iterated labour; down here in Devon my clock is nature's clock—the sun.

Here is the daily task in Scarecrow Cottage. When a pale light explores the room, invariably I awake. Somewhere outside rasps the hoarse scream of a stag-bird. (This is Devon for cockerel.) It is dawn, the time when wild creatures wake and begin their search for food. I am a wild creature, and have to get my food like "Poor Tom" in "King Lear".

Perhaps you can imagine me leaping from my bed of bracken and sacks, fully dressed, rushing downstairs, and out into the cold dawn, seizing a hunting spear and pursuing the hedgehog, the frog, the rat, and other small deer? Nothing of the sort.

When Stag-bird shrills in the grey light I wake up; I yawn; then I turn in the bracken, pull my sheepskins over my uncovered toes, and muse.

MOTIONLESS SPECTRES

After a while everything in the room is visible. On the beams over my head are white, still things. They look like moths with their wings ripped off. They never move. They have heart-shaped faces, long and thin, and yellow backs speckled with ash-brown. On the beam they doze away the day, motionless and apart from life. My beautiful, mystic owls!

Of course, my three spaniels are in bed with me. And my two kittens. But not the buzzard hawk, Mewliboy. He sleeps in the oven downstairs—a cavernous hole beside the hearth, and long since disused. Diogenes, the carrion crow, sleeps on a chair back, and Zoë, the otter, lives in an outhouse, a wild thing, nervous and shy, yet fierce and very strong.

Well, Stag-bird (beastly cocky little creature, lord of dust heaps and dingy Orpingtons!) having crowed himself silly, I fall asleep once more. I awake some time later, and upbraid the dogs and cats for being so lazy. I pitch them out, and they promptly creep back again. I pitch them out once more; they yawn, stretch their legs; then begins the morning scratch (of the animals, I mean).

Downstairs there is an enormous pot. Our food. Containing rabbits, hedgehogs, potatoes, beans, peas, oatmeal, carrots, parsnips, a conger eel or two, and anything else that comes to hand. Once, I suppose, I was fastidious and finnicky—the idea of hedgehogs would have appalled me. You try them yourself, and I bet you will want more.

After breakfast we clean up, and sweep with a besom broom; we shake the blankets (these being sacks, newspapers, and sheepskins). Newspapers are great things for lighting fires and for use as blankets. Did you know this? I give the tip without fee.

IN THE LANES

Zoë clears off to her woodshed. The crow, the buzzard, and the other birds fly away on their own business, or sit in the elms and cheek the rooks who are now noisy at their old nests. The seagull creeps into Mewliboy's oven for warmth. The kittens go to sleep on my little bookshelf. I go for a walk with my dogs. How they leap and bark in the lanes, and explore the rabbit holes! How blue the frosty sky and the cold sea. From the solitude of the hills I can look westwards to where sea and sky are fused together. The sun of winter sparkles the rime on grass-blade and blackthorn, already a lark is singing high in heaven, the gorse bloom is yellow in sheltered hollows. Flocks of goldfinches rise with drumming wings from old thistle-heads, their sweet twitterings and reedy notes of song telling of the spring that will soon bring the blossom to the apple trees and love to their little hearts.

CONGER EELS AND WHIST

Sometimes I go fishing for conger eels. At night I play whist in the inn with my human friends, and quaff with them the tawny home-brew. Often we talk; and their talk is better than the talk of townspeople. They know much more, their brains are more resourceful. It is not the "chawbacon" who is a "girt vool", or wooden-pated, but the Londoner. Even the great writers of fiction do not seem able to create a *real* countryman. You've got to live with them, and share their hopes and sorrows, to know them even partially. It is the Devon labourer who has restored my faith in humanity.

Later on, if "Barkis is willing", I will tell you how.

'Ham': Henry Williamson's Village in the 1920s

Peter Lewis

The village of Georgeham near Braunton in North Devon is a central element in the life and writings of Henry Williamson. This examination of the village is offered as a background guide to our understanding of the *Village* writings.

Henry Williamson moved to Georgeham from his childhood home in London in March 1921, and lived there until 1929, when he moved to Shallowford, a hamlet near South Molton about twenty miles due east, where he lived until 1937, when he bought a farm at Stiffkey on the north coast of Norfolk. Although he returned to live in Georgeham in 1946 and lived there almost until his death in 1977, it is his first period in the village which is the subject of this article.

Williamson tells us in a preface to *The Old Stag* (1926) that the editor of a London magazine had said to him in 1924, 'But surely in your village and round about are many happy people, who still believe in romance and clean, healthy living. Why not write about them? Why waste ink and paper, why burn the midnight oil writing about animals? I feel it is a tragedy – a waste of a real talent.' Well, Williamson did go on to write about his fellow villagers in due course. Although they were not very happy about it at the time, it was gradually come to terms with as time passed.

Country villages and the people who lived in them featured in nearly all of Henry Williamson's books – nothing is more natural, or inevitable, than that Georgeham and its inhabitants should have inspired him. The main protagonists of most of his books, if indeed not all of them, are clearly autobiographical – the 'H.W.' of Skirr Cottage in the Devon village (never named) in *The Sun in The Sands* (1945), 'Willie Maddison' in Scur Cottage at 'Speering Folliot' in Devon and 'Phillip Maddison' in 'Valerian Cottage' at 'Malandine' are all of course Williamson himself at Skirr Cottage in Georgeham, Devon. Even the village of 'Rookhurst' in Dorset, the home of the 'Maddison' family in *The Flax of Dream* and the *Chronicle of Ancient Sunlight* novels probably has an element of Georgeham in its makeup.

Up until now it has not been clear why Williamson came to Georgeham. This is addressed in Anne Williamson's biography *Henry Willliamson, Dreamer of Devon* (Alan Sutton, 1995). It is understood that one of his aunts lived in the area, and he spent a wonderful holiday at Ham in 1914 – in May, according to the story 'First Day of Spring' in *The Village Book*, and in the same story we are told that he spent his leave there, with a friend, in 1916.

After demobilisation from the army in 1919, and a short-lived career as a journalist in London, Williamson resolved to earn his living as a writer, and rode down to the West Country on his motor cycle in March 1921, aged 25, where he rented a small thatched cottage below the church at Georgeham for £5 a year which was about two shillings a week – 10p in today's money! The cottage, once called Church Cottage, was renamed Skirr Cottage by Williamson after the noise made by the barn owls who lived in the roof. Within a few months his first novel, *The Beautiful Years*, the first book of *The Flax of Dream* tetralogy (the story of 'Willie Maddison') was published. In 1922, *The Lone Swallows*, a collection of nature stories, was published and also the second of the *Flax of Dream* books, *Dandelion Days*. In 1923 *The Peregrine's Saga* (more nature stories) was published, and in 1924 *The Dream of Fair Women*, the third novel. It was at this time that he began *Tarka the Otter*, not published until 1927, after having been rewritten several times. And also in 1924, Williamson started writing his fourth novel, *The Pathway*.

In May 1925 he married Ida Loetitia Hibbert, a Devon girl, and soon afterwards moved to the nearby Vale House (since renamed Crowberry Cottage), rented from Aubrey and Ruth Lamplugh. The following year their first child William ('Windles') was born, and *The Old Stag* (nature stories) was published. In August 1927 the immensely successful *Tarka the Otter* was published – this book won the prestigious Hawthornden Prize in 1928 which enabled the writer to complete the purchase of his beloved field at Ox's Cross, above Georgeham, for a total price of £125. In 1929 he built a wooden hut there, which was to be his Writing Hut. (The adjacent 'studio' was not built until 1953, and belongs to his later period.)

Georgeham is a small ancient village in north Devon, a mile or so from the sea. It lies in a saucer-like depression, at the head of a valley, 250 feet above sea level, although its highest point, Ox's Cross, is at 600 feet. A small stream runs through the centre of the village on its short journey to the sea, where it loses itself in the golden sands of Croyde Bay. The inhabitants in the 1920s earned their living, as they had for centuries, from fishing in the nearby estuary, farming the rich red Devon soil, and labouring in the local stone quarries; their social life centred about the church, chapel, the two inns and the village Institute (built 1926), not necessarily in that order! There was no gas, electricity, mains water or sewerage. Communications were poor – there was no railway, and the narrow twisting sunken lanes turned to red mud in winter and dust in summer, being quite unsuitable for the omnibuses and charabancs which were beginning to grope their way towards the remote West Country beaches after the Great War.

Georgeham was always 'Ham' in Williamson's fiction, as indeed in the 1920s it was known, and still is to a certain extent, to the villagers. It had in fact once been called Hamme, an old word for low-lying ground, which described Georgeham, of course, lying below its steep hills. In the story 'Washing Day' in *The Village Book* (1930), Williamson, atop the 14th century tower of St George's church, relishing the sounds and smells of his beloved village, describes what he sees:

> *The village lies below, formless and casual in winter, with dark brown thatch, uneven slopes of worn slate roofs, new red tiles, and pink asbestos roofs. Gradually the eye from this clear loftiness traces the shape of the village, which lies under the green hills, at the head of a valley. The valley opens into the sea a mile and a half to the south-west. Cottages and bungalows, cob and stone and brick and corrugated iron – ancient and modern – stand beside the roads, which reveal the village as in shape like an old-fashioned swan-neck spur. The slightly hollow space between the higher and lower lanes is divided by a stream, down to which slope the ragged and flat winter gardens, with their old pails and boxes; tubs; oval baths, broken and rusty, hiding early rhubarb; dung heaps; fruit trees lichened and dishevelled with wild wood, gnarled and blighted, never sprayed, never pruned.*

The tower that loomed over Skirr Cottage, with its bats, owls and screaming swifts, and of course its bells, often featured in Williamson's stories. If one climbs the tower steps and peers into the gloomy bell-chamber,[1] one can see the great tenor bell, said to weigh over a ton, inscribed 'My morning ring *doth* call them in', which was installed in 1926 as recorded by Williamson who was there, in a story called 'Surview and Farewell' in *The Labouring Life* (1932). It seems that he had been invited to suggest a suitable inscription for this, the largest of the eight bells (there had previously been six), and had submitted 'My iron tongue doth bid men come', which was rejected, he said, in favour of 'My morning ring *shall* call them in'. How marvellous it would have been if his words had been accepted, and now hung over his village, albeit in the dark, for a few more centuries. But through his books silver tongue still bids men come to Ham. Standing in the silent dust and cobwebs of that ancient bell-chamber from which for hundreds of years the giant bells have boomed over the medieval village below, one recalls the poignant story of Willie Maddison and Mary Ogilvie in the bell-tower of St Sabinus Church in Speering Folliot, in chapter five of *The Pathway*. This is where Williamson had imagined that they had once stood. On one bell Willie made out "Religion, death and pleasure make me sing". 'No, don't,' whispered Mary to Willie who had seized her, 'the ringers will be here soon.' They scrambled up the rest of the steps to the top of the tower, where vertigo quickly dampened Willie's ardour. From here, Williamson would have seen the whole village in which he lived from 1921 to 1929 and again from 1945 to 1975. Below him in the shadow of that old grey tower lay the tiny dark damp thatched cottage to which he had moved from a London suburb, and to which he brought his bride in 1925. Near the foot of the tower today is the dark blue slate which marks his final resting place.

On a map of Georgeham dated 1839, which I have seen, many of the buildings around the church have what appear to be dates alongside them, which may indicate when they were built – for instance, the school building 1826, the Rectory 1803, Crowberry Cottage (Vale House) 1829, Vale Cottage 1810, the blacksmith's forge 1833, part of the church 1835, and the cottages which include Skirr Cottage 1787. If these dates are correct it would seem that Williamson's claim somewhere that his cottage had been built in the time of King John (*c.* 1215) may be somewhat exaggerated! Incidentally, the map and later maps show that a Mr Winner owned property in Ham – we remember that the proprietor of Comfort House (Richard and Betty Maddison's first home in London) of whom we read in *The Dark Lantern* (1951) pp. 364-366 and 381-386 is a Mr Winner!

The village inns, the King's Arms and the Rock Inn,[2] called by Williamson the 'Lower House' and the 'Higher House', respectively, as well as their landlords and regular patrons, were freely interchangeable in his fiction. The Lower House appeared often as the 'Nightcrow Inn', but the interior of the Nightcrow Inn as illustrated by C.F. Tunnicliffe in the story of 'Redeye' in *The Old Stag* (1926) is obviously the bar of the Rock Inn, with its American wall clock and small inset cupboard in the corner (both still there).

The landlord of the Rock Inn, whose real name was Albert Jefferey, was portrayed as Albert Gammon, the landlord of the Nightcrow Inn in *The Dream of Fair Women* (1924), and as Albert Hancock in the *Village* stories. The Nightcrow Inn itself was moved around from village to village at the whim of its creator!

Williamson's readers can sit in the King's Arms and the Rock Inn today and recapture the atmosphere which so enthralled him seventy years ago, but not many will know that there were at one time two other public houses in Georgeham besides these well-known institutions, namely the Ring o'Bells and the Victoria Inn. Both however had ceased to trade well before Williamson came to Ham. In common with most public houses of the 19th century these inns brewed their own beer and cider, particularly cider in Devon. The Ring o'Bells, where cider was made in an outbuilding in the garden (called Scamps Garden, after Mr Scamps the farmer, where now are the eight new houses called Williamson Close), was situated at West End Farm, now no longer a farm – it seems that the farmer was also a publican. West End is at the lowest part of the village (Netherhams) called locally 'the Dip'. Williamson must have known that West End had once been the Ring o'Bells, and although this is not an unusual name for pubs in Devon, we remember that the pub in 'Malandine' is the Ring of Bells, and this is a further clue that 'Malandine' was modelled upon Georgeham. Members will recall the hilarious story 'Devonshire Cider' in *The Labouring Life* (and *Life in a Devon Village*) where Williamson made his own barrel of cider in a 'barn', not identified. But in the story 'The Life of a Stream' in the same books the writer tells us that it was at West End that he had made his first (and last) barrel of cider.

The Victoria Inn had once been called Church House, where beer had been brewed and sold, the profits going to church funds. When the Victoria Inn ceased to trade it became Victoria House (or possibly Victoria House had become the Victoria Inn). It is thought that the outbuilding where the beer was brewed had at one time been the village mortuary. Victoria House/Inn is now 'Millies Tea Rooms' (or lately, Millies Cottage), directly along the road from the King's Arms.

In 1929, Vale House (Crowberry Cottage) proved to be too small for the writer's growing family. *The Pathway* had not been well received by the Rector,[3] Williamson's friend, and had been criticised in *The Church Times* because of the unorthodox religious views expressed by the novel's semi-autobiographical protagonist, 'Willie Maddison'. There was also some little difficulty over the mild vandalising of the village sign by Williamson and his friends.[4] Williamson tells us in chapter one of *A Clear Water Stream* (1958) that in 1929 he 'had wanted to escape from the noises of a village about which he had written all he knew in two books'.[5] 'Tarka' and 'Willie Maddison', too, had been laid to rest. In October the family moved to Shallowford, near Filleigh, Devon.

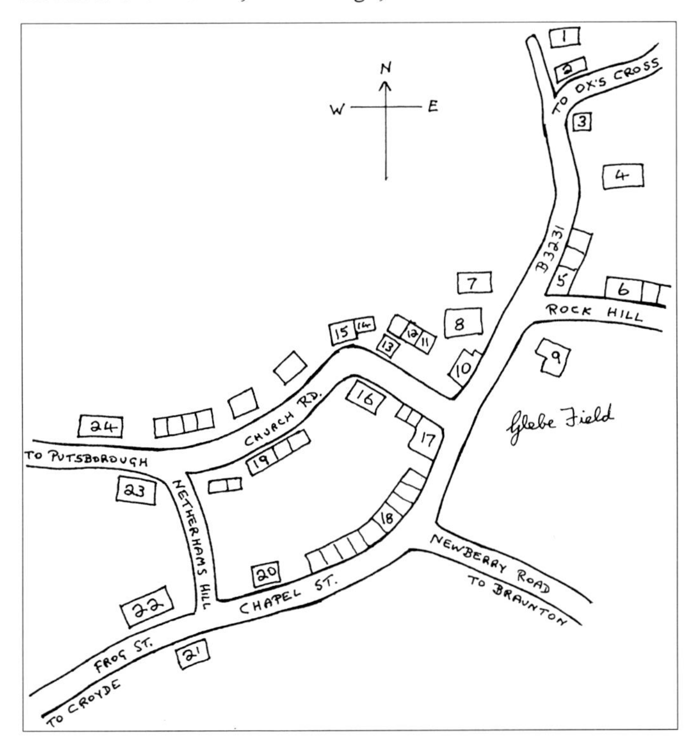

1. Kentisbury Cottage
2. Incledon Farm
3. the Well
4. Incledon House
5. Post Office/butcher's
6. Rock Inn
7. the Rectory
8. St George's Church
9. coach house/stables
10. Victoria House/Inn/'Millies'
11. Skirr Cottage
12. Clare Cottage
13. Vale Cottage
14. Billy Goldworthy's barn
15. Crowberry Cottage
16. Foote Farm (Hole Farm)
17. King's Arms
18. Faulkners (Village) Stores
19. Barn Guest House
20. Chapel/Baptist church
21. Blacksmith's
22. Village Institute (Hall)
23. West End Farm ('Ring o'Bells')
24. School

Before discussing Williamson's characters in detail, let us turn to another writer who lived for a short time in Georgeham, R.W. Thompson, who fell in love with the village and its people, and wrote a book called *Home in Ham* (1938), thereby affording a fascinating glimpse of Georgeham only a few short years after Williamson's first time there, during which little or nothing had changed. Strangely, perhaps, although the writers were well known to each other, neither mentions the other in his books – Williamson did not actually live in Ham when Thompson was there. (In chapter three of Thompson's book Mrs Thorne, his prospective landlady, tells him in a disapproving tone, 'There was another author in the village,' although possibly this could have referred to the American writer Negley Farson, who lived for eighteen years at nearby 'Vention').

When Thompson first moved to Georgeham he rented from Aubrey and Ruth Lamplugh a corner cottage with a stone garden wall that buttressed the hillside against the road. From a tiny balcony he could look up the lane along by the churchyard wall to the sign of the King's Arms across the way. Farmer Norman (of Foote Farm) lived across the road. The cottage, of course, was Vale House – Crowberry Cottage; strangely, too, neither Williamson nor Thompson ever refers to it by name. Williamson preferred his readers to believe that he had lived all his time at Ham in Skirr Cottage.

Thompson found Georgeham to be a happy place with its 'cottages rambling up and down the slopes of the sheltering hills around the grey stone tower of the church which was the heart and body of Ham'. In chapter six he discusses briefly the history of Ham provided for him by the Rector. Hama was the Saxon word for homestead and when the church gathered a village around it the Hama became Hamme, dedicated to St George – Hamme Sancti Georgii, its name in the 13th century. When a Rector tried to rename the village Ham St George he found the change was stoutly resisted by the villagers, including Williamson.[6]

Thompson was a regular patron of the King's Arms and was friendly with the landlord and proprietor Charlie Ovey and his popular Missus. The bar parlour regulars were Tom Willis and his son Alwynne, Percie, old Brownie (William Brown) and his son Alec, Jack Bourchier and Stanley, all glad to see the summer visitors go so that they could settle down by the firesides of their beloved pubs to enjoy a song or wo and a game of table skittles. Alwynne Willis lived next door to the Rock Inn and played skittles there with Butch (Arty) Thomas. Alwynne took Thompson around Baggy Point to the great cave there called Baggy Hole which was supposed to be inaccessible.

Thompson soon moved to Kentisbury Cottage in Higher Ham, rented from old Mrs Thorne (Mrs Jonathan Furze in Williamson's stories). He was introduced to Cap'n Chichester, a patron of the Rock Inn, and was invited on a trip on the Cap'n's ketch Enid from Appledore to Braunton Pill after which they visited the Mariners' Arms (my favourite pub in Braunton). On the walls are photographs of old Braunton, the lighthouse at Crow Point demolished in 1960, the isolation hospital ship moored there in 1895 which had become a hulk in Williamson's time – the ketch Enid, the stranded whale, etc. Charlie Ovey took Thompson to Barnstaple Fair, fully described by Williamson in his story 'The Fair' in *The Village Book* (and *Life in a Devon Village*), and they visited the boxing booths well known to Charlie, himself a retired professional boxer. (Williamson described one of the boxers as Boy Ovey from Cardiff.) While strolling around Baggy, Thompson saw the whale skull displayed on the greensward on the southern slopes with its great eye-sockets. Some bones are still there, protected by the National Trust. He tells us that it was Tom Willis and Aubrey Lamplugh who formed the first soccer teams in Georgeham in the 1930s – see the many photographs on the Walls of the Rock Inn. He tells us too of how Stanley of the King's Arms sang 'Will the Weaver', an old village ballad (sung by Gammon the blacksmith in Williamson's story 'The Village Inns' in *The Village Book*, during the amazing Rabbit Supper, and also by old Brownie in *The Dream of Fair Women*, chapter twelve).

Thompson and his wife went to South America in 1938, leaving their children in a school in Ilfracombe, and finally left Georgeham in 1941.

David Stokes, veteran HW Society member, lived with his parents at Incledon Farm House from 1936 to 1951 and so was a neighbour when Williamson returned to live at Ox's Cross in 1946. He was also contemporary with R.W. Thompson. In October 1984 Stokes led Society members around Georgeham, and recalled his life and times there, 'scratching only the surface'.[7]

Stokes referred to Mr Gammon the blacksmith whose Smithy was opposite the Institute (now thankfully called the Village Hall). He pointed out the Barn Guest House where fat German visitors used the sunbathing and nudist club there behind a twenty-foot fence, and referred to the cider-drinking prowess of the villagers in his day. He mentioned the lovely tall elms around the churchyard, alas no more, but some of the stumps are still there (1955). The felling of the fifteen trees was witnessed by Williamson, who described it in his story 'The Sawyers' in *The Village Book*. Stokes pointed out Foote Farm opposite Skirr Cottage and noted that a Mr Norman still farmed there (still there in 1955). In Williamson's time, he said, a Mr Lovering farmed there – he was the 'Stroyle George' in Williamson's story 'A Farmer's Life' in *The Village Book*. In the village stories Foote Farm was 'Hole Farm'. (R.W. Thompson in chapter six of *Home in Ham* talks of Tetbald a local landowner after the Conquest being known as the Lord of Hola, which has become Hole.[8] Stokes referred to the King's Arms being Williamson's Lower House or Nightcrow Inn, and the landlord as being Charlie Ovey, an ex-boxer. The front door in the 1930s faced the church, but this door is now partly bricked up, being now the middle window of three. The gentlemen patrons emerging from this door at closing time relieved themselves against the churchyard wall opposite, much to Williamson's disgust. (The villagers also threw all sorts of rubbish into the stream running past his cottage and through the village in spite of his repeated protests.)

David Stokes mentioned that a Mr Hyde (a retired barrister who lived with his sister at what was until recently Baggy Hotel) had given land for the new extension to the churchyard and was in fact the first to be buried in it. The story of the new cemetery is told by Williamson in 'Cemetery or Burial Ground', and of its consecration in 'Consecration of The New Burial Ground', both in *The Labouring Life*. In the latter story the elderly Bishop Trefusis, white head bowed, murmurs, 'I, who am old, and soon to die, have seen the graves of those I have buried pass away in time, forgotten or lost, until nothing is left but grass, and a lessening mound. Such is God's intention for all living things: to be, to bloom, to mingle in earth and air, in the hope and faith of resurrection in radiance beyond the hills of our mortal mornings grey.' This simple message is very poetic. The sexton, added Stokes, was a Clibbert Thomas caricatured by Williamson as Old Clibb, and also as Jan Mules in *The Flax of Dream* novels.

Stokes pointed out the corner building at the foot of Rock Hill as having been the village shop, butchers and Post Office run by Arty Thomas (Clibb's brother) and his wife and daughter Zilla. Sheep and pigs were slaughtered on the premises. There was a public water pump outside used by the gossiping village women, most of whom had no running water, electricity, bathrooms or toilets in their homes. The Rock Inn further up the hill (called Stony Hill by Williamson), Stokes said, had been greatly enlarged since the 1930s, but the front door was still the same. It still contained photographs of Old Browner (William Brown, but Gammon in the stories). Past the pub had lived Middy Hancock with her twelve children, all named after national disasters! He said that Jacob Thorne occupied Incledon House in the 1930s (in the *Village* stories 'Jonathan Furze' lived at 'Inclefell'). A fine avenue of elm trees, now gone, had lined the main road.

The main character in the four books that made up Williamson's *Flax of Dream* tetralogy is 'Willie Maddison', born in December 1896 at Rookhurst, Dorset. In the third novel *The Dream of Fair Women* (1924) we find Willie, in April 1920, in north Devon, renting a dilapidated cottage, called 'Rats' Castle' by the villagers, at Shelley Cove (perhaps Croyde), near Braunton. The village pub is the Nightcrow Inn, the landlord Albert Gammon. The bar, with its dark beams and smoke-yellow ceiling, is lit by a paraffin lamp hung on a bent nail beside the small American wall clock. Wooden benches are placed around a polished table, the beer being fetched from the barrel room. A regular patron is William (Brownie) Brown who has a glass eye. The pub is of course the Georgeham King's Arms, whose landlord was Albert Jefferey.

Willie has two spaniels (one called Billjohn), an otter cub and other pets. He uses Vention sands at 'Bag Leap' to bathe. He meets Mrs Evelyn Fairfax. Eventually he goes to Folkestone to continue his liaison with Evelyn, and later to Rookhurst to visit his widowed father. He drinks at the local pub, the King's Arms, then goes back to Folkestone to finish his book, *Policy of Reconstruction*. Three years later, after living in London and working in France as a labourer attached to the War Graves Commission, he returns to north Devon and in *The Pathway* takes up with the Ogilvie family of Wildernesse, a grey thatched manor/farmhouse near the Braunton Burrows, in the parish of 'Speering Folliot'. He rents a small damp thatched cottage, below the church wall, which had been empty for some time. It was called Scur Cottage and rented at £4 a year from 'cousin Billy's widow'. The end wall of Scur Cottage could be seen through the elm trees above the western wall of the churchyard. Fifty yards from the cottage is a pub, The Plough. The church at 'Speering Folliot' is 'St Sabinus', a sister church of St Brannock, Braunton. The vicar is the Reverend Aubrey Garside, a forty-year-old bachelor who had until recently been a curate in a northern suburb of London.

After a very moving romance with Mary Ogilvie whom he had known when a child, Willie was sent packing by Mary's mother who disapproved of him. He walked to Crow Point to be ferried across to Appledore to begin his long lonely walk to London. The salmon boats had just stopped operating for the season – no boat picked him up from the 'Sharshook Ridge' in the estuary, and he was drowned by the incoming tide.

The 'Sharshook Ridge' is often mentioned in Williamson's fiction, and on the river trip on a sand-barge, organised by the HW Society in October 1987, the skipper pointed it out. He said it was called Shellock Ridge, and he indicated its approximate position (it was covered by water at the time) very near the Appledore shoreline. He thought it extremely unlikely that anyone could walk or even swim to it from Crow Point, the currents being very fast and dangerous as we saw for ourselves.

'Phillip Maddison' is the main protagonist of Williamson's immense fifteen-volume *Chronicle of Ancient Sunlight.* In chapter two of *The Innocent Moon* (1961) (practically a rewrite of an earlier novel, *The Sun in The Sands* published in 1945 but written mostly in 1934, in America), 'Phillip' takes a holiday at 'Malandine' in south Devon, undoubtedly modelled upon Georgeham. For the first two nights he stays at the Post Office (when Williamson first went to Georgeham he stayed at the Post Office). He then rents 'Valerian Cottage' at £5 a year. This cottage has, like Skirr Cottage, one room downstairs and two upstairs. Valerian Cottage has no gas, electricity or water. The time is June 1920. His immediate neighbours are Mr and Mrs Walter Crang and a small child, drawn directly upon Mr and Mrs 'Revvy' Carter who lived at Clare Cottage next door to Skirr Cottage at Georgeham. The village pub is the Ring of Bells. In chapter seven of *The Innocent Moon* 'Richard Maddison' tells his son Phillip, who has been out of work for eighteen months after leaving the army, to 'leave the house at once'. (This was of course the fate of the writer himself.) Phillip rode down to Malandine on his motor cycle in April 1921, aged twenty-six, and took up residence in the thatched Valerian Cottage for which he had paid a year's rent ten months before. 'How wonderful to be living in such a romantic place. London was of another world, gone forever.' In chapter ten Phillip meets his future wife, then a fifteen-year-old schoolgirl, Barley Lushington, staying with her mother at Verbena Cottage (there is a Verbena Cottage in Georgeham, some fifty yards from Skirr Cottage). Most of the characters in *The Innocent Moon* first appear in *The Sun in The Sands*, and the anonymous village where they live in *The Sun in The Sands* is clearly also 'Malandine'. Valerian Cottage is identical to Skirr Cottage in Ham. The better of the two pubs in Malandine, Phillip tells 'Julian Warbeck', is 'to the left when you get to the top of the street, and then first on the right up a short steep hill' – a glance at the map will show the route from Skirr Cottage to the Rock Inn at Ham. Phillip meets Barley again, while walking in the Pyrenees. They marry suddenly, Barley being just eighteen, and spend their honeymoon at Malandine. One year later (see *It Was the Nightingale* (1962) chapter four) Barley dies giving birth to Billy. Phillip moves out of Malandine at once, aged thirty; his tame otter escapes, and is seen no more.

In chapter seven of *The Phoenix Generation* (1965) we read that when Phillip had lived at Malandine he had bought a field above the village for £100, in which was a derelict linhay (cattle shed) which he converted into a 'studio', with sleeping accommodation. He planted trees to make a windbreak. He called this building, with its views of the distant sea, the 'Gartenfeste' (the Garden Strongpoint), and filled its lower room with bookshelves. The 'Gartenfeste' at Malandine is of course drawn directly on the field at Ox's Cross above Georgeham. Later still, in *Lucifer Before Sunrise* (1967) (chapters seven and eight), we read of Phillip going down to Malandine from Norfolk to cut timber from woodland near Malandine on which he had taken a ten-year lease in 1931. This episode is based on real life.

The Rector of Georgeham while Williamson was there in the 1920s (except for a few months in 1921) was the Rev. Alfred Rose, but I don't think that Williamson ever referred to him by name, in fact or fiction. We read a good deal about the Vicar of 'Speering Folliot', the Rev. 'Aubrey Garside', in *The Pathway*, but too little is known about the Rev. Rose to be able positively to identify him with his fictional counterpart in Speering Folliot. About the Rector of 'Ham', though, we read *inter alia* in the story 'On Scandal, Gossip and Hypocrisy Etc.' in *Life in a Devon Village* that he 'was new to the parish from a London suburb'.[9] We know from chapter six of *The Pathway* that the Vicar of Speering Folliot, too, came there from a London suburb, so it would seem that the Rector and the Vicar were one and the same. I believe that the Rector of Georgeham is portrayed, brilliantly, as the all-important Vicar of Speering Folliot in *The Pathway*, and the long but fruitless discussions about religion and philosophy between 'Willie Maddison' and the Rev. 'Garside' very possibly reflect similar conversations between Williamson himself and the Rev. Rose. When *The Pathway* was published in 1928, it may be that Mr Rose recognised himself and his beliefs (especially if he had 'come from a London suburb', for which we have no evidence) in the weak Rev. Garside and his feeble responses to Willie's radical outpourings, and this may account for the coolness that existed between Williamson and Mr Rose in 1929 before Williamson left the village. (Mr Rose himself left the village shortly after Williamson.)

The Vicar, hardworking and conscientious, sincere and willing to talk (but not too intelligently), tried hard to understand Willie but in the end urged him to abandon the material world, concentrate on his art and write about birds and their beautiful free lives in the sunshine. Mr Garside had been impressed but not converted. In chapter seven of *The Pathway* Willie tells Diana Shelley that Mr Garside thought him an idiot, and he agrees that he was indeed an idiot, to talk to him. In chapter 10 he tells her, 'Poor Garside, he hasn't the faintest glimmer of the historical Jesus,' and she responds, 'He's a half-wit.'

Williamson's *Village* stories were contained mainly in *The Village Book* (1930) and *The Labouring Life* (1932), and also in *The Peregrine's Saga* (1923), *The Old Stag* (1926) and *The Linhay on The Downs* (1934). In his 'Notes' in *The Village Book* and *The Labouring Life* Williamson strove, tongue in cheek, to assure his readers that 'his characters were not meant to represent any living persons, and the actions were imaginary; the books were imaginative work and should not be read as the history of any particular village, and certainly not of any man or woman'. These two books were in fact published after the writer had left Georgeham. Most of the characters of 'Ham' in the 1920s are now long departed this world, and their way of life has gone forever, but their names, changed, muddled, and only thinly disguised, have been marvellously immortalised by Williamson's pen. Many graves in the churchyards and cemeteries of Georgeham and neighbouring Croyde bear the names of the characters who appear in the *Village* stories – Gammons, Browns, Tuckers, Hancocks, Loverings, Badcocks, Zeales, and many others, about some of whom there follows a brief description as Henry Williamson, their friend and neighbour, saw them, with humour and compassion. These word-pictures (all the words are Williamson's, albeit scattered throughout his books and novels) of some of the indigenous folk of the village in the 1920s, are in no particular order of interest or importance – they all had lived, worked, talked, argued and drunk with Williamson, long ago, in Ham.

WILLIAM GAMMON, whose name in real life was William Brown, called Browner or Brownie, was the fifty-year-old father of ten sons and four daughters, of whom he was very proud; some of his descendants still live in Georgeham. He had been a stonemason for thirty-five years. He was the most popular man in the village, but he owned no property and was a grief to his tall handsome father John who thought him a poor stupid fellow. He was kind, gentle and sympathetic, with a sweet voice which sometimes became 'loud and groaning'. He was given to using bad language for which he was always apologising. He was a Celtic type, with a small head, hands and feet. He had black hair and a black moustache. A pink patch sometimes concealed an empty eye socket. In *Home in Ham* by R.W. Thompson the small sketch of Brownie shows a large moustache and a pipe but no eye patch, but this is clearly shown in the portrait and photographs on display in the Rock Inn.

In *The Dream of Fair Women* he is Billie (or Brownie) Brown, a man with a glass eye who on Sunday nights in the Nightcrow Inn wore his best outfit, an army tunic and a bowler hat. He was a man entirely without pretension, physical or spiritual, a man who had never saved a penny and passed most of his evening hours in the village pubs. He used to keep score for the table-skittle players and was rewarded with beer. David Stokes said that he had lived two doors up from the Rock Inn.

Brownie's wife said that he was a Methodist, and he admitted to being 'chapel through and through', although he did like to ring the tenor bell in church. One night at the Nightcrow Inn, wearing his bowler hat and partnering Willie Maddison at whist, he sang 'Will the Weaver', got drunk and took half an hour to get home. He was soundly scolded by his wife, a stout woman from Cardiff, whose Welsh blood, said Brownie, could make her 'speak politically (particularly) fierce'. Brownie's youngest son is 'Tikey', and his eldest daughter is Megan ('Revvy' Carter also had a daughter Megan), a tall girl of fifteen with dark eyes and adolescent figure. I believe this girl was Daisy Brown, a village beauty. In St George's cemetery (the 'extension') there lies a William Brown who died in 1957 aged eighty-four. This is almost certainly 'Brownie'.

TOM GAMMON (Tom Brown, brother of William) was a mason who had been born in the village and knew every tree and stone. He was a thin, blue-eyed, narrow-headed man, a generous spendthrift, proud of his many children. He lived a mere thirty steps up the hill from the Rock Inn (perhaps next door to Brownie). He kept lurcher dogs for poaching, and knew more about rabbits and ferrets than any other man in the parish. (Fitch is a country word for a ferret – possibly 'Tom Fitchey', owner of the dog Redeye in the story of that name in *The Old Stag* was Tom Gammon/Brown.)

JOHN GAMMON was Brownie's father. He had a handsome old face with a strong jaw, firm upper lip and 'John Bull' side whiskers. He was a splendid physical specimen of a man, hale and active at seventy-five. He had recently proposed marriage to a girl of eighteen. 'Heaven knows how many grandchildren and great-grandchildren he had in the district – over a hundred, it was said'. They were all vital, quick, passionate beings.

ERNEST GAMMON was another, younger brother of Brownie. He was a church warden, and never went near a pub. He was an employer of labour and an owner of increasing property. His eyes were always guarded and it was impossible to talk to him man to man. 'Poor brother Ernest', said Brownie, 'he hath no more voice than a dib-chick, he was always a timid boy.'

HARRY GAMMON was one of Brownie's sons. Now a mason, he had been seven years in the Army. He had a fat Maltese wife Emma, and a three-year-old son Henry, who was always being chastised by his mother. This small family moved into Skirr Cottage when the Williamsons moved to Crowberry Cottage. Emma eventually went mad and died in an infirmary. It was Harry Gammon who sealed up the entrance of the owls' nesting place under the thatch of Skirr Cottage, on the instructions of the owner.

TIKEY was yet another of Brownie's sons. Tikey was a bold, bad, brave boy. He stole Farmer Rodd's apples and then sold them to him to make cider (at West End Farm). He stole flowers from the graves in the churchyard and sold them to the living. He was merry, nervous and strong. His sister Marty was the girl hanging around the workmen in 'The Sawyers'. 'Marty' appears once or twice as Daisy, a real Brown, noted by both David Stokes and R.W. Thompson as a village beauty in later years.

ALBERT HANCOCK or ALBERT GAMMON, whose real name was Albert Jefferey, was the tenant and landlord of the Higher House (the Rock Inn), and sometimes landlord of the Nightcrow Inn which is sometimes identified with the Lower House (the King's Arms). He was a short sturdy little man, with a round face and small clipped moustache, face and elbows brown with the sun, forehead bald and shiny. He had an honest face, and had been born and bred in the parish, where everybody liked him. He was never quarrelsome, but quiet by nature, and thrifty, and wont to become quietly philosophical and poetic. He was a regular churchgoer. Every moment of living was a grand moment for Albert. There are one or two poor photographs of Albert in the Rock Inn – in one of them he is labelled as Nobby Jefferies. He had been a corporal in the North Devon Hussars, and as such he is addressed by Willie Maddison in *The Dream of Fair Women.* He worked in the fields until six o'clock, and was truly of the soil, having the natural courtesy and charm of a countryman. Albert Jefferey died in 1946, aged sixty-five, and lies in St George's cemetery.

ARTY BROOKING, whose real name was Arty Thomas (nicknamed 'Butch'), was the village grocer and butcher. Arty butchered animals on the premises, while his wife looked after the shop and his daughter Zilla sat behind the Post Office grille in the shop, which was on the corner of Rock Hill. It was Arty who fetched the eighteen-year-old Williamson from Braunton station when he first came to stay at Georgeham in 1914 – the boy Henry stayed at the Post Office/shop. Arty liked his pint of scrumpy (cider) and a game of skittles at the Rock when his day's work was done. Arty was a most amiable fellow. His older brother was Clibb the Sexton.

CLIB or CLIBB BROOKING, whose real name was Clibbert Thomas, was the village sexton and grave-digger for some fifty years. He doubled as a postman and chimney sweep. He also doubled as 'Jan (John) Mules' in the same role in 'Speering Folliot' (where Mrs Mules was the postmistress). In his spare time he tended the garden in the churchyard set up by Miss Hyde. He was a shy, thin, shambling figure, all elbows and knobbly fingers. He had close-cropped red hair and sandy eyelashes. He was gentle and tender-hearted, the most innocent man in the parish, too shy to look people in the eye.

STROYLE GEORGE was Farmer Lovering of Foote Farm (Hole Farm). Gaunt, worn, irritable, argumentative, deemed morose and bitter by many, his farm was failing. He was a lonely, solitary man, a widower. He was the best ploughman in the parish, but the worst farmer. He had side-whiskers and a nose like a sparrow's beak. His farm was too big for him, and his son, disabled, was unable to help, although little 'Boykins' Brown lived in the farmhouse and did odd jobs. When 'Stroyle' was unable to pay the rent the farm was auctioned and bought by Charlie Tucker. 'Stroyle' George's character was uncannily similar to that of 'Clibbet Kifft'.

CLIBBET KIFFT, original unknown, seems to have been another 'Stroyle George' type. He was a tall, thin farmer, with a red prominent nose, intensely blue wild bloodshot eyes, a loud cracked voice, and a small head on a scrawny neck which made him look like a woodpecker. He was 'a raving bliddy madman', dressed in ragged clothes. His father in Frogstreet Farm had thrashed him, and his own eldest son had run away from home. He had several children, and although kindly and generous when drunk, when sober he was violent with his children and farm animals. His wife left him, taking the children. For cruelty to the shaggy pony (which he rode bare-back about the village) he was sent to prison for seven days, and shortly afterwards, starving, a failed farmer, he shot himself. The story of his dog Ship ('Stroyle George's' dog was a Ship, too) in 'A Crown of Life' in *Tales of Moorland and Estuary*, cruelly beaten and starved by its master but faithful unto its own death in the church on Christmas Day, is particularly moving.[10]

MISS VIRGINIA GOFF was in real life the formidable Miss Hyde, who lived with her bachelor (or possibly widowed) brother, a retired barrister, in the big house (until recently the Baggy Hotel) on the flanks of Baggy, overlooking Croyde Bay. Her age uncertain, she was tall, with big hands, a thick figure with a brownish face. She walked with a man's stride. She was 'a big pillar of the church' in 'Speering Folliot'. She was the richest woman in the parish, and was the village benefactress. The people to whom she gave coal, food and money thought her 'a proper lady, real good to poor folk'. In the *Village* stories she is portrayed as Lady Maude Seeke (Hyde and Seeke!), or Lady Maude Bullace. She had a fur coat and with her own hands planted five hundred daffodil bulbs there. Her horticultural work in the churchyard was occasionally praised in the Rector's 'Monthly Bulletin'. (The churchyard is still full of daffodils and primroses.) It was Miss Goff who turned Mrs Ogilvie against Willie Maddison, and consulted her solicitors with a view to having Willie prosecuted under the Blasphemy Laws. Also, she had been appalled to see him (though her binoculars!) bathing naked with two small boys. The real Miss Hyde planted many trees and shrubs and built rustic bridges at Baggy to 'improve' the rugged landscape there.

WILLIAM (REVVY) CARTER of 'Ham' (and WALTER CRANG of 'Malandine'), real name William Gammon and his wife, known only as Mrs Revvy Carter, and their three children, Madge, Megan and Ernie, lived in Clare Cottage, next door to Skirr Cottage. (The three cottages which now constitute the row were clearly once four, two of them in recent years having been made into one – once there may have been five cottages, for there are still five chimneys.) William was a middle-aged farm labourer often out of work, a slow rheumatic fellow who wore a potato sack for an overcoat. Although the Carters pinched his coal and firewood and clogged up his drains, Williamson got on well with them. Little 'Ernie' was a great favourite of his. William was called 'Revvy' because he had once worked for his reverence the Rector.

GRANFER JIMMY CARTER was Revvy's father and therefore William Gammon's father in real life, who lived 'across the road' (this may have been opposite the church gate). He was old, bent double, happy in his garden, but miserable because he could no longer work. He was probably the James Gammon who died in 1925 aged seventy-nine, buried in St. George's churchyard. Granfer and Mrs Jimmy Carter looked after Babe (Vivian) Carter, Ernie's cousin, who had mysteriously 'appeared' in the village, aged two years.

WILLIAM (VANDERBILT) CARTER (real name Gammon) and his wife and spinster sister Bessie lived in the other thatched cottage, next door to their cousins 'Revvy' and his family. 'Vanderbilt' (so called because of his supposed wealth) was also variously known as Farmer Bill, Billy, Rumbling Willy and Thunderbolt!). He was club-footed and almost deaf. He was thrifty, stingy, shy, a 'proper miser'. He owned and worked a seven-acre field which he eventually sold for £300, supposedly in small silver. His wife was an elderly London woman with no children. It was rumoured that she had been 'found' through an advertisement in the 'Matrimonial Times'. She was a big-faced stupid woman, a little deaf, but she spoke' grammatically'. She had been a dressmaker at Croyde. Her sister-in-law quietly resented this 'new' woman in the family home. Bessie was a tall, thin, pale woman who ran the spotlessly clean dairy. She had woeful eyes, and walked stiffly with rheumatism, and spoke with 'craking' voice.

JOSEPH RUSH, a widower, lived alone in the cob cottage at right angles to the three cottages in which lived Williamson and the Gammons. The cottage is now called Vale Cottage – the bootscraper in the 'drang', about which we read in the story 'A Weed's Tale' in *The Peregrine's Saga* with its true-to-life illustration by Tunnicliffe, is still there. Known as Uncle Joe, he was seventy-one years old and had six sons. He was rheumatic and simple-minded. A retired railway porter from Bristol, he spoke with a slow, thick voice. A lonely figure, without cat or dog, he drank his fivepenny pint every night at the pub, his words not much heeded. He clipped his beard three times a year. His cottage was dark and rarely ventilated and smelled of musty wallpaper and mouldering clothes. His proposal of marriage to eighty-year-old Mrs Hector was promptly rejected. "Oo, well, tidden no odds," he said. When he died the cottage was bought for £250 by Sam Pidler, a retired coastguard, who rented it to the mysterious 'Captain' Cannon and his sinister Borstal-boy companion who was soon arrested by the village bobby, PC Bullcornworthy, a big man with a face like a large round cheese, admired by all.[11]

MUGGY, whose real name appears to have been John Smith, was better known as 'Muggy of Croyde'. He was a trapper and odd-job man. Williamson was proud to call him 'friend'. He was over seventy years old, with weather-worn face and hands. For generations, we are told, his family had lived in the 'village' – from the context of the passage I think the village was Croyde. He and his family before him had owned the Manor Inn at Croyde. 'Muggy' sold the inn and moved to America, coming back to Devon in his old age to live in a shanty. He had been in most places on earth, happy in the open air with his simple livelihood. He gathered and sold watercress, crabs and mushrooms, and acted as an agent for fertiliser firms and fire insurance companies. He was the most honest man in the village, and refused to repeat or listen to gossip. He delivered telegrams from the post office in Croyde, and was the best whist player in the 'Nightcrow' Inn. He was never without his stick and handyman's basket. He had no convictions about life, having outworn them all. His usual seat in the pub was the corner seat under the clock in the 'Higher House' (the Rock Inn). He died in August 1929.

ALICE (of 'Hole Farm') was the daughter of 'Stroyle George', so probably her real name was Alice Lovering. Aged twenty-seven, slightly built, hair drawn tightly back, she had been a shy little girl. She was a hard worker, and would not leave her widowed father and crippled brother. She was never unkind or angry, and was always ready with a smile and cheery words. We are not told what became of this small family when the farm was sold.

FARMER 'CHAMPION' HANCOCK was a strong and successful farmer, broad-bodied and ruddy-faced. He was married, with no children. He always wore a bowler hat and breeches with leather leggings. He used to tie his horse outside the Lower House (the ring is still there). He was a good business man.

COLONEL 'HARRY PONDE' was really Admiral Biggs, says David Stokes. Retired, he was a newcomer to the parish but was already a Parish Councillor (we remember that the parish consisted of Georgeham and Croyde). A stream ran through his property and with immense labour he made and maintained fish ponds by damming the stream (hence his name, of course). The Rector, who had called him Captain Ponde by mistake and annoyed him, hoped that he would stick to his mud and not go near him again. His house is now the beautiful thatched Kittiswell Hotel in Croyde.

REAR ADMIRAL BAMFYLDE, DSO, RN, RET'D, was not, as I once thought, drawn on the real Admiral Biggs. Admiral Bamfylde was the owner of Pidickswell Manor at Pidickswell (Pickwell). A bluff, red-faced man, who wore a monocle, he had a jovial word for everybody. He was unaffected and friendly. He was a District Councillor and a 'proper gennulman' – he was rich, generous and courteous to all.

CHARLIE TUCKER was a Parish Councillor and rate collector. He was a farmer and a master builder and carpenter. He was tall and strong, a rapid solitary worker. His only life was work. He lost his temper easily. He did not get on well with his wife, and they had no children. He bought Foote Farm (Hole Farm) when it failed.

BILLY GOLDSWORTHY, real name not known to me, was a dairy farmer aged about sixty-five. A bachelor, he lived with his widowed mother 'down by Zeales' (Netherhams Hill). He owned four acres and rented another farm. He owned the 'barn' attached to Crowberry Cottage (still there). He was a quiet little man (but made a lot of noise in his barn, even at night), lean, long-armed, with a greyish face, long nose and little eyes. He was a 'proper old owl', annoying the neighbours. He did not drink or go to church or chapel. His sister, after their mother's death, wore her mother's clothes, period 1880.

JONATHAN FURZE, real name Jacob Thorne, was a keen, energetic farmer. He was elderly (but only fifty-nine in 1925), with a nice expression, open and kind. He was a cheery hardworking yeoman whose fortune (he was the richest man in the parish) was based on industry and good judgement. He was quiet and aloof, and the biggest landowner in the parish, One-time Chairman of the Parish Council, he was 'chief' of the Chapel Brethren and did not smoke or drink. He had a rolling, unsteady gait. He was disliked in the village for he worked while others talked. His business and his pleasure (which were identical) was the buying and selling of bullocks. His was a prickly character at times, for it was said of him that he was 'furze by name and furze by nature'. Jacob Thorne of Incledon House died in 1935, aged sixty-nine.

CHARLIE TAYLOR, whose real name was Charlie Ovey, was the proprietor of the 'Lower House' (the King's Arms) which he bought for £450 in 1920. David Stokes described Ovey as a rugged individual who had been a professional boxer, and who owned a famous (fox) terrier called Mad Mullah which he used for badger hunting. In the *Village* stories Williamson tells us that Charlie had a 'prize-fighter's head'. He spent his money easily and used to sing in a high falsetto voice. Out of his joviality, anger and rage were liable to burst. He was one of the best skittles players in the parish. He could eat eels and pigs' trotters all day and all night! He always wore a cap on his mat of white hair. Thompson, in the 1930s, describes him thus: 'his face was square and strong, a rugged-hewn face. He had a great barrel of a chest, muscles like iron on his thick arms, gnarled like old trees – broad shoulders.' There is a good photograph of the real Charlie in *The Children of Shallowford* (1939). He stands behind his bar in the King's Arms, about 1936. Williamson had not liked him at first, and thought him a brutal and unimaginative boozer, but they became friends, and Charlie became mellow and humorous. In the story 'The Fair Morning' in *The Labouring Life*, one of the champions at the boxing booths was 'Boy Ovey' from Cardiff.

In the story 'The Epic of Brock the Badger' in the first illustrated edition of *The Old Stag* published in 1933, the badger-digging landlord of the local pub (the Rising Sun at Colham) is Mr Tinker (Tinker, Taylor?) whose bar, illustrated by Tunnicliffe, is obviously the bar of the King's Arms in Georgeham, as photographed in *The Children of Shallowford.* Among the 'sportsmen' in 'The Epic' are a Charlie and a Mr Ovey and a Mr Corney whose terrier is called the Mad Mullah! In the story 'The Goldfish' in *The Linhay on The Downs*, the landlord of the local pub (not named) where Williamson enjoys an occasional supper of eggs and bacon, says, "I've gaffed scores and scores of salmon. Thousands I've took! And spent twenty years in Cardiff fish market, too." This sounds like Charlie Ovey. The photograph of Charlie in *The Children of Shallowford* also shows three of the Williamson children.

In chapter eight of *The Sun in The Sands* (1945) Williamson writes, 'There were three brothers in the village (not named), each spelling his name differently: Zeal, Zeale, and Zeele.'

SIDNEY ZEALE was a stone-quarrier, gardener, one-time railway worker, elder of two brothers. He was dark, hook-nosed, a man of thrift and ambition. He worked hard on his two acres of garden. Netherhams Hill (the 'Dip') was referred to as 'Zeales Lane' as so many Zeales had lived there for generations. Sidney was a somewhat sinister character, unpleasant and even violent when drunk. He liked a neat home and 'everything regular'. He was very 'masterful' in some ways, but 'had no more heart than a gosling'. He and his obedient wife Liza, however, had never had a bad word since they had been at school together, where apparently he had been a virile lad. It seems that he had taken advantage of his brother's absence at sea to take his girlfriend Liza from him and marry her. In a jealous temper he had pulled off the head of a goldfinch his brother had given her. He could no longer tolerate his drunken brother lodging in the house and literally threw him out during a supper at which Williamson was a guest.

'SAILOR' ZEALE was 'Sidney's' brother, never named. Ex-Royal Navy stoker, he worked in the stone quarries, and lodged, until he was thrown out, with his elder brother. He was a good-natured, lumpy sort of drunk, an unshaven oaf. He quickly spent his monthly Navy pension and was forced to work in the quarries for the rest of the month, but he 'always paid his way'. His timid long-haired girlfriend had ditched him for his brother. Even after he had been thrown out he often came back to Ham and tried in vain to make friends with his brother. We don't know his name, but it was not Stanley, who was another Zeale. Covered with fuel oil, he had been rescued after a day and a night in the sea after his ship had been sunk during the Battle of Jutland in 1916. Until his pension ran out he sat in the village pubs, his eyes with an ox-like stare. He is the man who had to share his bed with 'Julian Warbeck' when that gentleman had at last been thrown out of Skirr Cottage!

HARRY ZEALE, one of the chapel 'Brethren', purchased a motor-car for use as the first taxi cab in Ham.

JACOB LEY (Sparker) was ninety-four, the oldest man in the village. He lived in a tiny thatched cob cottage up the hill from the Rock Inn. Short and sturdy, with a long nose and strong, regular features, he carried nearly a hundred years with stowed strength. He spoke a slow and beautiful dialect, the broadest Williamson had ever heard. He carried a thick ash staff in his mittened hand; his trousers were hitched up below the knees with string. He had been the district wrestling champion between his twenty-fifth and thirty-first years (approx. 1856 to 1862) and had won prizes, usually silver spoons, at the annual Ham Revels,[12] presided over by the formidable Parson Hole,[13] whose hounds 'Sparker' had looked after in his youth. The wrestling must have been a nasty business, the contestants apparently trying to kick their opponent's legs from under them with iron-capped boots. Sparks flew and legs broke.

Williamson took Sparker into the Upper House for a pint on his ninety-fourth birthday, but he had lost the habit of going to the pub and preferred to be at home listening to his grandfather clocks striking. He died shortly afterwards, and was laid out in the all-wool nightgown which had been given to him years before but which he had never worn, keeping it for his coffin. At the auction of his effects, Williamson bought his old pint pot, a grandfather clock and a fireside chair, ready for his imminent marriage.

NOTES

1. I was conducted up the tower by a gentleman from the St George's Christian Holiday and Activity Centre, which operates at what used to be the large rectory next to the church.
2. The Rock Inn was known for a short while in recent years as Rock House – see the photograph reproduced in HW Society *Journal* No. 4 (p. 26).
3. In the Preface to an edition of *Tales of Moorland and Estuary* (reprinted in the 1981 Futura paperback edition) Williamson tells us that when he moved to Shallowford he was "shaking the dust of rectorial criticism of *The Pathway* from his shoes".
4. See Lois Lamplugh 'The Georgeham Village Sign Incident', HWSJ, No. 29 (March 1994) pp. 44-46 and the accompanying reprint of a newspaper article about the incident, p. 47. The double-sided village sign (now no more), on its post near the village hall, was designed and painted by Margaret Kemp-Welch, who lived locally. It is illustrated in HWSJ, No. 28 (Sept., 1993) p. 10 – the side we see there shows us St George slaying his dragon, with the words VILLAGE OF GEORGEHAM. I have seen a poor photograph of the reverse side, which depicts a Saxon chief and his dog, and bears the legend HAMME OF ORDGAR (or similar) THE SAXON, and what appears to be a date, 1026.
5. The two books of course were *The Village Book* and *The Labouring Life* which were later adapted to become *Life in a Devon Village* and *Tales of a Devon Village* (now in paperback *Village Tales*), both first published in 1945.
6. The village was called Hamm, or Hama, in the *Domesday Book* (1086). The Parish Register of 1571 records that 'the plague was in Georgeham'.
7. See David Stokes, 'Living in Georgeham', HWSJ, No. 12 (Sept. 1985) pp. 41-49, plus map on p. 40.
8. 'Hole' was the name of the local manor, recorded in *Domesday Book*, owned by Tetbald, who also owned the manor of 'Hamma'. There are today two farms between Georgeham and Croyde called North Hole Farm and South Hole Farm. The latter has vestiges of a medieval chapel. My wife and I stayed at South Hole Farm (B&B) in 1987 – when the farmer Mr Shapland learned that we were 'Williamson people' he told us that when he was a lad on the farm Williamson often came to the farm to study the owls in the barn there, sometimes staying all night.
9. In the original story 'Scandal and Gossip' in *The Village Book*, the words 'from a London suburb' do not appear. Both *The Village Book* and its successor *Life in a Devon Village* were published after *The Pathway*.
10. 'Be thou faithful unto death, and I will give thee a crown of life' is a quotation from the New Testament, Revelation 2,10.
11. In the 1880s the real village bobby was stabbed when patrolling Church Road, and died of his wounds. The drunken old man who stabbed him died before he could be brought to justice. I don't think that this tragedy is mentioned anywhere by Williamson – he may not have known of it.
12. I have been unable to find out much about the 'Ham Revels' but I read somewhere that they took place in April annually. They had ceased to be held when Williamson came to Ham. But in the story 'The Fair' in *The Labouring Life*, he tells us that the revel had been an August Fête held in the Glebe Field nearly every year to raise money for church funds. "'The Revel," he said, "brings to mind wrestling, balm cakes, white-pot, ale, skittling for a live pig, 'tanglilegs' (courting) and the rough fun of olden time."
13. A list of the Rectors of Georgeham going back many years is displayed in the church. It seems that Rectors were sometimes hereditary Squires, entitled to receive village tithes (taxes), and were not necessarily ordained clergymen. This applied to the Parsons (from 'persona', a Person) of Georgeham until modern times. Thomas Hole was Rector in the late 18th century, succeeded by Francis Hole. Soon another Thomas Hole became Rector, and he was succeeded by another Francis Hole! The second Francis, the last Parson Hole, was Rector from 1831 to 1867. I have been unable to discover whether the Hole family was connected in any way with the ancient manor of Hole.

* * * * *

The Society is planning to publish a small booklet containing all the relevant information about Henry Williamson's Georgeham. If you have any information which would add to the above and would further our knowledge of the village and its surroundings, please contact the Editor.

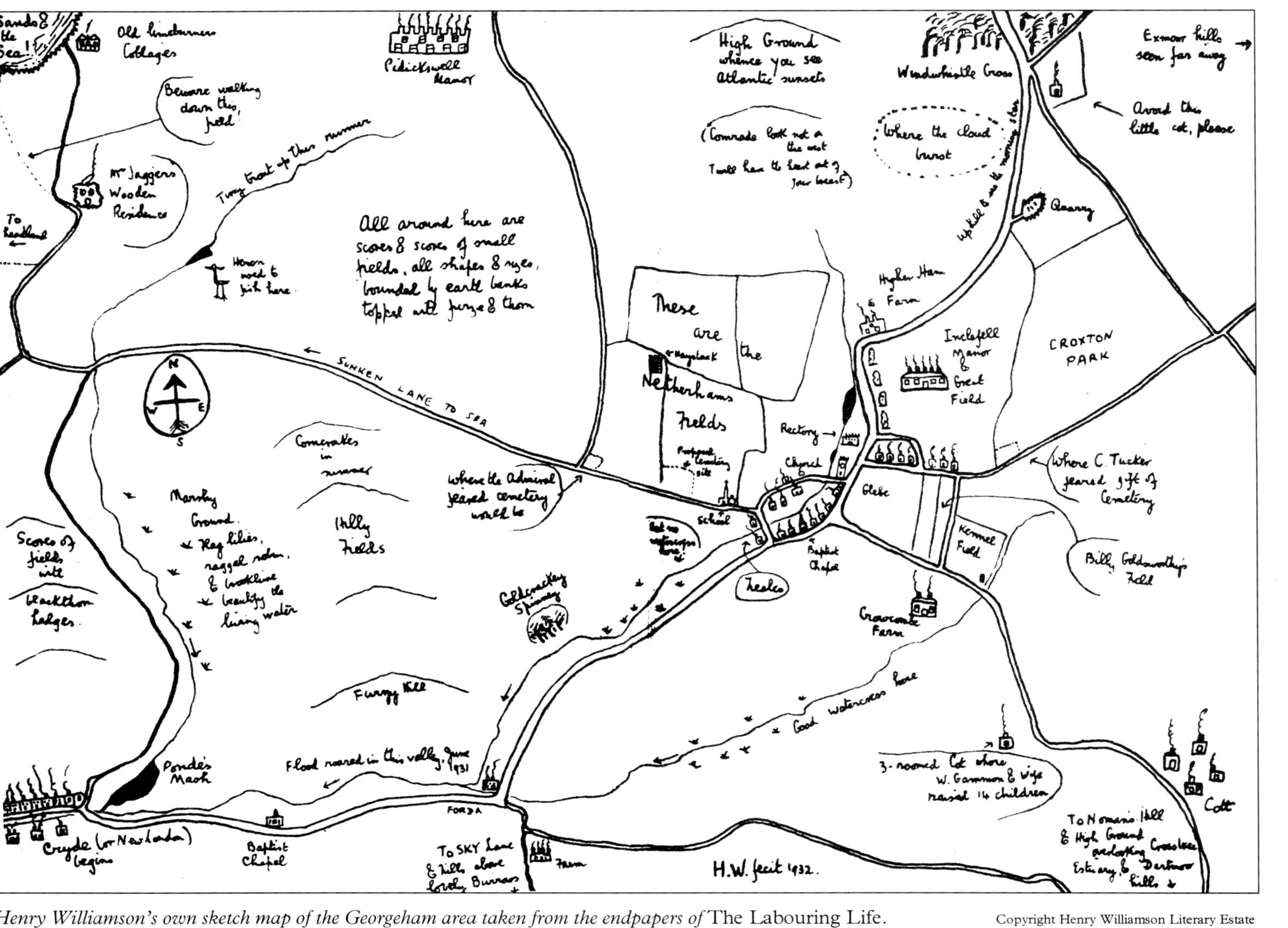

Henry Williamson's own sketch map of the Georgeham area taken from the endpapers of The Labouring Life.

T'chackamma

This fragment of manuscript from the literary archive makes interesting comparison with the printed story which appeared in *The Old Stag* (1926). In a 'Preface' printed in *Collected Nature Stories* (1970) Henry Williamson states that T'chackamma had been 'suggested by a crude pen-and-ink sketch of African baboons being attacked by dogs on the lower slopes of a mountain. I imagined all of the incidents in this story . . .' (*Collected Nature Stories*, pp. 149-50.)

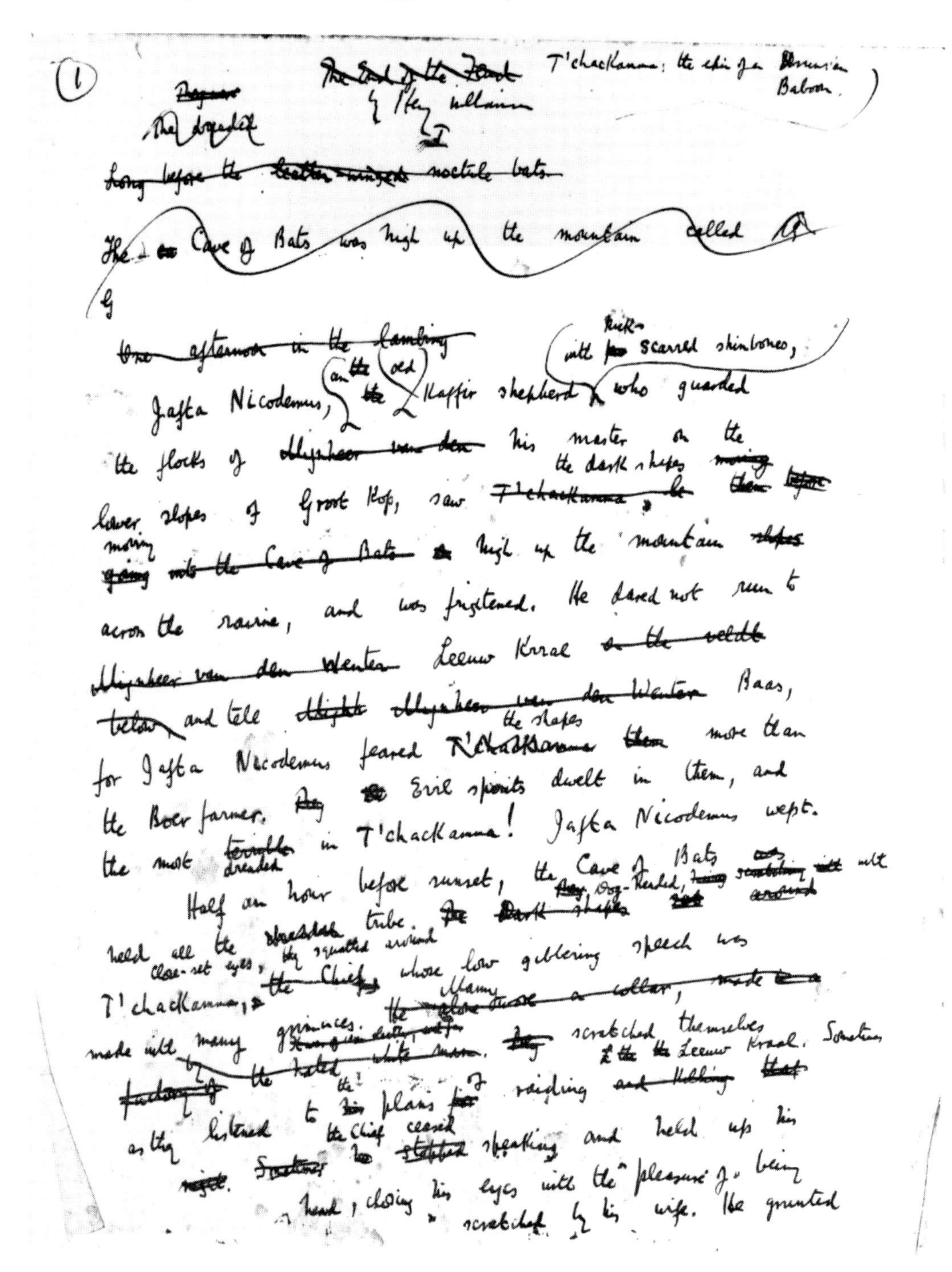
T'chackamma: the epic of a Baboon.

by Henry Williamson

Jafta Nicodemus, an old Kaffir shepherd with scarred shinbones, who guarded the flocks of his master on the lower slopes of Groot Kop, saw the dark shapes moving high up the mountain across the ravine, and was frightened. He dared not run to Leeuw Kraal and tell Baas, for Jafta Nicodemus feared the shapes more than the Boer farmer. Evil spirits dwelt in them, and the most dreaded in T'chackamma! Jafta Nicodemus wept.

Half an hour before sunset, the Dog-Headed tribe held all the close-set eyes, they squatted around T'chackamma, the Chief, whose low gibbering speech was made with many grimaces. Many scratched themselves ... Leeuw Kraal. Sometimes ... the plans of raiding ... as they listened to the Chief ceased speaking and held up his head, closing his eyes with the pleasure of being scratched by his wife. He grunted

(2)

with ecstacy, fluttering his white eyelids, and the upper
lip of his massive face, curled back
from the teeth. Such teeth! They had been magnificent; but
T'chackamma was growing old and the years of captivity
spent behind iron bars, and the unnatural food, had
ruined them. Brown tartar nicked the necks of the four
incisors.

Many eyes watched T'chackamma, but none so fixedly
as the eyes of T'je. The little male, who had
left his mother only a few months, sat at the

T'chackamma (from The Old Stag*) Charles F. Tunnicliffe (Reproduced with the kind permission of his literary estate.)*
The correspondence between HW and Charles Tunnicliffe was extensive, of great interest and frequently amusing; as is shown by the following sentence about the drawings for the story of T'chackamma.
'By the way, I hope you don't expect me to take a little trip to South Africa to get authentic baboons. Please, please may I study them at the Belle Vue Manchester.' (Tunnicliffe's local zoo.)

The Dreamer of Devon

Herbert Faulkner West

"All theory, my friend, is grey,
But green is life's bright golden tree." —Faust.

OUTSIDE it rained. This was the first rain in Devonshire for six weeks. The trout streams were almost dried up. So low was the water that the salmon were unable to come up from the sea. The grass of the pasturelands was shrivelled up and brownish in colour. Across the hills and fields blew a south-west wind from the sea, carrying the rain like clouds of smoke between the valleys. It was not bitterly cold, for it was early March, and spring was just around the corner. Crocuses were in bloom and birds sang. Rooks were visible on the hillside opposite the window from which I sat. Nearby was the rookery of the Castle Hill, in the beech trees of Lord Fortescue's deer park. This situation was exactly the sort of place that I expected to find Henry Williamson living in. One could scarcely find a more peaceful spot in all England than in this remote corner of North Devon.

Shallowford! The name of Henry Williamson's cottage, and the name, too, of the four or five cottages clustered here between the hills on the immemorial estate of the Fortescues. Over beyond rose the Exmoor hills, where men hunt the wild red deer. Nine miles to the west is Barnstaple at the end of the estuary. Devonshire!

I thought of Sir Francis Drake and the countless generations of simple people who had lived and died here, most of them never having been further away than a radius of twenty-five miles from the place where they were born, and whose one big day of the year was when they attended the Barnstaple Fair described with such fidelity in Williamson's *The Labouring Life*, the proofs of which I read for him all yesterday. Still the sons of these Devonshire people travelled. Many never came back, as each village war memorial testifies. Many crossed the seven seas, and many, too, went to Flanders and France. At my left, near an open fireplace, where a beech log burns (dry after three years' seasoning), hangs a helmet picked up on the battlefield by Lieut. H. W. Williamson. It is riddled with pieces from a 5.9. Bits of hair cling to the inside. The brains that once clung there have dried up and left only brownish stains. Who was the poor devil? Did he once walk over these nearby hills ? Did he, too, once love ? What was he thinking when he was struck down so blindly in a sudden crash of flame? Always the war! A boring subject! But the war remains for Henry Williamson and his generation. They are the war neurotics! Poor chaps, too bad they cannot forget. The ghosts of countless dead pass like fitful shadows through Williamson's memory, but happily, since the war, his shell-shocked and depressed spirit has been lifted and, as it were, purified by the peace of these Devon hills, by his three lovely children, by his keen feeling for Nature here perfectly satisfied, by his love for the clear trout waters of the stream in the deer park, and through his loves. The ghost which haunted Hamlet was a weak, thin wraith compared to the ghosts which haunt Sassoon, Blunden, Tomlinson, Williamson, Graves, and others not so well known. Over the fireplace is a war etching by his friend, C. R. W. Nevinson. Nearby a fine Kermode woodcut. Always the war. Would that Williamson's generation could forget. Hear for a moment what Edward Thomas wrote (I see the helmet hanging there) :

A PRIVATE

This ploughman dead in battle slept out of doors
Many a frozen night, and merrily
Answered staid drinkers, good bedmen, and all bores:
"At Mrs. Greenland's Hawthorn Bush," said he,
"I slept." None knew which bush. Above the town,
Beyond "The Drover," a hundred spot the down
In Wiltshire. And where now at last he sleeps
More sound in France—that, too, he secret keeps.

Upstairs in Williamson's study there are many books about the war. The best of the war books are in his collection, which is quite complete. Two of them are his own. One, *The Patriot's Progress*, is a simple story of Private John Bullock (good ironical name), who ended up minus a leg and after the war became once more a humble clerk. It is a well-planned, unhysterical story written around Kermode's graphic and biting woodcuts. The second, *The Wet Flanders Plain*, is the record of a journey back to the old front line after the war, written in the form of a diary, and readers of these books will see what happened to William Maddison during Armageddon.

There has been for some time past a reaction against war books of the Sassoon, Blunden, Tomlinson, Remarque type. Too long, say the reactionary critics, have writers represented the soldiers as a mere "pack of complaining drunkards, egotistical whimpering cowards, and foul-mouthed lechers, led by incompetents." Mr. Ressich's recent book *Gallop!* is one of these, and he implies that the ordinary man enjoyed the war, that there was something ennobling in his experience, that he considered it as the greatest adventure of his life, and that to die for one's country is beautiful by the nature of things. All ends happily in Mr. Ressich's book. For men of little imagination this may have been the case, but unfortunately for men of Williamson's type this could not be. On their shoulders they carried the massed grief of the nations. Post-war neuroticism has been, I think, too glibly blamed on the war. That it was the primary cause I would not deny for a moment, but Williamson's own restlessness, his seeking the inevitable anodynes which sensitive men seek, is due, I think, to the world as it is rather than any phase in its local history. His nature has always been a sensitive one. Readers of *The Beautiful Years* know how the author depicted the relationship between William Maddison and his father. Neither understood the other, and the boy was thrown too much on himself. Williamson was Maddison and Maddison was a dreamer, a lover of beauty, of birds and animals, and a sensitive youth longing for a time when Christ's simple tenets would govern the world. His mind, turned too long upon itself, enjoying in its own solitude the inner landscape of the soul, the prey to imagined fears, dreaming of some Utopia which would give it adequate and complete compensation, soaring to a belief in an impossible and unearthly love, had woven for itself a set of ideals which clashed inevitably with the compromises the world of experience forces upon all men. So he was unhappy and indulged in a great deal of self-pity. Still the Maddisons exist. Williamson now smiles, I suspect somewhat cynically, at the various incarnations of his past self. Maddison is dead. There is no doubt about that. No other man can judge in any accurate degree the shadows and half lights of the mind or personality of any other man. His real self remains partly hidden even to himself. I can only surmise what the war did to Williamson, and my guess is based partly on my own reactions. Like most men who saw four years of service, Williamson talks little about it, but I know he can never forget it and that the front line part of it seemed to him senseless, brutal and useless. The comradeship, the man's life part of it-the greater part-he enjoyed, he says. He was a private soldier only during the first six months, and an officer thereafter. But the scenes of the Somme, of the Passchendaele battles have left upon him their brand. He did tell me once about the famous English Guards' regiment whose discipline was so perfect that once given an order to go forward nothing could stop them. They went forward like implacable robots, no matter how full the air was of flying steel. This iron discipline made them perfect soldiers, but there is an element of sadness in their machine-like movements. Imagination and individualism (two of the keynotes of Williamson's character) could play no part in their lives. When training methods make of men automatons they cease almost to be men. Waterloo may have been won on the playing fields of Eton, but I have never been certain that this catchy phrase did not contain within itself a boomerang. Flogging boys may make them men, but Shelley resisted at Eton as all individualists must always resist tyranny. Williamson and Sassoon resisted too. They could not do otherwise, for they were sensitive individualists with agile minds, and they instinctively resisted the bludgeoning effect that war has on the human spirit. It is not by chance that Williamson lives in a remote corner of Devon far from the disintegrating effects of cities, nor that he chooses many hours of solitude for himself either in his writing-room or along his beloved trout stream, the river Bray. Still the ghosts are with him. The nervous shocks sustained during the war will never wholly be wiped out. It was for him the way of revelation, and what was revealed was not always good. So he writes of Nature, always indifferent and always itself, and of simple people who are close to the soil.

I first met Henry Williamson in the winter of 1931 in Hanover, New Hampshire. He had come over from England in August, 1930, to go on a fishing trip with his American publisher, John Macrae. A friend and colleague of mine, Professor W. K. Stewart, happened to share his state-room, and had invited Williamson up for the winter sports at Dartmouth College, which were to take place in February. After two or three weeks' fishing in Canada, Williamson went to New York. There he rewrote in an incredibly short time, sometimes at the rate of 10,000 words a day, *The Dream of Fair Women.* The loneliness one feels in a city like New York struck particularly hard at Williamson, for his is a personality which cannot stand complete and forced solitude in a city for long periods of time. He lived alone in an unfurnished down-town apartment. He finally cabled for his wife, and in due time after her arrival in New York they arrived in Hanover. This delightful college town, on the banks of the Connecticut River and at the foothills of the White Mountains, was in February a world of white. The pines weighed heavily with snow. The ski trails through the woods and on the many hills nearby were worn and fast from the skis of many runners. The air was crisp and the thermometer stood around zero. Williamson loved it all. He had skied before in the Pyrenees, and once in Devon (which has about four great blizzards every century), and I procured for him an outfit. The second afternoon of his visit we set out for a trip across country. It was evident that he had not ski-ed for a long time. We went for two or three miles and he showed signs of weariness. I turned toward home. He came to a short but steep slope, went down, his skis stuck suddenly at the bottom of the grade so that he fell sharply forward, his face buried in the snow, his arms spread-eagled to stop his fall. He finally extricated himself, said nothing to my roars of laughter, took off his skis and walked home. Later on he became proficient and enjoyed the sport immensely. Several days later he turned an ankle on a particularly fast slope of hard crust, and was able to ski no more.

During his stay he gave a lecture at the college on the war and its effects on his generation. He had written out the lecture, and from my own experience of listening to lectures for ten years in Dartmouth Hall I never heard one so well written, or as sincere and moving. This is not faint praise, for there I had heard such English writers as Hugh Walpole, Rebecca West, Frank Swinnerton, Bertrand Russell and many others. He introduced to the audience some war literature quite unknown to most of them, as, for instance, the war poems of Wilfrid Owen. I hope that this address, which he gave also at Harvard and Yale University, will sometime be printed.

Before several log fires, at home and at the Outing Club, we talked many nights of books, authors, and of other subjects men of the same age and with like interests discuss in confidence.

I did not see Williamson again until March, 1932, when I came to England. I gladly accepted his invitation to visit him in Devon, for I wanted very much to renew our friendship and also to see, with him as guide, the country which he had written about in several of his Devon books, notably *The Pathway*, *Tarka The Otter*, and *The Village Book*. I wanted to see the Torridge, the Taw, the estuary formed by these two rivers, and the villages of Saunton, Georgeham, and Croyde. I knew the works of the other writers who had used northern Devonshire as the background for their books. Kipling had written *Stalky and Co.*, and I knew Kingsley's *Westward Ho!* The Hon. John Fortescue's *The Story of a Red Deer* had done for the stag what Williamson in *Tarka The Otter* had done for the otter. Both are little classics and are among the finest animal stories in the language. So it was with a good deal of pleasure that I set out on my quest.

Williamson met me at Taunton, in Somerset, and we did the forty miles to his home in considerably less than an hour, for he drives his Silver Eagle sports car well, and (down hill and over cliffs, as he has put it) it can do eighty miles an hour.

Shallowford is a long-thatched Elizabethan cottage with walls made of mud and straw called cob, two foot thick, and built to last. Once it had been three labourers' cottages, separated only by a thick wall between each section. Now their houses have become one. There are many fireplaces in the house, for North Devon is cold and windy many months of the year. At one end of the house is a kitchen, roomy and altogether worthy of the food it sends out to hungry guests, for the Devon air breeds lusty appetites. Next to the kitchen is a dining-room with a long oak refectory table, solid as the men who many years ago hewed out its oak planks by hand. It is highly polished, and recently had absorbed two gallons of linseed oil. At one end of the table is a hand-carved Elizabethan press. The living-room, separated from the dining-room by the entrance hall, contains books, a gramophone, tables, and comfortable chairs. The first night of my visit we sat around the fire and heard the grand passionate music of the third act of *Tristan and Isolde*. I must confess we played other music than Wagner's, for his music threw us all into too profound a silence to make the evening at all sociable. As a relief we played records made by the playboy of New York, Rudy Vallée, whose crooning voice Williamson liked and had heard in a New York night club the year before. There was nothing highbrow about Shallowford. Williamson sat reading the papers while I read a book which Williamson swore by: Wilfrid Ewart's war book, *The Way of Revelation*. Ann Thomas, the author's secretary, daughter of Edward Thomas, killed in 1917, was knitting by the fire. Gypsy, Williamson's wife (who is Mary Ogilvie in *The Pathway*), sat quietly and serenely by the fire, her hands moving rapidly, making a sweater for Windles, the oldest boy. The light from the fire reflected a red glow on their cheeks. There was silence for a while, and after London, an astonishingly satisfying peace. Here at Shallowford Williamson lives, as Thoreau lived at Walden Pond, in his own silences amid quiet and lovely surroundings.

In the morning I went up to Williamson's study, where he works. The room contained an old three-legged round-top walnut table, a fireplace, a radio, and many cases full of books. Some are his own, and he has saved sets of first editions for his children when they grow up. Here I saw several of his manuscripts, proof copies, and other items to delight a bibliophile, and an unpublished manuscript which contained the genesis of the four novels comprising *The Flax of Dream*. Here, too, was the manuscript of *The Star-Born*, the fragment left behind by Maddison when, Shelley-like, he was accidentally drowned. I noticed that Williamson had all the writings of Richard Jefferies, his first great allegiance, many of W. H. Hudson's superb nature studies, several of Conrad, Galsworthy, the late Arnold Bennett, who had been kind to the young author, H. M. Tomlinson, Edmund Blunden, T. E. Lawrence, Siegfried Sassoon, Frederick Manning, Wilfrid Owen, Rupert Brooke, Robert Graves, White's *The Natural History of Selborne*, and countless others. It was the library of a most discriminating kind, and from our talks together he clearly had a deep appreciation of his books.

I left him to his writing, and at ten o'clock went for a walk. Behind the cottage I climbed a long hill up to Bremridge Wood to get a view of the hills and valleys of Devon. The sea is not visible from Shallowford. I met no one and saw no one in the paths of the dark fir-tree woods and in the fields beyond. After an hour or so I returned to rejoin Williamson on a dam-building expedition.

Near his house, and running through the deer park, wanders the river Bray, two miles of which Williamson has the exclusive fishing rights. He is an ardent fisherman and knows how to handle his 2½ ounce fly rod with all the delicacy of a swordsman. He prefers dry fly fishing. Around noon time, dressed in gumboots and Burberry to keep out the driving rain, we walked through the deer park to the river, where Williamson had built several small dams. These dams he hoped would form better trout pools. With crowbar and pick-axe, wading up to our knees in the swift running water, we swung 500 pound sacks of gravel-concrete into the stream. Then we tipped buckets of gravel at their bases. The water was rising fairly rapidly, due to the rain on Exmoor, for the Bray is fed by water running down the Exmoor slopes. At two o'clock we came back for a hearty meal, washed down with generous gulps of brown Burton ale. Whether the dams will stay in the terrific floods or not I don't know, but he and his "labourer" Ann Thomas certainly enjoyed making them.

After dinner that night Williamson asked Ann Thomas to fetch *The Star-Born*. The Christ-haunted Maddison wrote it, readers of *The Pathway* will remember, some months after the war. Parts of it were lost, some sheets were burned, but enough remains to recreate the gentle Maddison. *The Star-Born*, parts of which Williamson read to us with all the feeling he is capable of, is an allegory of the second coming of Jesus, who brought the spirit of love to all living creatures.

It would be a mistake to give a summary of *The Star-Born*, for the book itself is to be published. Williamson very generously gave me permission, however, to quote from some scattered notes of Maddison referring to his manuscript. These will give the reader some idea of this now long looked-for allegory. They follow:

The S-B

Time. *Not stated; all clock time, days, months, etc., ignored. Story is meant to be on verge of 4th dimension as it were; cf, simplicity of Einstein, and his "revolutionary" remarks on "educating" the child-mind.*

Place. *Not stated, but locality is drawn roughly from Lydford Gorge, and ruinous castle keep on western edge of Dartmoor.*

Theme. *The mind of a poet (natural man who is himself, unaffected by social strata, unaffected by 'education') —mind of natural modern man who needs no stimulants of child-misery-memory, etc. nor possesses any* geist *to urge him to 'fulfill' himself. Has never been mentally tortured when young—he grows and finds strength with the 'Spirits' —a marvellous or 'ideal' childhood.*

Those he encounters when he returns to the 'world' again are kind to him in their various ways, but only with his 'twin' is he able to be as he was formed by the Spirits.

His sufferings begin, but as he sees life whole (tree, animal, man, water, sky, etc., all making the harmony or balance of nature) he doesn't see in the natural world any cruelty—for no one was cruel to him as a child. He doesn't need to escape into nature—no self-identification. He is just the Star-born, or Sonny, or Starr—just himself.

But *Esther (symbol of the human world) isn't herself: and she, unconsciously, would alter him to her own image. Did she try and reform her husband and—and is this why, in a moment of anguish, he 'returned to Beyond '?*

There is never any cry of heaven forsaking him; for he has never postulated anything but natural facts. Wanhope is a lost Star-born in Beyond; even as the Star-born is a lost Lightbringer when he returns to the earth. But the powers of darkness are conquered at his giving up the ghost: and then Wanhope, through brotherhood or strength with S-b, becomes the Son of the All again. The book is a Fifth Gospel.

Those who read *The Star-Born* will see that Maddison had drawn Esther from Mrs. Ogilvie of *The Pathway*, and Mamis, *The Star-Born's* "twin," from Mrs. Ogilvie's daughter Mary. Robert may be recognised as Howard in the same book. The Christian symbolism is fairly obvious throughout. *The Star-Born* is beautifully conceived and discloses a soul too fine to stand for long the ravages of this life; Maddison has left a fine legacy which cannot but help appeal to the gentler spirits who still revere in their hearts the person and spirit of the Christ-child.

After Williamson had finished reading parts of Maddison's manuscript he told me a few things about it. It has been lying, completed, in a drawer since 1924. He thought he would write an introduction for it and perhaps publish it. This introduction has been written, and we even got so far as to discuss publishers and what kind of an edition it should be. We grew facetious as a relief perhaps, from the high intensity and seriousness of Maddison's manuscript. Should there be ten copies on all rag vellum, bound in Australian kangaroo skin, and made by the Garibaldi Printers who work backwards? Or should there be, suggested Williamson, twenty copies hand-engraved on sardine tins, and bound in boards laid over with slices of the first editions of his old tryst books? We temporarily decided on 1,500 copies printed by some good press at a price that Maddison lovers could afford, for I felt sure that they would be people of moderate circumstances. Maddison himself, I am sure, would have laughed could he have heard us talking about his book. He would have wanted ordinary paper on copies so cheap that they could almost have been given away. Maddison was a believer in the Wiclif doctrine of evangelical poverty!

One afternoon a day or two later, Windles had returned boisterously from school. We were having tea, and John, the younger boy, aged three, tried to come into the room. Windles said loudly, "Keep out." Williamson rebuked the lad, "Let him. in." Windles did so. "You are like a big trout," his father continued, "who sees a little trout coming and cries, 'Keep out, this pool is mine. All the food here is mine. Keep out!' and swishing his body angrily chases the little trout away. Later on the big trout grows fat, is caught, and the little trout takes his place. Don't be like the big trout, Windles." Williamson is very fond of his children, and keeps close to them, remembering perhaps, his own childhood so charmingly described in his first book. He often crawls on his hands and knees, making faces and uttering strange noises, chasing them from room to room. John follows his father whenever he is about the house, and watches his every movement. Though Williamson is highly strung, I never saw him once show any irritation toward his children, and watching him play with them one sees the really human person that he essentially is.

Williamson is tall in build with flashing brown eyes. His small head and face are deceptive, for he looks very thin ; actually his body is wiry and muscular, like that of a long-distance runner he used to be at school. His dark hair is slightly tinged with grey around the temples. He is quick and nervous in his movements, and walks with rapid strides. He is very impetuous and acts very often on sudden impulse. I witnessed an example of this while visiting him. He had read an advertisement in a fishing journal of the sale of half a mile of salmon water with a cottage and several acres of land. This fishing site, which he pictured glowingly in his imagination, immediately became the one great object in his mind. He must see it at once. "Ann, Ann, see the radiator is full! Gypsy, cut sandwiches! Windles, take off muddy boots, put on clean ones! Herb, get your heaviest coat on!" After hustling, we drove south to see it. The genial and charming owner showed it to us. It was a fine half mile of the Torridge, a river famous for its salmon, and had several fine pools and that rapid water in places which delights the real fisherman's eye. Williamson thought that it would be fine for trout too, and he would rather fish for trout than salmon. The cottage was attractively remodelled, and its only drawback to me was that it faced north and would never get the sun. In Williamson's mind it became at once a retreat where he could come by himself to write and to fish. I felt all along, more or less by instinct (for I knew nothing then of the high price of private salmon fishing in England often reaching, I believe, anything from £1,000 to £10,000 per mile and then only one bank!), that Williamson should not buy it. My reasons were based primarily on the economics of the case. I fully realised that it was none of my business, and whatever damping of his ardour I attempted was done with all the subtlety I could assume. I feel certain now that if he had bought it he would have regretted his action the next day. Now, a month later, he has probably forgotten it.

I remarked one day to him that he who had written *Tarka The Otter* didn't seem to like otters very much because they killed his trout. He corrected me, "I like otters but I wish they would stay in big streams. They come up my small stream, breed here year after year, and completely clean it out. I merely destroyed their breeding place as a matter of self-defence. It was in that big stick-heap under that clump of alders washed up by many years' flood at the bend I showed you yesterday." I had noticed that morning in the bathroom that there was on the wall a German poster advertising the German translation of *Tarka The Otter*, and Williamson had written on it that in August, 1931, otters had killed 450 little trout that he was rearing in a garden pond for his stream. This particular pond, fed by a tiny brook, was only about twenty-five yards from his front entrance. I could understand his feeling.

One afternoon we followed the Bray about half a mile down to the large weir at Stag's Head, watching as we walked every pool for trout and possibly salmon. We saw many trout, but no salmon, due to the low water, for they could not come up from the sea over the weirs until there should come a flood. When the trout saw our shadow they would dart like arrows, faster almost than the eye could follow, to some secure retreat beneath a rock or underneath the bank. "Lovely water," Williamson would murmur as he saw a likely looking pool, and suddenly, "Look!" and he would show me, visible often only to a trained eye, a beauty of two or three pounds. Months of this sort of observation prepares Williamson to write his best Nature studies. He is planning a book to be called *The Water Dreamer*, about a trout. After months, and in this case years of observation, he will write this book in an incredibly short time; meanwhile it grows in his creative consciousness. Reaching a saw mill, we were told that up the valley there was a stag hunt and that the stag was running this way. The first Exmoor hunt was on! We retraced our steps, and climbed the iron fence which enclosed the deer park through which his stream runs. "A bad sight, the end of a stag hunt," he said, pointing out to me where a stag was killed a year ago. "They shot him as he stood exhausted after about a thirty mile run and then cut his throat. They threw his entrails to the hounds." I could visualise the scene, and thought it cruel and unsporting. I failed, perhaps, to realise the thrill the hunters felt during their wild riding over the moor, avoiding bogs, sliding down steep, rocky hills, mile after mile. "Most hunting people hate the idea of the stag being killed," said Williamson, "but it is a fact that they owe their existence in modern times only to the hunts themselves, who pay for their damage. There are too many of them," he went on, "they ruin the crops." Williamson published last year a very sensible defence of stag hunting in his little book, *The Wild Red Deer of Exmoor*. He wrote there in one place that "the deer owed their survival, in this present time, to their swiftness and shyness developed and maintained during the thousands of years they have been hunted pitilessly by animals of prey, and men of prey, and because for hundreds of years they have been hunted—but only when mature—by staghounds, and protected by the staghunters . . . it will be historically true that for a great many years the hunts practically befriended the wild red deer of Exmoor. I, for one, a mere imaginative friend of the deer, shall always be grateful for their practical benevolence." We heard from afar up the valley the sound of the horn and the deep baying of the hounds. I never found out whether the stag got away or not, for we did not see the end of the hunt. We continued up the river for a couple of miles, picking out likely looking pools, to see if we could find any big trout. In the morning he had fed them, and in one fine pool, at a bend in the river, we had seen a large one swiftly and gracefully turn to snap the food. They were too thin at this time of year to catch, but they fatten up when the flies begin to hatch. In April or May, Williamson begins his fishing, and, as I have said, he is not only an ardent devotee but an expert. The Bray winds up the valley, and we followed it, our feet sinking in the rushy bogs by the riverside, and so on under the viaduct of the Great Western Railroad to the Brayley Bridge, where his fishing rights ends. He suspected that the village boys came at night and fished the trout out with worms. Poaching goes on, of course, as it has from the legendary days of Robin Hood, and it will go on until the end of fishing.

The next morning the page proofs of Williamson's newest book, *The Labouring Life*, came from his publisher. It is, perhaps, his best book, with the exception of *Tarka The Otter*, which will always remain personally for me one of the finest books I have ever read. His newest book is of the earth, and comes direct, with long roots, from the Devon soil. It is a human book, reflecting the dry wit of the natives with an amazing fidelity. Williamson was rather comic as he stood in his slippers before the table, comparing the galley proofs with the page proofs, at the same time beating rhythm with his arms and his body, his pencil weaving spirals in the air, to the divine music from *Tristan* which I was playing on the gramophone.

Tristan: *Ach, Isolde! Isolde! Wie schön bist du!*
Isolde: *Tristan! Ha!—horch! Er wacht! Geliebter!*
In dem wogenden Schwall, in dem tönenden Schall, in des Welt-Atems wehenden All—
ertrinken, versinken—unbewusst,—höchste Lust!

He hummed and he sang under his breath, "Wie schön bist du!" He corrected his proof. He noticed my preference for the music sung by Isolde, and said that he saw only Tristan's side, but that I was less selfish and less self-centred, and that my liking for Isolde's part augured well for my future. Divine music . . . the less said the better.

I continued to play as he went on with his proof-reading. He worked rapidly and made no mistakes. He does whatever he does well, and is a master for detail and exactness, whether he is dealing with writing, correcting proofs, keeping the hearth clean, or seeing that his automobile runs perfectly. He takes great pride in his house and its management, and those who think that he must be as impractical as Shelley was supposed to have been, with whom one naturally compares his Maddison days, are most decidedly wrong.

We had a picnic tea that afternoon about six o'clock at a bend in the Bray by the deep Tree Pool. Gypsy and I had carried the tea things, and we built a small fire to boil the kettle. Piles of small driftwood washed up by a previous flood furnished the fuel. Williamson and Ann Thomas were working on the dam. The evening was cold, and after tea we heaped the fire high and soon a huge blaze was leaping toward the sky. Williamson showed me some otter tracks and expressed concern that they had probably taken his big trout, the Loch Leven five-pounder which he had been feeding for years and which came into the shallows when it saw him. "The trout probably swam down the stream, found my dam, got all excited at the strange obstacle, for trout are very highly strung, darted here and there, flapped desperately into the shallows, and was caught," he said. "The otters," he went on, "eat only while the fish is alive. They kill for sport. The bitch otter is probably over there underneath that oak. I'd like to see her." We noticed, too, some tracks of the heron. They kill many fish, standing on one leg motionless, and spearing the fish with their long beaks, which they move with incredible speed. "Blast them!" he said, "they think I am softhearted so they come here and take all I've got. But one day they'll get a charge of No. 4 shot!"

The moon and the evening star appeared in solitary loveliness over Castle Hill. Williamson suddenly said, "Come here," and he showed me the moon through the smoke of the fire. "In *The Beautiful Years* there is a phrase, 'and the smoke hanging vaguely overhead tarnished the little moon,' " he quoted. This book, his first, was written when he was twenty-two, under the spell of Jefferies' *Bevis*. Though lacking, perhaps, a little in form, it was charming in its spontaneity, and showed the promise the writer has already fulfilled in his later books. Only a mind keenly tuned to the myriad beauties of nature could have caught such a perfect phrase. The moon, a pale silver, did look tarnished through the smoke. We waited for the fire to burn itself out and walked home in silence with that melancholy man sometimes feels before the loveliness of the stars.

The good, clear weather continuing, came the day when Williamson was to show me some of the landmarks of his books. Driving between Bideford and Barnstaple, we skirted the river Torridge. Here Tarka lived, and Williamson pointed out to me the place where he was killed. Having seen Williamson climb a tree beside the Bray to watch for hours the movements of the trout in the pool below, I could understand why he had caught so well the life of Tarka. For years he had followed the otter hounds. He had watched patiently for days and weeks their movements. He knew every square yard of the estuary formed by the river Torridge and the river Taw, where Tarka lived his joyful water life. But his book is more than the result of his observations. These are strained delicately through the poetic tapestry of his creative imagination. Williamson became Tarka, as he is now the water dreamer, and yet escaped the pit of many Nature writers who endow their animals with the thoughts and feelings of humans. Williamson did not commit this pathetic fallacy in his book. Tarka is an otter, and behaved always like an otter.

When *Tarka The Otter* was published in 1927, Mr. Edward Garnett sent a copy to his friend, Colonel T. E. Lawrence (Aircraftsman Shaw), who was then serving in the Royal Air Force in India. Lawrence wrote a letter from Karachi, in his minute handwriting, about 7,000 words long, about the book, and suggested to Mr. Garnett that the author might like to see his letter although it was only from a "prentice hand." This Mr. Garnett did. Since that time Lawrence has written to Williamson a most faithful and penetrating criticism of each book published since, with the exception of *The Pathway*. This criticism Williamson freely acknowledges to have been of great help in his development. "More than anything else, the influence of Lawrence has, invisibly, helped me to become my true, strong, natural self in writing," said Williamson. "He may write once a year; but I find myself as a soil wherein seeds have been planted; and they grow and grow, and lo! I have discarded a weakness; I write with simpler, more workaday truth. The way Lawrence was behind Prince Feisal in Arabia during the war; he is certainly a great aid to me—and never sees me, remember. It is like the stars, each in its orbit."

Any future study of Williamson's work will assuredly trace the change from the subjective idealism of *The Flax of Dream* to the objective realism of, for example, *The Labouring Life.* I saw in an oak chest at Shallowford, seldom unlocked and seen by few, if any, before, a diary kept by Williamson just after the war. It was begun I should guess in 1919, just after Williamson's brief and unsatisfactory excursion into Fleet Street. The chest also contained the proof sheets of several of his books, letters, original manuscripts and other literary items. When Williamson gave me the key to it he did so with a feeling of, as he expressed it, the freemasonry of friends. With his friends he is always very frank, and is not averse to expounding a good deal of self-criticism. The diary was for me to read, but it was so intimate in describing his inner life that I read little of it, and, though I should have liked to do so for this paper, transcribed none of it literally. I disclose, therefore, very little of what a casual glance gave me. The diary is most essential in understanding the genesis of, particularly, *The Flax of Dream,* those four novels describing the life of William Maddison. The diary included many youthful and poetic outpourings of adolescent yearnings for an unattainable and unreal woman. Like many idealists, sensitive and shy, Williamson (or Maddison) idealised various girls that he met, put them on pedestals where they not only did not belong but did not, I suspect, even care to be placed. Naturally, disillusion followed and several of his idols fell. It takes men of Williamson's nature about ten years longer than the average, insensitive male to wake up to the earthy nature of women. They are Cybels rather than Rimas. The disillusion of Maddison was quite common, I suspect, to many young men brought up in the post-Victorian period in homes where sex education was not discussed. In his early youth, and during the period of this diary, Williamson was suffering, I think, from a lack of healthy sexual experience, and this repression or sublimation broke out in a certain amount of self-pity depicted in the character of the noble Maddison. I use the word "noble" in no ironical sense, for Maddison was a noble character. This repression, too, explains some of the sentimentality visible in the earlier version of *The Dream of Fair Women,* and to a certain extent in *The Pathway.* There is throughout these books a softness, or a "tender mindedness" as William James called it, which the realistic or "tough-minded" reader of the post-war epoch reacted against. This may explain why his novels never approximated a "best seller," even though *The Pathway* did have considerable success. Maddison's reaction to Evelyn Fairfax in the first version of *The Dream of Fair Women,* first published in 1924, differs a great deal from the same affair in the 1931 version of the same book. Williamson, I am sure, would now read the diary with a slightly ironical and humorous contempt that one reserves for the silly, but none the less genuine and real and unhappy, days of his dead past. Indeed, he said to me, "Two sentences are enough to make me sick." The diary revealed the tremendous idealism visible in Maddison and best seen in his unpublished work *The Star-Born.* Maddison sublimated his natural desires for a woman (or the biological urge, if you will) in the Christ-Lenin philosophy implicit in his last testament of faith, *The Policy of Reconstruction,* printed in part in *The Dream of Fair Women.* Had Maddison lived until now he would be much happier and saner than he was in 1919. Last year, at Dartmouth College in Hanover, New Hampshire, Williamson took my copy of the early version of *The Dream of Fair Women* and crossed out the entire title page. I understand now why he did so. The old Williamson is dead and the new one wants to be judged by the version written in New York in 1931. Maddison had grown up in the interval. The second version is not only more realistic, but Maddison has become an objective creation. The author now sees Maddison as someone else, and not as himself. Though the four novels comprising *The Flax of Dream* are frankly autobiographical, in the latest versions Williamson did not, as do most Romantics, weave the plot from his own entrails.

Though from a point of view of his progress as a writer it may have been a mistake to rewrite his earlier books, I can quite understand why he did so. They were to him, and somewhat wrongly I think, standing reproaches to an ego now mature. Critics who judge Williamson only on the first versions of *The Beautiful Years, Dandelion Days,* and *The Dream of Fair Women,* do the author an injustice, and when they cry "We are sick of Maddison," they are referring to the earlier Maddison and not to the later one. I have no doubt that from the point of view of sales Williamson has lost temporarily by rewriting these early books and not continuing after *Tarka The Otter* and *The Village Book,* with *The Labouring Life* or the planned *The Water Dreamer,* but I think that in the long run, when Williamson is judged years later, he will have proved to have been right in rewriting these books. I noticed, too, in the diary a long and generous acknowledgment to Richard Jefferies as his *Master.* Although he would still acknowledge his debt to this writer, especially Jefferies' *The Story of My Heart,* he has now outgrown his influence, and now relies entirely on his own experience. Indeed, the other day a bookseller said to me, "He has knocked Jefferies into a cocked hat."

The diary contained, too, many fine Nature passages, many of which he expanded later in his volumes of short stories and sketches in *The Peregrine's Saga, The Old Stag*, and *The Lone Swallows*. Any real study of Williamson as a writer must refer in great detail to the contents of this journal, and also to his unpublished first novel mentioned at the beginning of this essay.

My last day with Williamson was spent on a trip to Georgeham, where I met some of the characters who are in *The Village Book*. On the way he pointed out Sharshook (sometimes spelled Shrarshook), an island in the estuary, invisible at high tide, between Appledore and the Braunton Burrows. This is the gravel ridge where Maddison drowned, due to Mrs. Ogilvie's fatal oversight. The Burrows, as Mr. Girvan has pointed out in his bibliography of Williamson's writings, has been used by Blackmore in his *Maid of Sker* and to a lesser extent in Barbellion's *Journal of a Disappointed Man*. Williamson's Nature descriptions in *The Pathway* are faithful and sensitive recreations of this part of North Devon.

Georgeham is a rapidly changing village with new mushroom camps springing up for the summer "tourists" who have discovered the place, and new stucco houses for weary and heavy-laden Londoners to spend their holidays. Thus it seems to me fortunate for lovers of the simple and unpretentious to find how amazingly well Williamson has caught and preserved the true and real village of Georgeham and its inhabitants, which at the present rate of change will cease to exist in another twenty-five years. There is no sentimentality in *The Village Book* or in *The Labouring Life* that one occasionally finds in Williamson's earlier books. These books are the work of a conscious literary artist, the master of his medium, with an eye for essential detail, and a perception of "things as they are in themselves." The realist is now at work and the subjective, self-pitying idealist of the past is dead. The island where Maddison drowned is as real to Williamson as Baker Street, where the late lamented Sherlock Holmes lived, is to me, and I still inevitably think of that gentleman whenever I am in Baker Street.

In Georgeham I met old Billy Brown in a pub called "The Lower House," or "The King's Arms," winking with slightly crossed eyes, and talking most comically after a load of several pints of "bitter." You will find him in *The Labouring Life*, and Billy Brown, though he does not know it, has been faithfully preserved for a long, long time. Readers who demand "escape" literature will probably not find much to their liking in this latest of Williamson's books, but those who like Hudson, Borrow, Bourne, Jefferies or Gilbert White will read with deep pleasure this book about old England. The villagers regard Williamson as a famous man. Once when he left his pipe, by chance, in "The King's Arms," on his return several weeks later he found it hung up on the wall and labelled "Henry Williamson's Pipe." He retrieved it.

In the afternoon we sought the heights above Georgeham, where Maddison wandered and indulged his love for Nature. On the hill overlooking the Downs and the sea, Williamson has built a hut of strong English oak. He has planted trees, dug a well—successfully in spite of sceptical villagers, surrounded his acres with a hedge, and there in my old age I expect to find him, glancing wistfully and perhaps a little sadly over the domain he has so well made his own.

What Edward Thomas wrote of Richard Jefferies may, I think, be applied with equal fitness and truth to Jefferies' disciple, Henry Williamson. I am indebted to the poet's daughter Ann Thomas for permission to quote this brief but succinct passage. Thomas wrote: "He drew Nature and human life as he saw it, and he saw it with an unusual eye for detail and with unusual wealth of personality behind. And in all of his best writing he turns from theme to theme, and his seriousness, his utter frankness, the obvious importance of the matter to himself, give us confidence in following him; and though the abundance of what he saw will continue to attract many, it is for his way of seeing, for his composition, his glowing colours, his ideas, for the passionate music wrought out of his life, that we must chiefly go to him. He is on the side of health, of beauty, of strength, of truth, of improvement in life to be wrought by increasing honesty, subtlety, tenderness, courage and foresight. His own character, and the characters of his men and women, fortify us in our intention to live. Nature, as he thought of it, and as his books present it, is a great flood of physical and spiritual sanity, of 'pure ablution round earth's human shores,' to which he bids us resort." Readers of Williamson's finest work, much of which is still to come will find for themselves this heritage of Jefferies, visible in Williamson, which is theirs as readers of the best in English literature.

LONDON, April 1932.

(Privately printed in a limited edition of 250 copies by The Ulysses Press, 1932, Prof. Faulkner's essay is reproduced here with the kind permission of his son, Herbert West, Jnr.)

The Man Who Did Not Hunt.

BY

HENRY WILLIAMSON.

An otter-hunting story by a brilliant young writer whose novels "The Beautiful Years" and "Dandelion Days" have attracted considerable attention.

Illustrations by Lionel Edwards.

SHE screamed as the shot tore a welt in her side, and splashed into the water which immediately was turned red. She screamed for her mate who was hunting eels upstream; she thought of her babies in the drain-pipe. A man shouted, a spaniel barked. The dying otter swung listlessly her brown rudder, made a few feeble paddles with her legs, rolled over, and was borne away in the current.

The farmer who had shot her ran downstream to the falls, where he could recover the body. His dog rushed around him, barking and leaping up. In the April evelight a tall man was sitting by the falls, chin on hand, in an attitude of meditation.

"Gude evening," said the farmer shortly.

"Good evening," replied the other looking up. His face had the sickly pallor of an invalid.

"I don't know if ee knaws it, measter," began the farmer, "but you'm traspassing on my land. I'll trouble ee tew get out."

"I beg your pardon. I was under the impression that this field belonged to Mr. Angell."

"That there below belongs tew th' squire," informed the farmer, "and this here belong tew me, Jacob Morte. If you'm permission to go below thik falls, it ban't no business o' mine. But this here is mine, bought and paid for by honest work, and I'll trouble ee tew get off—an' be quick about it, or I'll zet my dog on tew ee. Thik likes o' yew gentry think yew can go anywhere but you'm mistaken."

Captain Horton-Wickham got up unsteadily, his spine was injured. A German machine gun at Bullecourt had caused wounds that resulted in his being bed-ridden for two years; he was a doomed man.

"Is your name Morte?" he asked quietly.

"It be. Why?"

"I've heard about you; that's all! Good evening."

He turned away, and commenced to descend the path, helped by two sticks, when an exclamation from Farmer Morte made him turn round. Farmer Morte had flung his gun on the grass, and was crawling over the boulders. He seized the dead otter by its rudder, lifted it dripping from the river, and carried it to the bank.

Captain Horton-Wickham stared at him.

"Did you shoot that otter?" he asked coldly.

"That be naught to do with you. My trout be more valuable than vermin. I ban't no otter-hunting gennulmun; I'm a working man."

"That otter has cubs," replied the other. "You're a swine."

"Get off," bellowed Farmer Morte, "you lazy, good-for-nothing gennulmun. Pah! You kills un wi' hounds, and I shutes un. Where be th' difference? If I could find thik cubs I'd shute un tew! Be off, fore I summons ye fur traspass!"

Captain Horton-Wickham limped away,

The otter, in her distress, came towards the scent of the man she loved. "Go away—go away," almost moaned the man on the bank. (*See page 232.*)

trembling at the exertion of the argument, his heart thumping in his ears.

THE little thing made a frail noise, half moan, half whine. It was caused by the pain of hunger. Bitten pieces of trout lay around it; beside it was its dead brother.

Something shuffled along the drain, and the little thing cried out. A warmness surrounded it; it pressed with tiny clawed pads into the hair of the warmness, and sought with its mouth that which it could not find. Later it was quiet. More trout were brought in the jaws of the dog-otter; but the whelp could eat nothing. The father was distressed; he could not understand the absence of his mate. Vainly had he been whistling for her; all night he had swum for miles, but her scent vanished at the fall. The cries of the whelp caused him to bring many more fish to it.

He was away when two men came with a pick and shovel, and one of them commenced to dig at the other's direction.

"It doesn't matter if you crack the pipe," said Captain Horton-Wickham, "because it is never used now, Abner. I know they must be here, because I've watched them going up dozens of times. That fellow Morte deserves to be shot."

"You'm right, zur," replied Abner. "I minds thik time when he were drowen into thik horsepond for beating Jearge Taylor's lill boy, because he found un picking mushrooms in his field."

Having unburdened himself of this memory Abner spat on his horny hands, seized the pick, and commenced to dig. After two hours' work, the pipe was exposed.

It was a little over a year since the invalid had come to the village of Corse Barton, lying three miles inland from the sea in North Devon. That he was a "crock" everyone knew. Beyond that they knew nothing. He was about forty years of age. If he was married, his wife never came to Corse Barton; few letters arrived for him. He was always playing his gramophone, or standing about in his garden. Abner's wife came in to his cottage in the morning, cooked, cleaned up, and waited upon him; he was always courteous and considerate; she pitied him, but he discouraged all sympathy or talk about himself.

Abner wondered what "thik Captain" wanted with the cubs, but he did not like to ask. He cracked the yellow pipe, and inserted the end of the pick into a small hole, using it as a lever. A shard, or fragment flew upwards, and he knelt down and put his arm into the hole, pulling forth a speckled trout.

"Ah, you old poacher," he grunted.

His companion asked to be permitted to examine the cavity, and Abner crawled aside. Captain Horton-Wickham rolled still higher his sleeve, exposing the wasted white length of his arm, and felt down the drain. Something sucked his fingers, and he drew forth a tiny drab brown animal.

"Got them," he cried, triumphantly. "Fancy hitting the right spot right away! There's half a gallon for you, Abner, tonight at the 'Foxhunter.'"

"Thank ee, zur," said Abner, satisfied.

They took out the dead cub, and Captain Horton-Wickham stroked its soft fur.

"Poor little fellow," he said softly, "died of starvation. But your sister is all right, aren't you, my pretty?"

THE pretty was about eight inches long, with a tiny flat head and beady eyes sunk into the brown fur; she had white whiskers and flat ears, webbed pads, or feet, a rudder—or tail—brown like a bull-rush head, but longer, and tapered. Languidly she explored the fingers of her rescuer.

"She'm hungrisome, Captain," said Abner.

"Where can I borrow an infant's bottle?" asked the other. "Or failing that, do you know of an old cat that's had kittens lately?"

"There be one at the 'Foxhunter,' Captain. A tarrible old grimalkin, her be. Her might give th' cub a dapp on the head, though."

"Let's try," suggested the Captain, "forrard to the 'Foxhunter.' You can have your half gallon, and Zoë—I shall call her Zoë—can be introduced to the tarrible old grimalkin."

At the first sight of Teeter one realised that the adjectival description was correct. She was tarrible—the Devonian dialect is more expressive than the conventional. Teeter had had more fights with dogs, female cats, stoats, had had more adventures with trap and gin, than any other feline in Corse Barton. One ear was so torn that it resembled a piece of frayed string; the other was depressed. She had one forepaw—and one stump—the result of a night spent in gnawing the limb held in a trap. One of her eyes was whalley, the other was inscrutable. She sat on the window-sill outside the 'Foxhunter,' content in the sunshine.

Captain Horton-Wickham and Abner approached. She did not move. They came to her, and held the whelp near her nose. She did not move. They placed the crawling thing on the ground. She did not even look at it.

The two men entered the inn, and spoke to the grey-haired landlord. "Gorbruggee, what 'ave ee there?" he gasped; "a fitchey?"

They replied that it was not a weasel, but an otter whelp.

"Gorbruggee, if I ban't dumbfounded, Captain!"

It is regretted that it has not proved possible to trace the source of this item. [Ed.]

A BIBLIOGRAPHY

AND A CRITICAL SURVEY OF
THE WORKS OF
Henry Williamson

By I. WAVENEY GIRVAN

Together with
authentic bibliographical annotations
By ANOTHER HAND
(This being Henry Williamson getting the itch out of a few old scars of his own seeking!).

THE ALCUIN PRESS
Chipping Campden
Gloucestershire
1931

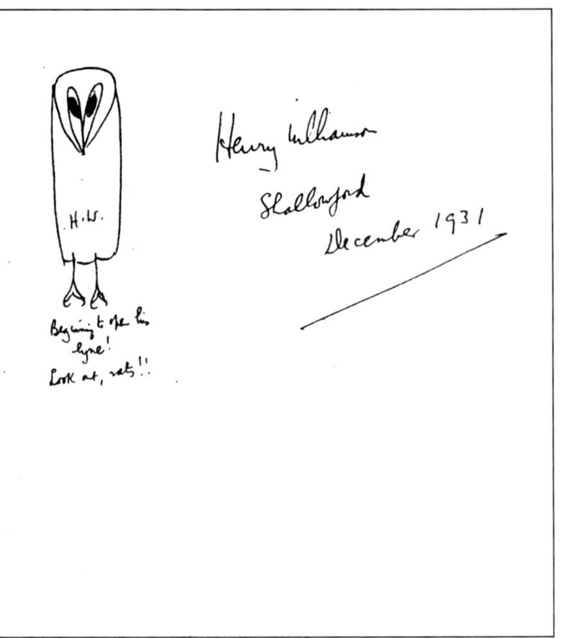

Introduction

. . . The Introduction is intended neither to flatter nor to disparage but is an attempt, in a short space, to trace critically Mr Williamson's progress and development as a writer. *I.W.G.*

In studying the work of Henry Williamson it is necessary to stress the name of Richard Jefferies, whose writings have greatly influenced Williamson's outlook and from whom he derived his early style. He has said that *Bevis, The Story of a Boy*, was the first book that he had really read and it undoubtedly turned his attention to his own boyhood and *The Beautiful Years* was the result. But another, the best, book of Richard Jefferies has had a greater influence on Williamson, for in most of his writings there is reflected the pagan philosophy contained in *The Story of my Heart*.

Henry Williamson was born in 1897 and his first book, *The Beautiful Years*, was published at the age of twenty-four in 1921. Later in the same year was published *The Lone Swallows*, which affords a better starting point for the critic in that it consists of Williamson's earliest essays reprinted from various periodicals. In these essays the style and spirit of Richard Jefferies is apparent to a marked degree: there is the same close observation of nature that Jefferies was inclined to abuse and the same random change of subject that constitutes much of Jefferies' charm, notably in *Round About a Great Estate*. This volume did little more than challenge comparison with Jefferies, although the essay *The Change* seems to contain the seed that was to become *The Flax of Dream*.

There was less of Richard Jefferies in *The Beautiful Years* though there is a superficial resemblance between this book and *Bevis*. Both are the stories of a remembered boyhood spent in the open air, written by men who wished to escape from present suffering by reconstituting their early years, but whereas *Bevis* was the work of a naturalist *The Beautiful Years* is the work of a novelist endowed with the naturalist's powers of observation. Jefferies the solitary was the first naturalist to study that peculiar animal Man; Williamson, whom circumstances had thrown more among men in privation, is able to bring into his writings a deeper sympathy and understanding.

The Beautiful Years, Book I of *The Flax of Dream*, has an underlying current of sadness and foreboding of the tragedy that was to culminate in *The Pathway* with the death of Willie Maddison. In its original edition *The Beautiful Years* was lacking in form, but this Williamson has remedied in the revised edition without losing in the process the spontaneity that is its charm.

The naturalist and the novelist in Williamson developed side by side in *The Peregrine's Saga* and *The Old Stag*, which contain short stories of animals, birds and men. *Stumberleap* is perhaps the best example of these stories, for in it is evidence of the powers of minute observation and, what is more important, of the good use his fictional mind can make of the material he has collected.

So far Williamson's work had won for him little recognition. A few critics had discovered individuality in *The Old Stag*, but it is safe to say that the remarkable *Tarka the Otter*, published in 1927, came as a surprise to most. *Tarka the Otter*, unlike *The Beautiful Years*, could not 'practically have written itself', for it could only have been the result of patient watching by day and night. Tarka's hunted life is recorded above and below stream, in fallow and on moor, and never is it apparent where imagination, perforce, supplied the details when observation failed. The further title of the book, *His Joyful Water-Life and Death in the Country of the Two Rivers*, indicates its quality, for throughout there is no concession to the sentimental and for this reason thefinal pages carry a stronger pathos for the sentient. Before a sentence had been written *Tarka the Otter* must have cost its author as much energy as most writers would care to spend upon a completed novel. In its writing there is evidence of months of care as arduous as the months of vigilance. Williamson seems to have attempted faultlessness of style and somewhat faultily to have achieved it: it is further testimony to the novel that it is able to carry its author's style successfully.

The naturalist and the novelist combined to make *Tarka the Otter* one of the finest and most moving of animal stories and Williamson here revealed himself for the first time as a conscious stylist. At least it won him critical recognition.

Mention of *Dandelion Days* and *The Dream of Fair Women* has been purposely postponed in order that *The Flax of Dream* may be considered as a whole. *The Beautiful Years* left Willie Maddison at the age of nine. . . . *Dandelion Days* is the chronicle of his schooling at Colham Grammar School where he reluctantly assimilated the teachings which were to cause him so much pain in their unlearning.

The spirit of the fields is here as much as in *The Beautiful Years*, but the purpose of the tetralogy is seen more clearly, especially in the revised edition.

The machinery that should have turned out the conventional 'old boy' (synonymous for 'decent citizen') distorts the imaginative and sensitive Maddison. It is in the fields that he escapes from the school and his unsympathetic father and receives his education and also his character. He leaves Colham only to be caught in the vaster machinery of the war. The actual record of his war experience finds no place in the tetralogy and rightly so. Its effect is intensified by this omission, for *The Flax of Dream* is the chronicle of an individual's reaction to the ideas of those who made the war possible and not to the war itself. In fact, as Williamson has pointed out, Willie Maddison's character was decided at the time of his leaving school and only his outlook remained to be enlarged.

The first two volumes, though passionately sincere, were written with the detachment necessary in a novelist, but *The Dream of Fair Women* was the record of emotions without the tranquillity and seemed to have been written too closely upon the actual experience. In its revised form it is worthy of its place in *The Flax of Dream* though it still remains its most sentimental part. Williamson has removed the flippancy of the original version without destroying the humour that contrasts with the tragedy of Maddison's painful love-affair, and he has thus enhanced the emotional value of the novel. The story now flows evenly and naturally and is a fine example of the author's later development of his narrative gift. Most of the adverse criticisms of this novel resolved themselves into attacks upon the character of Maddison, but if *The Flax of Dream* is read as one volume these criticisms lose much of their point. His short life has been so powerfully presented that it is Maddison's individuality and not his attractiveness that is important.

The Pathway is Williamson's finest achievement and of the four novels comprising *The Flax of Dream* can stand best by itself. From the arrival of Maddison in North Devon, heightened by the dramatic effect of causing him to be discussed before his actual appearance, to his death by drowning with the leaves of his manuscript scattered on the shore, *The Pathway* moves with a melancholy and haunting beauty. The style that was inclined to be overloaded in *Tarka the Otter* is here, but is mastered and never used merely for its own sake. The book is also memorable for its descriptions of Braunton Burrows, a two mile stretch of towans,[1] alive with interest for the naturalist. The Burrows have made at least two previous appearances in literature—in Blackmore's *Maid of Sker* and to a lesser extent in Barbellion's *Journal of a Disappointed Man*. It is curious to note the points of affinity between Barbellion and Maddison. The descriptions of nature in *The Pathway* have been criticised as being unnecessary, but since Maddison's first and last love was for the fields, birds and animals, these descriptions seem to fit closely into the theme, and bring to the book a further distinction.

Reference has been made to *The Flax of Dream* rather than to the four component novels for it is certain that until it is published as one volume it will not receive the recognition that it deserves. The perspective is lost by the separate publication of its parts and unity is essential to bring out to the full the tragedy of Willie Maddison's life.

The Flax of Dream is largely autobiographical, and in Maddison's attitude to the war may be discovered the author's. This is made clear by reading Williamson's two war books *The Wet Flanders Plain* and *The Patriot's Progress. The Wet Flanders Plain,* written in the form of a diary of a soldier who has returned to the battlefields, contains the same fervency that the author has put into the mouth of Maddison, but the bitterness is absent. It remains, however, pure anti-war propaganda and may lose some of its poignancy when the ideas it contains are more generally accepted, but it will always be read by those who can appreciate the frank expression of the author's personality.

The Patriot's Progress, written in the form of a novel, is much more effective, for the propaganda, though inferential, is as strong. Williamson has been wise to choose for his central figure an ordinary clerk with a stolid outlook, for he thus avoids the hysteria that has marred so many other war novels. It is terrible, as a war book should be, but Private John Bullock's reaction only goes as far as his crushing retort "We are England" when told that England will not forget her heroes.

Williamson has written a novel round the lives of three hunted animals, Tarka the Otter, Willie Maddison and John Bullock; the finer animals, Tarka and Maddison, lose their lives in the chase, but Bullock escapes with the loss of a leg. The lino-cut epigraph cynically suggests that the old stolidity will assert itself in John Bullock and that the war will have proved only an interlude in the more serious occupation of book-keeping.

There remains *The Village Book,* consisting of essays alternating under the headings of *The Spirit of the Village* and the *Air and Light of the Fields and the Sea.* Of the whole it is difficult to write, for the essays are of uneven merit. Their unevenness lies in the choice of subject; the writing is Williamson's best.

It seems a pity that in most of these essays Williamson should have divorced his two supreme gifts of story-telling and accurate observation of nature, for where they are combined, as in *The Badger Dig,* the result is one of the most moving things he has written. The author's object, to present truthfully the spirit of the village, is certainly achieved but in the process he seems to have lost some of the poetry inherent in his other writings.

HenryWilliamson's remarkable powers are apparent in nearly everything he has written; especially in *Tarka the Otter* his detached yet sympathetic understanding of animals, in *The Pathway* his poetry and compassion, in *Dandelion Days* his humour, in *The Wet Flanders Plain* the sincerity of his beliefs, and in all his care and style. He has outgrown the early influence of Richard Jefferies that threatened at first to prove too powerful, and he has relied in his later work more upon his own experience.The novel has been his most successful mode of expression and it is evident that he is, and will be, preeminently a novelist.

Only in technique have his novels been traditional, though towards the end of *The Patriot's Progress* there is a hint that he may yet develop beyond his last convention.

I. WAVENEY GIRVAN

Liverpool, August 1931

NOTE

1. Cornish word for sandhills.

Illustration from Henry Williamson's The Old Stag *by Charles F. Tunnicliffe*

The Ironic Mode: Aldington and Williamson

John Onions

(Chapter Four from *English Fiction and Drama of the Great War, 1918-39*)[1]

Two well-known literary figures made significant contributions to the war-books controversy by taking to extremes the ironic narrative mode already employed, as we have seen, by numerous war novelists. Richard Aldington's two works, *Death of a Hero* (1929) and *Roads to Glory* (1930), together with Henry Williamson's *The Patriot's Progress* (1930), constitute examples, in their different ways, of what Northrop Frye terms 'naive irony':[2] they draw attention to themselves and to their highly egocentric natures. They invite the reader to share their self- conscious satire on human folly. Certainly *Death of a Hero* and *The Patriot's Progress* are two of the most overtly bitter attacks on the social hero which came out of the war boom. (The section on Richard Aldington is necessarily deleted. Interested readers should refer to John Onions' book, op. cit.)

THE PATRIOT'S PROGRESS: EVERYMAN AT WAR

The Patriot's Progress arose out of a suggestion by J. C. Squire that Henry Williamson write captions for a series of lino-cuts by William Kermode illustrating the Great War. He was to describe it as 'tedious work, forcing one bare word after another';[13] indeed, he abandoned it for a year, disgusted by the acclaim given to *All Quiet on the Western Front.* In 1959 he added that 'it helped to delay my own books on the war' and was now dated, 'mannered to the anti-Staff period of the infantryman's war of 1915–1917'. He further noted that he 'didn't want to use one sentence of P. P. prose'.[14] All this would suggest, as Holger Klein does, that the book is 'peripheral to Williamson's work'.[15] Yet in 1968 he reprinted in full the laudatory comments about it by Arnold Bennett and T. E. Lawrence, and it is not difficult to see how it is consistent with many of the ideas to which Williamson remained loyal. And while it may not be as significant as some of Williamson's other works, the extremely ironic mode which it so effectively employs seems wholly appropriate to Williamson, whose 'life and work', as Colin Wilson remarks, 'are mixed up together in a curious and complex way'.[16]

The Patriot's Progress tells the story of John Bullock who, as his name suggests, is a modern British Everyman. As the TLS reviewer noted, the book – coming at the back-end of the boom – covers very familiar ground:[17] John Bullock makes the ironic journey from romantic illusion to revealed degeneracy; his acquaintance with SIWs, the brothel and suicidal attacks puts it firmly in the category of what Graves in his droll way called the 'genre war novels'.[18] His army number, Pvte 19023, immediately – and hardly coincidentally – follows Frederic Manning's whose novel appeared in January 1930 under the pseudonym Private 19022. Williamson was already acquainted with T. E. Lawrence, who had fulsomely praised Manning's work; Williamson might even have seen a copy of the limited edition of The Middle Parts of Fortune which appeared the previous year. Both authors take the ordinary soldier as subject, but, though Williamson admired the other's book, their attitudes are fundamentally antithetical.[19] Manning's soldiers exist in their 'prejudices and partialities', as he put it in his Preface; John Bullock is deliberately anonymous.

He is emphatically not a character, and even less a disguised projection of the author. Only briefly, in the early sections, is he even called 'John'. Otherwise he is John Bullock, archetypal son of England, his ideas fathered by such influential parts of the press as Bottomley's John Bull. The opening line alone – 'John Bullock, a youth beloved by his parents, was a clerk in the City of London' – establishes his significance and the mode of narration. 'Youth' is unqualified by adjectives; that he is beloved by his parents confirms his normality and prepares to engage our pity; his job projects him as one of the archetypal figures in the war's fiction, overprotected and highly sensitive. The confidence with which Williamson offers such a generalised character points to the very functional nature of his descriptions. It would be foolish to search the opening pages for richness of detail or subtlety of implication:

> *Every morning John Bullock went to London on a train that took twenty-two minutes to reach Cannon Street Station – unless it were foggy. Except in the hot summer the windows of the train were closed; men and girls were sitting close together on the seats, seldom speaking. Puffing pipes, reading newspapers which formed the surface of their minds, 'wearing sombre clothes, usually shapeless, and hard bowler hats, the old and middle-aged men in the carriages were once like John Bullock.* (p. 1)

This is not a cameo scene; no middle-aged men nor girls can be imagined. It is a piece of history given in its representative data. Like the opening train-scene in *Parade's End*, it symbolises – ironically – the apparently secure world of pre-August 1914. Unlike the irony of that trilogy, however (and the comparison is not pejorative), the irony here does not chiefly arise from its place in the novel's structure or from the complications of character. Here the irony is overtly and verbally present in the knowing superiority of the speaker; it soon becomes particularly sardonic: these superficial, illusioned, controlled old men 'believed that they were of the finest race on earth, superior to all foreigners'. The whole narrative rests on John Bullock's innocence (and thus his continually hopeful but ironic ignorance of the future) contrasted with the narrator's omniscience.

The irony is one of circumstances, and these exist in essential and representative experience, stylistically handled through simple sentence construction, unexceptional adjectives and inventory-like description. The mark of the mainstream novel – the interreaction of character and circumstance – is absent. John Bullock, far more so than even Aldington's characters, is a personification of circumstances. He enlists because of the media, is scared by the war, disillusioned at the Somme, horrified at Passchendaele, and quite content after a few months' blighty. He is utterly unheroic, not simply because he is no great warrior, but because he is a creation of his surroundings. He moves from ignorance and illusion to ignorance and disillusion, but his innocence – like Candide's, to some extent – intensifies the bitterness of the book. John Bullock, one leg amputated,

> *grew fat and happy, and lost all interest in the war. Never wanted to hear of it again. It hadn't been such a bad time, taken all round: he wouldn't have missed it, really.* (p. 192)

Williamson's skill lies in sustaining the ironic narrative without the authorial wisdom grating upon the reader's moral or aesthetic sense. He does so by variation of voice and style within the limits of the narrative mode. Some war scenes are orthodox descriptive writing; often he is the omniscient narrator. On occasions he borrows the language of his subjects: ''The sergeant came along, shouting something, and waving his rifle. He looked pissed, as though he'd been half-inching the rum' (p. 115). At times he notes the deliberately shocking detail: 'Three in the hut were killed. They had to scrape one off the curved iron hut wall with an entrenching tool' (p. 132). The detail is again self-contained; the single fact of horror is the reality of the scene. Selective detail is often made functional by a dogmatic note: 'Every theft was exploited by the peasants' (p. 85); 'All thought of being allowed to sleep on the ground . . .' (p. 90). Some scenes are individualised by the skill of the writing but generalised in other ways, for instance by the avoidance of pronouns and articles:

> *Pay parade after tea:– waiting outside the Company office door: name called by C.Q.M.S.: stepping in smartly, saluting. Officer signing the slight brown-covered pay book, handing it back with a five-franc note in it. One pace back, another salute ignored by hatless subaltern holding out his wrist-watch'd hand for next man's book: and then about turn, smart steps to the door: relaxation. . . .* (p. 80)

Here the impersonality, speed and discipline of the affair are vividly conveyed with just sufficiently choice detail to bring the scene to life. Sometimes Williamson speaks through the superficial consciousness of John Bullock; on occasion he permits John Bullock's thoughts a looser rein:

> *Straw on the floor was pressed down, damp, muddy. Candles flickered beside cast-off boots, sodden packs, red cigarette spots. A bit of all right. Sleep, sleep, sleep, O lovely warmth and comfort, sleep until nine next morning, breakfast, no fatigues, sleep, sleep-ha, ha, blotto, he was the boy, rum was the stuff to give the troops. Good-night, Ginger, old man.* (p. 74)

There is something perhaps suggestive of *In Parenthesis* here, but Williamson cannot permit such a mode of narration to continue lest John Bullock achieve a stature and individuality which his author denies him. Indeed, even in this short revelation, Williamson is being ironic at the soldier's expense: John Bullock celebrates the very cause of his mental and moral blotto.

Ginger is one of several characters who make brief appearances in the book. He and 'Nobby' reflect some of the comradeship which Williamson so much admired. Inevitably both are killed. The padre emerges as a slightly larger and admirable character; he and his idealism are further victims of the war.

Kermode's lino-cut of his face evokes an overwhelming sense of pity. None of these are ever realised characters, for Williamson maintains a tight control of his art. However, at rare moments he briefly vacates his superior moral position. At one point, John Bullock perceives the war as 'something that kept millions of men like himself in slavery' (p. 151-2): an incredible insight in his circumstances. Similar insights by the mutineers at Étaples are also unconvincing (p. 127-8). Williamson's clearest loss of control is the very ending. Here the irony ('This good man is a hero') and John Bullock's proudly deliberate sentence – 'We are England' – are at odds with each other. Although the scene has autonomous power, it fails as an ending because John Bullock is given a moral stature beyond his achievement in the book. T. E. Lawrence, greatly though he admired the work, found the ending sentimental.[20]

The use of such functional characters is to make *The Patriot's Progress* a book about war: a risky business in that most First World War fiction is so obviously dated by its subject and by its own inability to see something about men beyond their circumstances. *The Patriot's Progress* is far more successful with its subject because its medium, as the title implies, is the morality tale. It cannot be judged simply within the tradition of the novel; indeed, part of its effect comes from the literal page itself, with its large strong print and Kermode's powerful lino-cuts. Williamson's stated intentions were to

> *write an entire story around them [the lino-cuts], pouring in a concrete of words making, as it were, a line of German mebus, or 'pillboxes'. . . . His lino-cuts would be shuttering to my verbal concrete.*[21]

His compact, highly expressive language accords perfectly with the illustrations; and the division into 'five phases' reinforces the simple directness which structures the tale.

Yet *The Patriot's Progress* is not an allegory and John Bullock is too passive to become a modern Christian. For Williamson's work, unlike Bunyan's, depicts the triumph of circumstances. In fact, *The Patriot's Progress* does not create a close relationship with the book whose title it so boldly echoes. The connection comprises two main elements: the use of an Everyman character, and Williamson's ironic manipulation of Bunyan's story. There is surprisingly little of the latter. Critics who point out the obviously intended allusion to Bunyan do not elucidate any close interweaving. Paul Fussell, who seems to imagine that no English writer can fail to make something of the Bunyan literary influence (just as no American, such as Cummings, could succeed), notes Williamson's sardonic use of it, but, despite a whole section on the theme, reveals little more than the obviously ironic use of 'progress'.[22] Each succeeding phase takes John Bullock farther from past ideals and towards a fresh degeneracy. He ends up back at home, the civilian population as ignorant as ever, and he missing a leg. This is the major irony of the book; specific ironic allusions have to be contrived by the reader. It might be that the Celestial City is parodied in the profiteers' notion of a land fit for heroes, and there is the religious implication of: 'On the sixth day they rested' (p. 86). Sometimes the literal pushes towards the symbolic and metaphorical: 'Darkness pressed upon each man, darkness sucked at him from the mud, often sucked oaths of blazing despair from his muffled, floundering being' (p. 100). Descriptions of the mud and horror of Passchendaele inevitably evoke pictures of the Slough of Despond or the 'dangerous Quag' of the Valley of the Shadow of Death where Christian 'thought he should be torn in pieces'. However, Williamson provides very little verbal manipulation, and *The Patriot's Progress* resists allusive inquiry. Nor does it need it. The book identifies itself as a morality tale, its hero a simple character who ultimately has undergone little change. It is a medium fertile for naive irony and well cultivated by Williamson.

THE AUTHOR AS GREAT MAN

Williamson's nature writing, autobiography, war works and political statements make a semi-digestible stew of ideas which would require, though perhaps do not deserve, a book of their own. Here, it might be worth suggesting simply why the 'naive irony' should so appeal to Williamson. Eric Hiscock described him as 'an oddball . . . . Always, like Byron, saying "I want a hero". He found him in T. E. Lawrence, then Hitler and Mosley. The 1914–18 war scarred his soul'.[23] Williamson's notorious but naive appreciation of Hitler certainly had its political origins in the war, though it took some while to formulate. He was not, like Jünger, a subscriber to the belief that war can strip man to his tragic greatness; for him, the dominant psychological and moral moment of the war – referred to throughout his writings – was the unofficial Christmas truce of 1914:

> *Three weeks after my eighteenth [it was, as we now know, actually his nineteenth] birthday I was talking*

to Germans with beards and khaki-covered pickelhauben, and smoking new china gift-pipes glazed with the Crown Prince's portrait in colour, in a turnip field amidst dead cows, English and German corpses frozen stiff. The new world, for me, was germinated from that fraternization. Adolf Hitler was one of those 'opposite numbers' in long field-grey coats.[24]

Williamson apparently suddenly discovered that 'the whole war was based on lies, and that, most typically, the lies were not deliberate, but arose from the obscurity or denseness of the average European's mind'.[25] Hitler's perception of the same circumstances, so Williamson hoped, would cause him to lead humanity out of the morass of fear and slavery.

Throughout such writing runs the theme of the innocent soldier. Addressing the Unknown Soldier in 1936, Williamson asks: 'Were you, like hundreds of millions of others in Europe, reared and educated in such a manner that you could seldom be your true self?'[26] The story of Willie Maddison in *The Flax of Dream* revolves around the Romantic theme of alienation and environment. From this to his misguided celebration of Hitler was a relatively small step, incorporating a notorious sentence penned on Christmas Day, 1935: 'I salute the great man across the Rhine, whose life-symbol is the happy child.'[27] Hitler, according to Williamson, 'perceived the root causes of war in the unfulfilled human ego'; his ideas were those of 'the ex-soldier, made coherent, real'.[28]

This Rousseauist understanding of man's goodness and society's wickedness points to the moral nature of *The Patriot's Progress*: John Bullock is continually the innocent and the victim, never the killer; at the end he remains blithely uneducated in the ways of the wicked, like the mass of the world which can never change itself. Yet he is also given, perhaps unconvincingly, moments in which he perceives the truth of his situation. Such moments are vital if a great man is to lead him to a better world: in effect, the political message of Under Fire and its Marxist author. Williamson greatly admired the book and, in fact, until 1927 'had seen hope only in Lenin's point of view'.[29] The functional descriptions of *The Patriot's Progress* owe something to those of Barbusse, but the latter also dramatises the role of writer as hero. In The Wet Flanders Plain (1929), his account of a return journey there, Williamson relates a perfectly Barbussean episode. He describes a visit to a peasant family whose son was mentally retarded by an English shell during the war; he mentions Barbusse's book:

Their eyes lit up; they exclaimed with enthusiasm at that name. That was reality, la verité! Only the week before a German soldier, looking for the grave of his brother, had come to the village, and it so chanced that he had read Barbusse, and had declared that it was true for the German soldier as well as for the French! He was a comrade, that Boche . . . no, Boche was a bad word, part of the old world: pas vrai! He was a man like themselves, but in the War his uniform happened to be a different colour. He was a brother!
(p. 136-7)

Williamson's belief in the man of insight who must lead the befuddled masses towards the light of a better civilisation lies behind his political position and underpins *The Patriot's Progress.* The superior knowingness of the narrator implies a role for the writer as Carlylean great man or Rousseauist legislator. In the later *A Chronicle of Ancient Sunlight,* Williamson did create a literary soldier as hero; like his creator, Phillip Maddison sees the war as the product of an unnatural society which he must lead, through his writing, back to its natural roots.

Williamson's change of political loyalties around 1927 was a result of perverse thinking rather than militarist sympathies (though his dislike of *All Quiet* reveals almost a militarist's indignation).[30] He somehow sustained his own tangled consistency, combining in *The Patriot's Progress* a morality tale and the Romantic tradition of the writer as hero.

NOTES

1. We are grateful to the author and the publishers for permission to print this extract from John Onions' *English Fiction and Drama of the Great War, 1918–39* (Macmillan Press, 1990).
2. Northrop Frye, *The Anatomy of Criticism* (1971), p. 41.
13. Henry Williamson, *Genius of Friendship: T. E. Lawrence* (1941), p. 37.
14. Epigraph to 1968 edition, p. 196. He did, in fact, use a brief example of P. P. prose in 1936 in *Goodbye West Country* (p. 348: cf. *The Patriot's Progress, pp.* 100, 103).
15. Klein, 'Projections of Everyman', in Klein (ed.), *T'he First World War in Fiction,* 84–100, p. 88. Colin Wilson's essay on Williamson in *Eagle and Earwig* (pp. 225-38) makes no reference to *The Patriot's Progress.* Klein's

comment is largely, though not entirely, valid; *7he Patriot's Progress* certainly seems minor when alongside the fifteen-volume, post-1945 *A Chronicle of Ancient Sunlight,* five volumes of which relate Philip Maddison's experiences in the Great War.

16. Wilson, p. 225.
17. *TLS* (5 June 1930), 472. Arnold Bennett's praise, however, led to it being serialised in the *Evening Standard;* the novel was also reprinted twice within a month. Opinions continue to differ: Greicus thinks it has doubtful literary merit; Klein supports Bennett's judgement; Bergonzi ignores it and concentrates on *A Chronicle.* Middleton Murry, who wrote a perceptive essay on Williamson, says that 'good *as Patriot's Progress* was, it was not good enough': *Katherine Mansfield and Other Literary Studies* (1959), p. 122.
18. Graves, 'The Garlands Wither', *TLS* (26 June 1930), 534.
19. In a 1934 postscript to his essay 'Reality in War Literature', he calls *Her Privates We* a 'good book' (p. 261), though not as good as *Winged Victory* by V. M. Yeates (an ex-comrade of Williamson's). In his 1968 Preface, he upgrades Manning's novel to the status of 'masterpiece'.
20. See Lawrence's comments in the Preface to the 1968 edition.
21. Preface to 1968 edition.
22. Fussell, pp. 137–44.
23. Quoted in Daniel Farson, *Henry: An Appreciation of Henry Williamson* (1982), p. 97.
24. Williamson, *Goodbye West Country* (1937), p. 9.
25. Williamson, 'Reality in War Literature', *The Linhay on the Downs* (1934), 224–62, p. 246.
26. Williamson, *Goodbye West Country,* p. 344.
27. Williamson, Foreword, *The Flax of Dream* (revised edn, 1936), p. 7. In fairness to Williamson, he was not the only literary figure from the war to sympathise with Germany in the mid-thirties. Bairnsfather, Lawrence and Blunden all expressed some degree of sympathy, though Williamson retained his belief in Hitler until he died. See Richard Criffiths, *Fellow Travellers of the Right* (1980).
28. Williamson, *Goodbye West Country,* pp. 228–9.
29. Ibid., p. 229. He calls *Le Feu* a work of genius in his Introduction to *A Soldier's Diary of the Great War* (1929), p. x. Williamson's sympathies with Hitler are dated to about 1927 in Murry, p. 129.
30. Preface to 1968 edition.

William Kermode – The Patriot's Progress. *Hand pull for title page. From Henry Williamson's literary archive. Apparently HW did not like this, as a postcard from William Kermode, 3.2.30, states, 'I'm sorry you don't care for the new title page cut.' No illustration appeared on the title page when published.*

Henry Williamson

Edward Seago

This title is misleading, for it implies a portrait of the man. That is not my intention. As well as I know how, I have done this in paint, and I hope that one day someone will do so in the written word. Whoever it is they will have a difficult task, for Henry Williamson will not be captured easily on paper. I think his biographer will find that he is writing the life of more than one man, and it will not be easy to keep them from getting muddled. But if he fails to do so the portrait will lose by it.

I remember once reading a little book by Dean Matthews which was called, I think, *The Adventures of the Angel Gabriel in his Search for Mr Shaw.* I enjoyed that little book, and I can imagine that Mr Shaw enjoyed it too. Briefly it described the difficulties encountered by the angel in his quest to find the *real* man. He met many in the guise of the playwright, but each in turn proved to be no more than part of his character. Finally he came upon a very little man sitting outside a tiny house. He was the *real* Shaw, and he told Gabriel that, because of all the others, very few people ever found him. . . . But, anyway, that was about Mr Shaw, and certainly not a serious biography. I only mention it because now and again one will hear people remark of someone, "I wonder what he's *really* like? You know, I don't think even his wife knows him!" which seems to me rather pointless, and, I should have thought, quite untrue. If a person is posing, surely one can usually tell? and there must be a reason for them doing so. Either they are play-acting for social reasons, or merely by inclination they have contrived to become artificial; in both cases I should have thought that one could form a conception of the character.

But if there are several sides to a person, each one entirely genuine, then why this conjecture of the real self, for are they not all of them real? I am certain that the various Williamsons are all of them very real, for I have never met a man more completely sincere, nor so steadfast in his search for truth.

No, I think we are apt to catch at the more lovable parts of a character, and say, "That is the real man," whereas the real man is composed of many parts, without any one of which his character would not be the same. And I believe there is no one to whom the weaknesses are more obvious than the person concerned. But there are probably very few who have the courage to face them openly, or who care to subject their actions to genuine self-criticism. I wish that I was one of them. I think that Henry Williamson is; few men could judge themselves more hardly.

And now what about happiness? Do you think the really genuine man, who follows without question the dictates of sincerity, has more chance of finding happiness? I don't. I think that what we broadly speak of as happiness will never really be his. By 'happiness' I suppose we mean 'contentment of mind,' and those more likely to possess it are those less exposed to the elements which disturb it. By this I do not mean that the lives of simple folk are untroubled, for indeed they are not; and moreover a more worldly conception does not necessarily develop sensibility. A lad will probably get no bigger thrill from his first motor-cycle than he had from his first toy engine in the nursery. But the child in the nursery is less exposed to outside disturbances than the lad setting forth with his girl-friend on the pillion.

There have been few writers and painters in every age who have refused to shut their eyes to the truth underlying the modes or conventional thought-patterns of their time; who have said, "These things are real; that is how we shall put them down. Beauty hand in hand with Ugliness, and sometimes apart, but never will we mask them with the cloak of conventional thought to make them more palatable." Such men to-day stand exasperated before the tender canvases of the Victorian painters depicting gentle motherhood. "Yes," they say, "there it is, fluffed like a soufflé to melt the public heart! But what's on the other side of the picture? the pain and the fortitude, the beauty and ugliness of man in the making!" And who say of the poet's ideal of spring, "Here are the rose-tinted spectacles to make the countryside more easy on the eye! But what of the verse unsung? the endless fight of the labourer on the land. And what of the ugliness which lay hidden beneath the blossom on the bough the unceasing cruelty of Nature. . . . No, you take the prettiness and let the other be."

For my part I choose to paint what I see in a simple and straightforward manner. Is this working with rose-tinted spectacles? I do not know. I can only paint as I see, as I feel. I love the beauty of the countryside, for me there is joy in every season of the year. Wherever there is beauty to be found I am content to go no farther. When I see the plough-team breasting the hill, to the jingle of the shackle chains, and see the great sky behind, the beauty of it fills my heart. To me it is a noble sight, and when I try to paint it, I try to put down what I have seen and felt.

Portrait of Henry Williamson, painted by Edward Seago, 1942. Taken from Henry Williamson's own copy of Peace in War. *His manuscript note states: 'The left hand was painted of the painter's father's hand. Ted left it like that!' (But Edward Seago specifically refers to making a study of HW's hands at the end of his essay, and the 'hands' sketch is included in* Peace and War.)

But what of the other side, which might scarcely show in the picture. Maybe it is poor land, each year growing poorer because the farmer is unable to put that goodness back which alone will enrich the soil. Gradually the land will lose fertility, and desperately he will watch it passing beyond his control. The fences will grow thin and the ditches become blind, his fields will not drain, and his premises will fall into disrepair; finally his men, his horses, his implements, and himself will abandon the unequal struggle. On Michaelmas day all that remains of his live and dead stock will be paraded in a meadow, and the farm will be sold by auction. That auction will be a picturesque affair, and I shall probably go there and paint it.

The average person will say, "There is enough unpleasantness in the world without bringing it all into pictures and books." I wonder. I think perhaps it is a very good thing for us now and then to be brought face to face with it. Surely only in that way shall we get our proportions right?

I admire those men who follow unflinchingly their own vision of truth, whether it be with, or though generally against, popular taste. But theirs is a hard road, and scarcely a happy one. Henry Williamson is one of them, and he, I believe, is not a happy man. I wish that he could find peace of mind, but I'm afraid that if he did the spark which burns fiercely inside him might die.

I suppose the Williamson most generally known is the writer of Nature and Animal stories. I wonder if I am wrong in supposing that these are more often his subjects, not because he is an enthusiastic naturalist, but because he finds in them the essence of truth and reality. With such things he is in sympathy, and with rare power he can put his profound understanding on paper.

I should like to have known the Williamson of the last war. From his books one can form a picture of the man. To-day there is Williamson the farmer. Several years ago he left his beloved Devon to farm in Norfolk. I think he left his heart behind. The farm of his ideal has not materialised. Perhaps it will do yet. I hope so, or perhaps the dream will become an encumbrance no longer bearable. Just now, in the second great war of his life, he is a tired man, toiling with his hands on the land; still steadfast to his principles, seeking 'orderliness' and 'regimentation,' believing that only through clarity, and universal comprehension of all points of view (through knowing oneself) can un-understanding and that mass un-understanding called modern war be avoided; and finding that he is a voice crying in the wilderness. Tormented always by the thought that he, himself, may be the discord, yet knowing that it is not within his power to strike a different note.

And then, on occasion, there is that other man, carefree and gay, with an almost slapstick sense of humour. I like his humour, and his nonsense would make the dimmest person laugh; unless they were too dim to realise that it was nonsense, and that I would like still more!

His passion for truth was even brought to bear on the painting of my portrait. I wanted it to be an outdoor portrait, with a rod in his hands and sky behind him. To do this Henry said we would have to go to a stream, preferably a Devon stream, on a hot summer day, and then we should get the real atmosphere for the picture. He was right, of course, but we couldn't, and stream or no stream I wanted to paint the picture. I produced a rod indoors, and suggested that he should stand with it in his hands. He protested that at least we should go outside in the sum, so we took the paints and easel into the garden.

I completed the head in one sitting, and was afraid to touch it again. But Henry was particular about the hands and the rod, and also about his little pipe, the shortest I have ever seen. He calls it his 'fishing pipe,' and he had it made specially, because a longer one got in the way when he smacked at the horseflies on his face. He says he killed scores on his cheeks and chin without disturbing his pipe, but the trout would not eat them when they dropped into the water, flowing away behind his heron-like stance in the stream. There is a great difference, he declared, between a blood-sucking horsefly and the authentic waterflies risen, Aphrodite-like, from the pure water. Those flies neither eat nor drink, and dance away their life in one day and die with the sunset. He talked of such things as I was painting, and of the music of his beloved Delius who, he said, was akin to Richard Jefferies, and, I think, to Henry himself.

A few days later, when we were over at his farm, he showed us his favourite trout-rod, weighing only two ounces. He pieced it together, and we took it outside to feel its perfect balance and make imaginary casts. That afternoon in his studio, with its books and scythe and hoes and neat built-up rows of thron-logs felled by himself and cut up on his circular saw, we sat smoking his home-grown tobacco, and I made a study of his hands and the rod. Afterwards I copied them into the portrait.

* * * * *

We are grateful to the Edward Seago estate for permission to reproduce this extract from Edward Seago, *Peace in War* (Collins, 1943). After Henry's death his family presented the painting of Henry Williamson to the National Portrait Gallery where it is currently on view. [Ed.]

No otter than this himself!

Henry Williamson's review article of *Peace in War* is pasted into the back of Henry's personal copy. Although it can be found in *Green Fields and Pavements* (HWS, February 1995), it seems appropriate to also reproduce it here. [Ed.]

GREEN FIELDS AND PAVEMENTS 28·6·1943

"Peace in War"

MY colleague Mr. Jacob Tonson, whose place I am taking in these Monday articles for a while, remarked in one of his articles how war turns things topsy-turvey, or words to that effect. When I read his list of paradoxes I thought of one instance on my farm, of how a small sample of weed-seed (charlock, or carlick as they call it in Norfolk) was declared by the buyer to be "spoiled" by a few barley kernels . . . and how it paid me, as a farmer, to put the carlick through the dressing machine and so remove the corn seeds which spoiled the pure weed-seeds.

The reason is that some cage-birds thrive on the small, round, oily seed of carlick, while the barley might stick in their throats and choke them. And the price of carlick seed, that curse of good husbandry? I got 64s. a cwt., but later on the price rose to £110 a ton!

Thus the farmer with land full of "rubbish," the slobberer of the pre-war period, was in a position to make a small fortune out of weeds, if he felt that way about things. The good farmer would, in my experience, rather have good, true crops and a moderate profit than receive a fantastic price for his wretched weeds.

The majority of farmers are good men; black markets don't start in the country, nor do international wars. Wars are a disease of the gold of the towns and cities, of pavements and offices, not of green fields and pastures.

* * *

These reflections arise in part because I have been looking at Major Edward Seago's new book, called "Peace in War." It contains about two dozen pictures which the artist has painted during rare periods of leave from the Army, in which he now serves as a Camouflage Officer. Each picture in the book is accompanied by a chapter describing how it was painted. At the beginning of the book the author-artist wins our sympathy by the modesty of his *credo.*

> There is a certain grandeur in the wide stretches of East Anglia, and a strange subtlety of constant change, which has inspired some of the greatest English landscapes. Each mood has a beauty of its own, whether in repose or raked by the sharp east wind. In the happy painting ground of Cotman, Crome and Constable, I am making no more than a modest attempt to follow in the tradition of the English school, which they endowed with such brilliance and harmony. . . I have only a simple perception, but the country is full of simple things of real beauty, and many of them may pass unnoticed by those more out of touch with a simple life

This is Edward Seago's belief and purpose, and with a quiet zest he sets out during various leaves with paint box and brushes and palette, and often a rug to keep him warm from the sharp east wind, to paint what he sees and loves. I have watched him on the uplands of my farm, huddled on a stool, painting for hour after hour. I have met him on the coast road coming from Morston Church, in the wintry twilight, lamenting in his quiet voice that the sky-tints are changing so rapidly, and each so marvellous, that almost by force he had to be brought home to drink tea and afterwards to smoke his pipe in my "studio" (where I am writing these notes) and talk about his beloved North Norfolk coast.

"Studio" is perhaps a pretentious word for this shell of an old small-holder's barn, with open hearth of bricks and made up with the aid of builders' oddments bought at various auctions before the war. Someone in the family, or perhaps a visitor, called it "a studio," and the name has remained, and it is too late now to change it. Writing-room it was supposed to have been; a place where the business of the farm would not obtrude. Yet all around me are paint pots and hammers, nails, hoes, an axe, coils of rope, old sacks—ranged tidily, yet still an obtrusion. No escape in the "studio" from the farm; no Jekyll and Hyde business, no complete metamorphosis from field worker to literary gent. It was intended as a sanctuary, in the days of toiling to reconstruct cottage and buildings and to reclaim weedy acres; the word "studio" held the promise of peace and reflection, so essential for literary creation, an escape from oil-grained hands and broken nails, from chaff-dust in nostrils and hair and worn-out overalls. . . Well, that is life, and here I am writing in the "studio," which is full of books seldom looked at, of hanging bunches of tobacco leaves seldom smoked, a deep leather armchair seldom sat in. There have been moments, however, as in that day when Ted Seago walked in, and we sat before the fire of "great old bull-thorns," and talked about a better England arising beyond the serrated horizon of war. I remember we discussed this very book, to be called "Peace in War," to be a record of his escapes into the world of colour and form and line. Which is not to say that the good artist cannot also be the good soldier. Here is Edward Seago.

> . . . the English countryside is threatened; a shield must protect it. The day will come once more . . . when the shield is lowered from the face of the land

There is his belief, quite simple, entirely firm; the simple artist is also the simple Englishman doing his duty.

* * *

In one of the pictures a figure lolls across an armchair in a cottage room. A cup of tea is on the table, a book in the figure's hands. The picture is called Moat Cottage. I know that room, that chair, that figure of a young man relaxed after his flying duties. The Moat Cottage is near a river in which trout rise in steady rings in the summer evening twilight. A few miles away is the air station. The figure is that of "Crasher," to whom the book is dedicated, with this quotation from the poem by Robert Bridges:

> O youth whose hope is high,
> Who doth to Truth aspire;
> Whether thou live or die,
> O look not back or tire.

Now, as I look at "Peace in War" in the quiet of the "studio," I reflect how apt, how prophetic, were the four lines of poetry; for "Crasher" did not look back, nor did he tire; but fell to death in his Spitfire on the day the book was published, a little over a fortnight ago.

Henry Williamson.

The Great Writers of Angling – Fishers of Men

John Bailey

SOME writers appeal only to the specialist angler, others take the general reader, the poet, the aesthete or the environmentalist by the hand and lead them all through hedges and copses, metaphor and allusion, across meadow and rill towards pool and riffle. They feed the fancy until it flows from chalk-springs as surely as Test or Wylye, or nurture the imagination so that it can stroll beside moorland water or glen-fed river. These writers are fishers of men.

When I was a child in the fifties streams still ran pure, fly fishing in Wiltshire was the preserve of the retired major who lived in the millhouse across the road and allowed me to dabble with my Sealey Octofloat in the pool by his lawn, cars overheated on Porlock and I met, and fell under the spell of, Henry Williamson on Croyde Beach. He brought me a plate of wild strawberries from the dunes and spoke to my father about Tarka. We had gone there by steam train but probably represented the growing invasion and crowding of North Devon which Williamson grew to resent in proportion to his disappointment at not being recognised by the literary establishment. His *A Chronicle of Ancient Sunlight*, a major sequence of novels, was never to bring him the OM or CH for which he longed, and it seemed that he would always be remembered for 'little Tarka' or Salar together with his stories about Georgeham, which had so alienated the villagers. His heavy drinking, loneliness and a misconceived popular conception of him as a Nazi-sympathiser were not apparent to me, clad in my knitted woollen swimming-trunks embroidered with a sailing ship, as I gobbled down the fruit and was aware of his baggy, khaki shorts and thin, suntanned and sinewy legs, which were the result of his long Exmoor walks and river wanderings.

I still cherish the postcard that he wrote on 1 January 1954, with its brownish twopenny stamp of George VI and a franking beyond deciphering. The sepia photograph of Morte Bay and Baggy Point has an inscription hovering in the air: 'You were down here between two promontories'. Everyone accepts that he had a marvellous way with children, and it may be that his relationships with them were more fulfilled and uncomplicated than those with adults. The text of the card is worth printing in full:

> *Thank you for your appreciation of little Tarka. There is a similar book, called* Salar the Salmon, *but more for bigger boys. There are also some stories,* The Old Stag *etc, written years ago. Meanwhile I am writing about the 1st battle of Ypres 1914. A change – far from little Tarka: though things seem to be catching up down here, now! All good wishes. H.W.*

Dame Julian Bernars and Izaak Walton remain touchstones of the literary anglers read by many who have never dangled a worm or cast a fly. In our own day the poet laureate, Ted Hughes, has been at the forefront of cleaning up the Torridge and his poem 'Pike' has captured the fear and apprehension of that special, charged loneliness of casting into the dark when the mist settles and imagined monsters cruise around a bait, maybe ready to strike as the hackles rise at the call of the owl or an evening gust rearranges the hovering mist over the ancient pond. At that time every nerve is alert, and ghostly steps walk over bridges as the glowing bite-indicator twitches and then is still.

> A pond I fished, fifty yards across,
> Whose lilies and muscular tench
> Had outlasted every visible stone
> Of the monastery that planted them –
>
> Stilled legendary depth:
> It was as deep as England. It held
> Pike too immense to stir, so immense and old
> That post nightfall I dared not cast
>
> But silently cast and fished
> With the hair frozen on my head
> For what might move, for what eye might move . . .
>
> Ted Hughes, 'Pike'

Of all sports, angling has produced the greatest literature. More books may have been written about cricket, technical manuals excluded, but fishing by its solitary nature has evinced all that it is most thoughtful and personal. Even the most dedicated trophy or specimen hunter has those moments of stillness and fear as the evening light fades and the river noises grow ever more unpredictable and uncanny. H.W., however, did not dwell on romantic notions of being alone with the elements, was not seduced by nymphs and dryads nor caressed into seductive notions of the literary angler. He looked beneath the surface film, was not carried along in the tense thrill of surface tension but looked through the glass darkly into the natural history of his great fisherman, Tarka, and the otter's occasional quarry, Salar.

We live in a 'green' age, and it has become more and more obvious that if man has reached the top of the food chain then to protect the environment and safeguard the continuance of species he must know what he is doing. Through our intervention, there are no longer wolves on Exmoor, to cull the weaklings amongst the deer. Otters have all but vanished, and the slower and weaker fish may well be the first ones caught as our baits probe the deeper pools and the slacks beyond. There are few fishermen, now, who are not conservationists and keen naturalists. If there are no dabchicks nor kingfishers, anglers are the first to notice and make this known. Farm slurry seems to be the cause of oxygen starvation, as Ted Hughes identified on the Torridge, and water extraction worries the keepers and anglers of the great sporting rivers.

We must hope that the indiscriminate killing of wild fish is now a thing of the past. Catching for the pot has a sound basis in man's hunting and sporting instincts and will only offend the most rabid and urban activists. Whilst H.W.'s most popular books amongst non-academics, *Tarka* and *Salar*, guarantee his continuing popularity amongst the young and old his occasional writing and particularly his *A Clear Water Stream* must surely make him required reading amongst those philosopher anglers who trace their descent from Walton and who now find themselves involved in environmental debate.

In Richard Jefferies' *A London Trout* it is now easy to see a harbinger of present environmental concerns: the account starts with 'sword-flags rusting at their edges'. As the doomed and fatal tale continues, the stream is gradually exploited by creeping civilisation (perhaps urbanisation is a better term) and inexorable silence gradually descends. Jefferies concentrates, in 1879, on the view from a abridge where he watches a trout still hovering over a sandy bottom 'at the tail of the arch'. We have all lingered on such a bridge, arches neatly constructed in stone or brick and reassuringly denominated as medieval. For these summers Jefferies had the simple satisfaction of seeing the trout 'day after day', which even survived the joint efforts of a keen-sighted navvy and questing angler. In the fourth season 'the brook was dammed up on the sunny side of the bridge, and the water let off by a side-hatch, (so) that some accursed main or pipe or other horror might be laid across the bed of the stream somewhere far down.'

With the diminished flow of water the pool below the bridge became shallow, and men with all sorts of spears and traps invaded it one, ironically glorious, Sunday but they did not land the beautiful, wild and aged trout. Jefferies asks, 'Is it possible that he could have escaped? He was a wonderful fish, wary and quick.' He hopes that the trout has escaped downstream to deeper pools and clear water. Nonetheless, and distressingly enough for us a century later, he ends his story:

I never failed to glance over the parapet into the shadowy water. Somehow it seemed to look colder, darker, less pleasant than it used to do. The spot was empty, and the shrill winds whistled through the poplars.

As a youth, I once followed the otterhounds up the River Bourne above Salisbury. The river, then, still had feeders which transected water meadows, even though I now realise that they were silting up and the golden, tigered, finger-long and surface-splashing pickerels were soon to vanish, as were red-bellied and hackled sticklebacks (which seldom survived in the aquarium for all their devilry) and lapwings, which always seemed to call and dummy near their nest in the doomed, lush water meadows of a boy who luxuriated in kingcups, frogspawn, and crayfish that back into the jar.

Of course, we found no Tarkas even if the huntsmen wore green and carried ash sticks. I had no inkling of death, knew nothing of supposed depredations on trout stocks and only knew the snickering laughter of otters which reached me, as I lay in my bed of innocence, from across the water meadows. In *Tarka the Otter* the controlled instincts of man in the veteran hound, Deadlock, finally kill off the untramelled joy of the protagonist in the last hunt. We are left with the knowledge of Tarka's offspring and of the elemental and often cruel nature of his life. Williamson presents a battle as glorious and heroic as that of Hal and Hotspur, but with the death of both combatants. Deadlock has been trained and exploited yet loved by man, and Tarka, though the moral victor with his three bubbles moving as

Bedivere's triple struggle to consign Excalibur to the water, proves the doomed, tragic hero.

Ted Hughes in his poem 'An Otter' captures this same mystery and nobility. He speaks of the animal bringing '... the legend of himself/From before wars or burial ... Like a king in hiding ...' His otter can 'outfish fish' and the great fishing writer can out-angle the angler and catch any reader.

Henry Williamson's abiding strength is that whilst giving names to animals he never sentimentalised their lives by anthropomorphic wizardry. He was a naturalist and observer. In his own attempts to find human happiness he never used nature as an emotional crutch: rather he saw in it instinctive loyalties and inexorable cruelty and unfairness when assessed by conventional standards. Life is unfair, but there are moments of glorious instinct and fulfilment.

In *Salar the Salmon* and *Tarka the Otter*, H.W. may have given infinite inspiration to artists and country lovers, and the economy and memorable richness of his prose may still make us all see a heron as 'Old Nog' or recognise a mended kelt as it is washed down and along an Exmoor stream. Williamson recalls for us the kingfisher's flash of halcyon blue, the uncontrollably nodding, brown-and-white courtesy of the dipper, the escape from a seal and all the other petty miracle which bring Salar to Tarka, salmon to the stream, and the resigned excitement of losing a grilse to the red power of the spate as the wild fish turns across the current and presents its silver flank to the force of Barle or Lynn.

Fortune may bring us the salmon of our dreams whilst application and a knowledge of ichtheology may land a ferox in the fastnesses of the Highlands, but H.W.'s account of *A Clear Water Stream* may well be the text that sustains us as we feast off roasted chestnuts and crusted port, staring into the hissing logs.

Some anglers are technicians and scientists, others are dreamers of dream who nod more than they cast and dream more often than they catch. H.W. was a London lad from a middle class home, who early on discovered the excitements and rewards of the countryside. After a formative and traumatic experience of the trenches, which was never to leave him and which was to inform his great novel sequence, he found himself settled in a cottage in a village in North Devon with a young wife and family, and with the control and keepering of a stream running from Exmoor and populated by trout and invaded by salmon. 'An advertisement in the local paper said that two miles of fishing were to be let with the place. A trout stream!'

H.W.'s water flowed through a deer park, was varied and included a three-arched bridge. Even as one reads H.W.'s account one can see, before he speaks, the water dividing and meeting in the pool and one can predict the slim, torpedo-shaped fish which he will see when he looks over the parapet.

> *There lay, sleepily, several trout, their hues varying with the colours beneath them: dark brown of back where they rested upon water-moss growing on rock-layers; brown over beds of gravel; and one, which had its stance by a little glacis of sand, was light golden yellow . . . While I stood there I experienced a feeling that the day was fixed immortally, for ever, in blue space. For a moment I was back in the summer of boyhood.*

Most trout anglers dream of their own stretch of water, whether single or double-bank. Depending on dreams or memories the river is moorland- or chalk stream-fed and runs within earshot of the perfect home where a rod can be left made up by the door and the evening rise can be addressed after a gentle stroll past ancient barns where owls call in the dusk. In this piscatorial arcadia there is no pressure to fish to the limit, the latter-day Walton can linger and watch and never cast to his own fish which hang beautifully below the clear pools. This dream underpins much of the imaginative energy of the true angler whilst grateful for an invitation to some remote and fecund stream he dreams of an underfished water, replete with wild fish, not the plump and gormless products of the stockists.

Early in his oversight of a trout stream H.W. found himself meeting an experienced angler and his assistant, who had a suspiciously successful fly called the Poacher. They had caught many fish in a morning, all the size of small herrings, and were very confident in their presence on H.W.'s stream. They felt that they had fished within their rights and questioned the definition of bank fishing rights. Reading H.W.'s account in the 1980s, one catches one's breath at the following:

> *He went on to say that if I looked in the fish book at The Fisherman's Arms, I would see an entry made by a visitor that he had already taken out of Devon streams one thousand, two hundred and forty-nine fish that season.*

H.W. makes mistakes over the introduction of ranunculus into a moorland-fed stream, stocks his river unsuitably, occasionally fishes his own river and presents an irresistible image of the relaxed gentleman angler of our childhoods. The water is relatively free of pressure, bottles of pale ale can be cooled in a stock tethered below a pool, split-cane rods and brass reels parallel a lost world of tweeds, leather boots and silk fly lines.

In H.W.'s world, which is not so far away, steam trains still shuffle warmly over the viaducts, the fishing hotels of Exmoor are as remote as Loch Garry is today, fishing is still courtesy of the lord of the manor, and only the author seems to realise the pressure on the streams and rivers which had always seemed remote and exclusive.

A Clear Water Stream is diminished by summary and report. It does not have the narrative drive of *Tarka* or *Salar*, but for even the most inexperienced game angler or the most endowed business executive it tells of the excitement and rewards of knowing a river. Every cast, perfect in itself and the result of skill or luck, may land a fish. H.W.'s account, when truly read, is that of a man alone with dipper and heron and otter. It may be no longer possible to reproduce his experience, but it is rapidly becoming overwhelmingly clear that anglers who have a sense of self-esteem and a love of the environment in which they pursue their applied skills are having to be more intelligent, well informed, and self-sacrificing. No longer can a huge butcher's bill be appropriate and a weighty deep-freeze quota be defensible.

Fishers of men seem to laud the challenge of the catching of the truly wild fish. The great fishermen go forth in the misty morn and the bat-haunted twilight to try their skill against the willow-shrouded shallow of moorland stream or the clear gravel-caressed lie of the chalk stream. All have doubts about their rods, the weight of their lines, the strength of their leaders and the appropriateness of their flies. Their doubt is universal. Each angler hopes that his choice is right and yearns for some fatherly local expert who can give him or her the key to success.

If catching a fish were easy then the 'finny race' would be left alone. If a salmon or wild trout were to turn athwart and succumb to the net at the first touch then we would not pursue them. It is their tragedy that, like their hunter, they fight against their entrapment with a vigour and courage that command the respect of the hunter.

To read Jefferies, Hughes and Williamson is to extend our humanity. To study them is to increase our stature as selfless naturalists.

* * * * *

We are grateful to John Bailey for permission to print this extract from Chapter 11 'The Great Writers' from his book *The Great Anglers* (David & Charles 1990). This book contains a wealth of entertaining and factual information with superb illustrations.

Drawing by Mick Loates

The Rural Tradition

A study of the non-fiction prose writers of the English Countryside.
Chapter 11: 'Henry Williamson'

Professor W. J. Keith

> People who don't see the earth and sea and stars plainly are spiritually corrupt – and spiritual corruption begets physical corruption. That is the real cause of the Great War.[1]

Henry Williamson, in his twenty-first year, had not yet begun to write when Edward Thomas was killed within a few hundred yards of him at the Battle of Arras.[2] Not unnaturally the First World War proved to be the crucial experience of his life, a horror to which he has returned angrily, broodily, ever since. Moreover he was a participant in the famous Christmas fraternisation between the British and German troops in the trenches in 1914,[3] and this event has remained the central point in his personal and literary life. It was an inspiring, fleeting testimony to what might have been, and its failure a tragic and permanent reminder of human folly. Williamson returned from the war a changed man. Like the Willie Maddison of his novel cycle *The Flax of Dream*, he was 'haunted by the ghosts of ten million murdered men of his own generation.'[4] By the end of hostilities he had come close to losing faith in mankind, and on being demobilised he determined not to be 'crushed into inanity by civilization' (*DFW*, p. 70).

The shock of the years 1914–1918 must have been all the greater for someone with Williamson's background and upbringing. 'There was,' he tells us, 'farming blood in me. My mother's family had been farmers; some of them had farmed the same land under the dukedom of Bedford for more than four centuries. My father's family had been landowners until comparatively recently, in the Midlands and North of England' (*SNF*, p. 38). From his early childhood, moreover, he had been fascinated by natural history in general and bird life in particular. The first two volumes of his *Flax of Dream* tetralogy, *The Beautiful Years* and *Dandelion Days*, though fictional recreation like Jefferies *Bevis* of a childhood that was in fact less rural and less idyllic, present none the less the essence of Williamson's early life, with its accounts of bird-nesting, fishing expeditions, wild pets, and – an early manifestation of his later talents – a detailed diary of natural observations (part of the original was printed in the 1945 edition of *The Lone Swallows*). 'As a small boy,' he writes, 'I lived a secret life in my grandfather's copies of *Bevis, The Amateur Poacher*, and *Wild Life in a Southern Country*.'[5] Like the young Willie Maddison, in looking forward to adult life he 'had dreamed of an existence in the woods and meadows, photographing birds' nests and writing in *The Field* an account of his observations.'[6] As one might expect, this somewhat unusual and naive ambition led to disagreements with his parents. His mother, about whom Williamson has written that 'the link between us, as in the case of D.H. Lawrence and his mother, had been stronger than is normal' (*SNF*, p. 39) was doubtless sympathetic, but his father (like Thomas's father) saw no practical use for his natural history interests, and as Williamson grew older this led to estrangement and bitterness.

After the war, of course, the clash became even more evident. For all their horror, the war years were 'years of such movement and excitation and comradeship that when they had passed the world had seemed poor and dispirited.'[7] The earlier 'dandelion days' now appeared remote, dead, embalmed in the pages of history; Williamson saw them as 'the Old World, the pre-1914 world.'[8] Yet at the same time it was the one possible world. He came to believe that 'only that secret part of myself that lived for watching wild birds and finding their nests in the fields and woods was an integral harmony in my life.'[9] The more he looked back in an endeavour to isolate the cause of the 1914-18 war, the more he found it in the separation of urban man from the natural life. 'Wars,' he insists, 'are made by the pallid mob-spirit, by mass-escapists from indoor and pavement living; the pale-faced men whose natural instincts are repressed' (*GWC*, p. 157). It was impossible for Williamson to relax after the armistice; he had begun during the war to feel 'the weight of the whole dark world on one's shoulders' (*LD*, p. 246) and the immediate post-war period was even more depressing: 'The years 1919 and 1920, their interior or mental life, were lived in a No-man's-land more bitter than that patrolled and crossed during the preceding years, for they were without companionship, and the enemy was world darkness, which must be created into light' (*LD*, p. 247). Consequently, after an unhappy period as a journalist in London, working for *The Times* and the *Weekly Dispatch*, and after a culminating row with his father, Williamson decided to make his own escape. But, unlike the mass escapes which lead to war, this was to be a solitary escape in quest of peace. Remembering a Devon cottage which he had rented 'on impulse' two years earlier,[10] he set out for the west of England in March 1921.

Basically, of course, this was an escape from the town into the country. Williamson persuaded himself 'that the inspiration of walls and pavements was false, bringing upon men the things of darkness.'[11] Devon was also a retreat where he could 'learn to write' (*SNF*, p. 37), but it was certainly no escape from the war mentality of 1914-18; there was no question of his forgetting the experiences he had gone through. In writing *The Flax of Dream*, the tetralogy which the war cuts cruelly but neatly into two pieces, Williamson relives the experience of his generation, despite the fact that the actual details of warfare are omitted. During the same period, as H.F. West has noted, he built up an impressive collection of First World War literature, two of the volumes (*The Patriot's Progress* and *The Wet Flanders Plain*) being his own.[12] And even his country books are haunted with memories of the war. The prefatory note to the first edition of *The Lone Swallows* is symbolically dated 11 November 1921, while that of *The Story of a Norfolk Farm* bears the armistice date nineteen years later, at the beginning of yet another war. References recur throughout the books written in the twenties and thirties – even his *Anthology of Modern Nature Writing*, is filled with wartime extracts from such writers as Wilfrid Ewart, V.M. Yeates, and Edmund Blunden. All this comes to a culmination, of course, in his ambitious novel cycle *A Chronicle of Ancient Sunlight*, in which five volumes are devoted to the First World War. Thus the Devon journey, if it can legitimately be called an escape at all, was undertaken not in order to forget, but to remember more clearly.

But the Williamson of 1921 was a mystifying, immature, contradictory, and often irritating figure. Even a photograph taken at this time, which appears as the frontispiece to *The Sun in the Sands*, shows an obviously intense and self-conscious young man. He was a romantic idealist, his mind filled with the visions of Blake, Shelley, Jefferies, and Francis Thompson, supremely convinced, on the surface at least, of his literary genius ('I am young and self-confident'[13]), and imagining himself as the much-needed prophet of a newer and better world. 'In those days,' he tells us, 'only one thought moved in my mind: the tragedy of Mankind, and the world's redemption through the truth I would reveal in my work' (*SS*, pp. 10-11). In Willie Maddison, hero of *The Flax of Dream*, Williamson presents his romantic, prophetic self in heightened symbolic form ('He felt himself a stranger, an outcast' (*DFW*, p. 86)), and in *The Star-Born*, the fantasy which Maddison is supposed to have written and which Williamson himself calls a 'Fifth Gospel,'[14] we find a similar semi- (or pseudo-) mystical version of the pattern. There can be little doubt that he moulded his own life in an attempt to encourage archetypal comparisons. He is the hermit in the wilderness, the visionary poet, the inspired teacher, the prophet without honour in his own country – even, at times, the suffering servant.

There is, however, another, very different side to the portrait of the young Williamson. He can write, with an eloquent gesture, 'I had rejected civilisation just as Jefferies had, I was going to be a hermit' (*SS*, p. 35), yet he made the journey from London to Devon on a racing motorcycle, eagerly intent upon setting a record time. Pausing en route to visit Stonehenge, he is soon complaining of 'the big-painted advertisement boards advertising a motor tyre' as a desecration of Salisbury Plain; they are 'offensive, a symbol of that materialism and negation of the spirit that one day would be altered through the Tetralogy about Maddison' (*SS*, p. 31). And so, back to what he had already described as his 'beautiful long-stroke, single cylinder Brooklands Road Special Norton!' (*SS*, p. 12) (The next time we hear of a visit to Stonehenge, he is himself driving a car; the advertisements are now ignored, and his indignation is reserved for the barbed wire fence and a tea-shop (see *LD*, p. 128)). He claims to have settled in the Devonshire countryside 'in order to find peace and quiet,'[15] yet he comes and goes 'at all hours of the day and night' on the motorcycle which, he claims with obvious satisfaction, makes a 'noise like a machine gun' (*LL*, p. 99). Despite his love of natural history Williamson belongs to the world of the motor-car which Sturt rails against in his *Journals*.

It would not be difficult to present the whole of Williamson's life and attitudes as a heap of contradictions. He holds an *odi et amo* relationship with so much. Despite the numerous passages of prophetic didacticism that clutter his work the reader often finds himself asking, in Auden's phrase, 'which side am I supposed to be on?' Or, to put the point even more crucially, 'which side does Williamson think he is on?' Sometimes, especially in his later work, he is prepared to face up to his own contradictions. On a visit to the north of England, for example, he finds himself bewailing the ugliness of industrialism, but suddenly changes his stance: 'You drive a car, and enjoy its speed; you are of modern life, enjoying its conveniences – so why this attitude because smoke hangs over the factories where your car, and the other things you use and approve, are produced?' (*LD*, p. 158) It is the kind of question that many of his readers must have asked years before. Although the older Williamson is often aware of the paradoxes and contradictions, there are only occasional moments when the young man realises how far he falls short of the artistic prodigy he believes himself to be.

These autobiographical details are necessary here, since Williamson employs his own experience in his writings more than any other rural chronicler with the possible exception of George Borrow. He is continually reliving or rewriting his past, viewing an incident from a different angle or with a different perspective. The same might be said of his countryside. From *The Dream of Fair Women* to *The Children of Shallowford* it is almost invariably north Devon, at first Georgeham and Braunton, later the river Bray around Filleigh; but it is recreated in varying literary genres – in fictional form in *The Dream of Fair Women* and *The Pathway*, in the animal stories such as *Tarka the Otter* and *Salar the Salmon*, in the numerous non-fiction works. The setting remains the same, but the treatment varies with the stance of the speaker, and even the genres tend to dissolve into each other. For Williamson also resembles Borrow in the way he mixes his imaginative with his real life so that it is impossible to separate fact from fiction. In *The Dream of Fair Women*, 'neither wholly fiction, nor . . . autobiography' (*GWC*, pp. 23-4), instead of insisting, with most novelists, that any resemblance between the characters and living persons is coincidental, Williamson goes out of his way to state that Maddison, 'like all the other characters of the novel, was based on a real person' (*DFW*, p. 441). On the other hand, *The Village Book*, though apparently non-fiction, is 'an imaginative work which should not be read as the history of any particular village, and certainly not of any man or woman' (*VB*, p. 9). A careful reading of the books of reminiscence such as *The Children of Shallowford* and *The Story of a Norfolk Farm* reveals sufficient discrepancies to suggest that, consciously or unconsciously, chronology and detail have been altered to increase the effect, while *The Sun in the Sands*, which is ostensibly offered as autobiography, is so well moulded and rounded as to suggest the contrivances of fiction. The description, 'novel autobiography,' to be found on its dust-jacket is appropriate and, one presumes, deliberately ambiguous.

In *Goodbye West Country*, with a profundity that we do not normally associate with him, Williamson has observed: 'All artists, to become real people, have to assume another self, and learn to discard it, lest it envelop them' (*GWC*, p. 63). Although intended generally, the remark has obvious applicability to his own work. Willie Maddison is clearly a mask, like Lavengro, and 'The Beard' of *The Labouring Life* at least allows for a certain distance between writer and character; but the Williamson of *The Sun in the Sands*, like the Borrow of *Wild Wales*, is problematical. We are never quite sure to what extent we should separate the 'implied author' from what we know of the actual writer. There is an important difference, however, between Williamson and Borrow (whom, by the way, Williamson had apparently not read at this time (see *SNF*, p. 206)): whereas in *Wild Wales* we are confident that Borrow is aware of the problem and is deliberately exploiting it for his own purpose, with Williamson – and this is true of a number of his 'non-fiction' books, not only *The Sun in the Sands* – we get the uneasy feeling that our judgements and responses are by no means identical with his own. The mask is donned more clumsily by Williamson; we are never fully convinced of the dexterity of the performer; and all sorts of questions therefore become important. Are the elaborate disguises deliberately put on to shield a personality who is basically unsure of himself? Are the contradictions already discussed attributable to the mask or to Williamson himself? How does all this complexity square with his much vaunted ideal of 'clarity'? I propose to consider, though not necessarily to answer, these questions in the ensuing critique. As in the case of Borrow, I shall make no attempt to confine myself to the ostensible non-fiction, since the rigid categories are irrelevant here. Instead I shall try to reveal the evolution of Williamson as a rural writer through an examination of the masks and devices he employs to conceal or reveal his essential self.

* * * * *

The Beautiful Years and *Dandelion Days*, which together chronicle the story of Willie Maddison from childhood to his leaving school on the eve of the First World War, might reasonably be described as presenting a portrait of the naturalist as a young man. In these years are sown the seeds that are to come to a brief and inevitably distorted flowering in the 'lost generation' Willie (the term is Williamson's, as well as Gertrude Stein's and Ernest Hemingway's) of the last two books of the tetralogy. In *The Beautiful Years* we are offered the vision of a potential rural paradise; the countryside around 'Rookhurst' is presented as an ideal environment for the growth of a healthy and harmonious soul. But even at this early stage threatening clouds become visible. Unlike Williamson himself, Willie is motherless and an only child; from the day of his birth, he is deprived of the affection to be found in a complete and natural family atmosphere. Unlike Jefferies' Bevis, whose enlightened 'governor' deliberately avoids interfering with his son's self-education in the world of nature, Willie is brought up by a bitter and unsympathetic father who is hopelessly incapable of understanding his child. The climax, in which Willie is accused of trespass and poaching because he has sprung some illegally set traps, brings him for the first time into harsh contact with the prejudice and power of what we have come to call the establishment.

Dandelion Days, in spite of the idyllic suggestiveness of its title, is a much sadder book than its predecessor.[16] School life, which was peripheral in *The Beautiful Years*, has now become central, and the policy of Colham Grammar School seems to be stamp out the imaginative spirit which Willie has developed in his natural surroundings. Shades of the prison-house begin to close in upon him. His world is now split, and the main subject of the novel is Willie's desperate attempt to preserve his love for the countryside against the concerted attacks of his father, his girl friend, and most of the boys and masters at the school. As Williamson recalls later, 'my theme was true: the natural development of the boy in the sunshine, contrasted with the unnatural spoliation of the immature mental and nervous tissues when shut away from the sunshine' (*SS*, p. 45). As Willie grows up, of course, the problem of human relationships becomes more complex. His boyish, romantic, helpless love for Elsie Norman is, like the rest of life, both beautiful and painful, and its inevitable failure, due not merely, or even primarily, to class differences, but rather to fundamentally opposed attitudes and temperaments, is more shattering to the shy and sensitive Willie than it would be to anyone else. Moreover the breakdown in their relationship takes place on the 'last day' before Willie is to leave Rookhurst and take a job in London. The 'beautiful years' in the countryside are over, though Willie's job at a city desk is almost immediately interrupted by the outbreak of war. 'The summer of 1914,' Maddison is made to write later, 'was to see the apotheosis of ideas and measures which everywhere had crushed the imaginative tissues of childhood' (*DFW*, p. 12). His own life provides the archetypal example. It is the end of an era; dandelions are replaced by poppies, the fields of England by those of Flanders. The book ends on a sombre note when in the final sentences of the so-called epigraph we hear of the death of Willie's best friend, Jack Temperley. Willie is now completely on his own.

The war itself, which becomes the focal point in *A Chronicle of Ancient Sunlight*, is not treated here. When we meet Willie again at the opening of *The Dream of Fair Women*, the date is June 1919, and, as the excessively romantic title suggests, the book is concerned with the young man's experiences of love and women in the depressing years of the early twenties. As the novel opens, he is living alone in a hut in north Devon, having exiled himself from a civilisation he despises in an attempt to write down his ideas in a ponderous manuscript, modelled on Jefferies' *The Story of My Heart*, and solemnly titled *The Policy of Reconstruction*. But soon he learns that such a hermitlike existence is not only impossible but vain; most of the book is taken up with his unhappy love affair with a married woman, Evelyn Fairfax, and the contrast between his own ideals and the pleasure-seeking but ultimately vacuous society into which his love for Mrs Fairfax leads him. The relevance of this volume to the earlier books – and to the rural tradition – lies in Maddison's apparent inability to find in the post-war world any connection with the dandelion days that seem lost for ever.

In *The Pathway* Willie Maddison finally emerges as a definite if not wholly satisfactory mouthpiece for Williamson's ideas; indeed his function may well remind us of some of the spokesman-figures in D.H. Lawrence's more pugnaciously didactic novels. Wandering about Devon, arguing with anyone who is prepared to listen to him, writing another prophetic book entitled *The Star-Born*, Maddison comes, as it were, into his ministry. His message, like Williamson's, concerns the relation between war and an unnatural life, and he it is who speaks the words that I have chosen as epigraph for this chapter. His despair verges on the misanthropic; only among the wild creatures of the countryside can he find peace. Like Hudson and Thomas before him he finds church-going constricting, and feels closer to God in the open air; unlike Hudson and Thomas he dramatically and ostentatiously walks out of the service. He is at one and the same time passionately sincere and painfully immature, yet Williamson deliberately offers his creation as the way, the truth, and the life – a quotation, incidentally, that he has called 'the most beautiful line in all literature' (*SS*, p. 165). Everywhere Maddison goes, of course, he finds selfishness, hate, misunderstanding. Finally, alienated from the family of Mary Ogilvie, whom he loves, he is drowned in a climactic scene that brings together all the romantic archetypes. The manuscript of *The Star-Born* is burnt as a signal of distress, but, like its message in the world, it is ignored. Maddison drowns, like Shelley, and an attempt is even made to burn his body on the shore à la Trelawney. At one time Williamson had contemplated a happy ending (see *SS*, pp. 53-4), but he wisely rejected it. The crusade of a post-war champion of the natural (rural) life, he seems to imply, can only end in failure.

The Flax of Dream is an impressive but infuriating near-masterpiece. Willie Maddison is, of course, a deliberately chosen name with equivocal overtones. Rhythmically it suggests the name of his creator, but at the same time it can readily and neatly be transformed into the undignified 'Mad Willie.' Like 'Stephen Dedalus,' one cannot easily decide whether it is a profound symbol or a complicated joke; unlike *A Portrait of the Artist as a Young Man*, the tetralogy suffers through Williamson's inability to maintain either a consistent attitude towards, or an appropriate distance from, his leading character. The first two books are acceptable in the sense that the young Willie's absurdities can be attributed to the inexperience of youth; but when in the last two volumes Maddison is in his early twenties and has still not grown up, and when, moreover, Williamson apparently offers his immature simplicity as a virtue rather than a failing, the reader finds it increasingly difficult to view him with the sympathy that is clearly demanded. As a result there is a fatal and undeniable flaw at the centre of the tetralogy which Williamson's drastic alterations and revisions have never been able to overcome. This is all the more unfortunate in view of Williamson's obvious gifts and the admirable boldness of his conception. Had he only been able, like Joyce, to remain 'invisible, refined out of existence, indifferent, paring his fingernails,'[17] he might well have written a comprehensive study not only of the *Weltanschauung* of the first quarter of this century, but of the uneasy modern relationship between man and the natural world.

⋆ ⋆ ⋆ ⋆ ⋆

The cottage to which Williamson retired in 1921 was in the north Devon village of Georgeham, which he always refers to under its earlier but still surviving name of Ham.[18] It was, in many respects , an ideal spot for one of Williamson's temperament and interests. 'A village of small property owners, without a resident "gennulman,"' as he calls it (*LL*, p. 474), the whole parish contained at that time a population of a little over eight hundred; still comparatively isolated, it preserved much of the traditional atmosphere of an old world (Williamson would say pre-war) village community. Moreover its environs were varied and scenically spectacular. It was an area rich in bird life, particularly the peregrine-falcons, buzzards, and ravens that Williamson loved. There were badgers in the woods, otters (and salmon) in the rivers, and, since Georgeham lies close to the western extremities of Exmoor, the red deer – Jefferies' red deer, the most imposing wild animals in England – were within easy reach. As for the local flora, Williamson is fond of alluding to the belief of the neighbourhood that every wild flower growing in England can be found on nearby Saunton Burrows (see, e.g., *LD*, p. 205). Georgeham had not yet been 'discovered' by tourists, and Williamson could explore the moors, wander along the beach with its cliffs and rocky headlands, and never meet another human being. The prospective hermit and follower of Jefferies could hardly ask for a more congenial or artistically stimulating locality.

Georgeham became Williamson's home for the next seven years or so. Here most of *Dandelion Days* and the whole of *The Dream of Fair Women* and *The Pathway* were written, but *The Flax of Dream* tetralogy was only a part of his work at this time, and it cannot even be described as representative. H.F. West forecast in 1932 that 'any future study of Williamson's work will assuredly trace the change from the subjective idealism of *The Flax of Dream* to the objective realism of, for example, *The Labouring Life*.'[19] The very different strands in his writing are obvious – indeed, one can imagine a critical study postulating two Williamsons in much the same way that Williamson has distinguished two Jefferies (see *RJ*, pp. 24-5) – but it would be a mistake to imply any kind of chronological development from one approach to the other. He is at one and the same time Willie Maddison and 'the Ham historian' (*LL*, p. 84), and the resultant portraits of a village society to be found in his twin volumes *The Village Book* and *The Labouring Life* show him making his own characteristic contribution to the rural tradition in a recognisable 'line' from Jefferies and Sturt.

At one time, apparently, Williamson had plans to write a book called *A Labourer's Life*, an account of 'Revvy' Carter, his next-door neighbour, that was to be 'a marvellous transcription of reality' (*LL*, p. 100). Unlike most presentations of the agricultural labourer, which are distorted and misleading, this would be 'so true and vivid that William Carter would be a hero for all time' (*LL*, p. 101). The book was never written, but, making the necessary allowances for Williamson's enthusiastic exaggerations that are yet another manifestation of the writer's mask, one suspects that it would have borne a close resemblance to *The Bettesworth Book*. Interestingly enough, the reasons he gives for abandoning the book are themselves extraordinarily similar to the difficulties that Sturt encountered. Williamson describes the problem as follows:

> *What was the theme of Revvy's life? Easy to make it pathetic: a poor man's struggle against rain and rheumatism, a poor man forced by an economic system to remain so poor that on a wet winter's morning he left his cottage with a potato sack over his shoulders, Hodge's usual overcoat. Or to make it dignified:*

the West Countryman's courtesy and natural charm, and in particular this man's sweetness to his children. How to lead into the story of his prejudices, his sudden bellowings at his children and wife, their taunts at their mother, the general disharmony of those first two years when almost everything that was spoken, and certainly everything that was shouted in bellow and shrill taunt, was heard through the thin lath-and-plaster wall that divided the cottages? Revvy was not a tragic figure; he was a happy man, like most men who work with their arms and muscles and thighs, happy men – except when out-of work. (*LL*, pp. 130-1)

Once again the difficulty lies in rendering the complexity of the whole truth, but Williamson was, in fact, in a better position than Sturt to present the realities of the labouring life. Where Sturt was the employer whose experience of Bettesworth was almost always confined to occasions when the old man was 'on duty,' Williamson, though an outsider in the village – a 'foreigner' in the rustic sense, and an eccentric one at that – is able to watch and record the daily routine. He talks to Revvy Carter on the road, in the public house, at church, in the labourer's own garden, not as employer to employee but as man to man. Indeed his enforced overhearing of conversation through the thin wall is reminiscent of that classic example of accurate recording, J.M. Synge with his ear to the cracked floorboard on the Aran Islands.

But even under these circumstances, which seem almost ideal, Williamson is dissatisfied, and abandons the project in its original form. Little seems to have been lost, however; most of the material appears to be contained in *The Village Book* and *The Labouring Life*, though these books attempt much more besides. They are written (and here, in view of the result, I think we can accept the somewhat exalted authorial statement) 'that the spirit and letter of village life in the decade following the Great War be contained for future students of English country life' (*LL*, p. 9). Together they form an impressionistic collage of village events, a pot-pourri of descriptions, stories, anecdotes which, though originally separate sketches written for newspapers and magazines, present when united a convincing, rounded picture. Despite the obvious differences of style and treatment we come away from a reading of these books with a feeling of intimate familiarity with the inhabitants not unlike that experienced in *Our Village*.

At first sight, the books seem artless. They are chatty, jagged, uneven, and sometimes repetitious, but, as Williamson is anxious (perhaps too anxious) to point out, this is all part of a conscious design. His own description, '"true but imaginary" local history' (*LL*, p. 144) is probably the best. Like most rural writers, the closer he comes to actuality, the more reluctant he is to admit it. Carefully worded statements of limited liability abound:

'The village of Ham' does not exist in the world of reality, nor are any of the human and other beings described in it real beings . . . I cannot truthfully declare that any baby was buried, that any tract was awarded, that any sermon was preached, in the manner I have written. (*VB*, p. 255)

Even the 'I' and the 'zur' and the 'Mr Williamson' of certain pages . . . are but devices of story-telling. (*VB*, p. 9)

The characters are not meant to represent any living persons; rather are they essences of personalities. (*LL*, p. 9)

One can readily appreciate Williamson's reticence in these matters; none the less, the amount of straight reporting is considerable. For example, H. Stevenson Balfour, in his *History of Georgeham and Croyde*, testifies to the essential accuracy of Williamson's hilarious account of the dispute over the new churchyard by inserting a footnote reference to *The Labouring Life*,[20] and his lists of local names indicate that Williamson made few alterations in the interests of 'story-telling.' Moreover H.F. West claims in his memoir to have met 'some of the characters' in *The Village Book*.[21] Above all, whatever he may say about 'Mr Williamson,' the 'I' of these books admits to being the author of *Tarka the Otter, The Pathway*, and *The Old Stag*, and complementary accounts in his other writings point overwhelmingly to biographical foundations. Granting the inevitable 'touching-up,' these books may be accepted as a record that is 'true' in all but the most narrow sense of the word.

None the less, Williamson is here much more than the mere observer. The books are, for instance, painstakingly arranged and constructed. Not only is there a seasonal division, *The Village Book* representing winter and spring, *The Labouring Life* summer and autumn, but within each book the village stories are interspersed with short descriptive essays concerning the non-human world. It is typical of Williamson that the birds and animals are not neglected in favour of the human villagers. Their fortunes continually overlap, but – and this is part of Williamson's point – the outcome is generally fatal. The slow-worm is stoned to death (*VB*, p. 207), the ackymals (tomtits) are ruthlessly shot by John Kift (VB, p. 273), Billy Goldsworthy's cow dies on the same evening as his mother (*LL*, p. 406). Moreover those parts of the - village in which there are no houses, where the natural inhabitants are buzzards and water ouzels and foxes and stoats, are as relevant to Williamson as Inclefell Manor or 'the Lower House' or the parish church. We are, indeed, offered a human view of the wild life and 'a starling's view of Ham' (*VB*, p. 52), and it is appropriate that Williamson's Georgeham years resulted not only in these books but in two collections of animal stories, *The Peregrine's Saga* and *The Old Stag*, and the book that is still regarded as his masterpiece, *Tarka the Otter*.

One commentator, Denys Thompson, has complained that there is no indication in *The Village Book* and *The Labouring Life* 'that any particular change has happened to English life in the last hundred years,'[22] but this is hardly fair. It is true that there is no sociological analysis that can compare with Sturt's *Change in the Village*; Williamson, however, is attempting something very different. His is an impressionistic, almost documentary approach, and the evidence of change exists in the very fabric of his anecdotes (which Thompson too hastily dismisses as 'mainly pointless'[23]). Williamson's real subject, we might say, is the extraordinary juxtapositions of modern and ancient in the rural society of the 1920s. The Ham villagers are aware both of age-old superstitions and of the latest scandals in the *News of the World*. The controversy over the new burial ground necessarily involves not only the parish meeting but the urban bureaucracies of the county council and the ministry of health. Means of transportation have, of course, changed completely; attempts are made (not always successfully) to introduce buses and taxicabs, and by the time Williamson writes the second book aeroplanes are 'scarcely heeded' when they fly over the village (*LL*, p. 460). Even the guillemot that Williamson finds on the beach with its feathers smeared with oil from passing ships (*VB*, pp. 43-4; cf *DFW*, p. 69; *SS*, p. 49) is a victim of the modern pollution that some call progress. It is a strange, transitional, uncertain world that Williamson presents here, and 'The Beard' is a suitable commentator to catch the ironies, since he is himself with his motorcycle and his genuine love for the old England, his passion for the simple life and his weakness for dance-halls and gramophones, a classic embodiment of the pull between old and new. He is a less obvious but in many respects more subtle persona than Willie Maddison. They share many attributes, and even some adventures, but there is none of the Christ *manqué* about 'the Ham historian' and only occasional traces of Maddison's self-important naiveté. A new type of rural observer, he is looked upon with amused interest and cautious mistrust by the villagers, and, more important, is viewed with a good deal of ironic detachment by Williamson. Moreover he does not play the role of solitary hermit for long. In a few years he acquires a wife and child, symbolically shaves off the beard, and by the end of *The Labouring Life* has left the village and blended imperceptibly into the Henry Williamson of the thirties, the author and broadcaster who rushes about the countryside in the 'Silver Eagle' instead of on the motorbike, and, in books like *The Linhay on the Downs* and *Goodbye West Country*, has apparently dispensed with any mask. Writer and man are now virtually united.

* * * * *

When Georgeham became 'too popular,' and Williamson's increased family and literary profits made a change necessary and possible (*CS*, p. 25), he moved inland to Shallowford, to 'one of the most secluded villages in England' (*GWC*, p. 194). The future biographer of *Salar the Salmon* was, in fact, following the salmon route from the world of Tarka to the spawning grounds of the river Bray. Here, close to the deer-park of the Fortescues and a 'clear water stream' offering excellent fishing, Williamson lived for seven years in the 1930s. Now established as a novelist and rural writer, winner of the 1928 Hawthornden Prize for *Tarka the Otter*, he is a very different man from the war-scarred 'hermit' of Georgeham, though he is still haunted by the horror of 1914-18 and worried for the future. But experience and maturity have tempered much of the youthful ambition. He is now prepared to see himself not as an inspired prophet but as 'a mere detached observer of animals, for the purposes of amusement and money' (*LD*, p. 46), 'a minor writer of country things' (*GWC*, p. 149) – even, in a retrospective memoir of these years, 'an eccentric literary tramp' (*CWS*, p. 178). He is now sufficiently detached that he can exclaim: 'Thank God I've got away from my pretentious self – it's the devil to one's life' (*GWC*, p. 63).

None the less, the literary record of these years is unquestionably disappointing. *Salar the Salmon* (1935) is the only work written and published in this period that can confidently be described as up to Williamson's standard. *The Linhay on the Downs* and *Goodbye West Country* both contain excellent writing, but can hardly be regarded as satisfactory wholes. The two pot-boilers *On Foot in Devon* and *Devon*

Holiday were disasters, while the notorious 1936 dedication of the one-volume edition of *The Flax of Dream* to Adolf Hitler 'whose symbol is the happy child' might well have proved the last nail in the coffin of a dead reputation.[24] Williamson was himself conscious of a decline in literary quality. As he writes in *The Story of a Norfolk Farm*, 'with the exception of the salmon book, the last three or four books I had published, while as good as most country stuff, were not much good' (*SNF*, p. 13). Portentousness, his weakness in the early writings, has now been replaced by a cynical flippancy. Thus at the beginning of *On Foot in Devon*, which he accurately describes as a 'sneering, jeering guide,'[25] we find this: 'I don't know if the reader will be interested in these and similar scraps of information; but that's how I intend to write this book; and for those who don't care about following us, there's always a sharrabang round every corner of the main and minor roads. We're going by cliff paths, sheep and deer-tracks, yes, and even rat-runs; we're going in the lowest pubs and by the highest tide-lines, too' (*OFD*, p. 4). This belligerent take-it-or-leave-it attitude would be detected as false even if one were not acquainted with Williamson's better work. *Devon Holiday*, we are told at the outset, was written 'in a spirit of slapstick and knock-about,'[26] and the creator of the humourless Willie Maddison is once again out of his depth. He presents himself in the book as 'Henry Williamson,' but has to project the impression of an eccentric – moody, angry, misunderstood; it is all very self-conscious and more than a little silly. One cannot help feeling, however, that the facetious tone, like Thomas's bitter ironies, masks a helpless but genuine despair. The sarcasm against charabancs, litter, main roads (to confine the list to subjects in *On Foot in Devon*) is understandable, but the forces and unsuccessful jocularity surely covers a realisation that to them belongs the wave of the future.

Williamson's literary, if not his financial, position had now reached its nadir. One of the reasons, as he was quick to realise, was that he had 'worked out' his Devon material and needed to make a fresh start. Writing of north Devon in *The Linhay on the Downs*, he comments: 'I had exhausted this country, or it had exhausted me. I had stayed here too long' (*LD*, p. 177). But his dissatisfaction in these years was not confined to the quality of his work; it extended to the very nature of the literary and artistic life. As early as his pamphlet *The Wild Red Deer of Exmoor* (1931) he had claimed that his only real happiness was achieved during 'periods of activity when I was sailing, walking, planting trees, or working with my hands.'[27] The same point is made more positively a little later: 'When I am in good form, that is well and happy, and fishing in the Bray, I enter into another world – the natural world – where senses and instincts are harmonious and co-ordinated to one purpose. The consciousness is no longer a house divided against itself' (*LD*, 215). Several years later in *The Story of a Norfolk Farm*, an account of his radical response to this challenge, he continually reverts to the same argument: 'Writing is not living . . . It was unnatural to sit hour after hour, day after day, week after week, getting more and more dyspeptic, while projecting life and vitality into an imaginary world. Much easier to be normal and natural, to go with the tide' (*SNF*, pp. 40, 42).

The last phrase is ironically inappropriate, for Williamson's solution was to go dramatically against the tide of commercial thinking dominant in the 1930s. At a time when, as H.J. Massingham was later to write, 'English agriculture reached the lowest ebb in all its history,'[28] when three hundred acres were going out of cultivation in Britain every day (see *SNF*, p. 65), Williamson decided to return to the land in the most literal sense of the phrase, and in 1937, without any farming experience, he became owner of a run-down farm near Stiffkey on the north Norfolk coast. While he did not abandon his literary career – he found, indeed, that he had to subsidise his farming venture by articles and broadcast talks prepared after a full day's work in the fields – the land now claimed the centre of his attention. The story, as Williamson tells it, is one of disappointment, frustration, and unending toil – but there is also a sense of achievement, of difficulties overcome, of a creative act more basic and satisfying than that emanating from the study. This is Williamson's answer to the sense of failure so characteristic of later rural writing. The dilemma of Sturt, separated from his wheelwright's shop, finding his own vocation trivial and dilettante compared with the humbler but more natural work of Bettesworth and Will Hammond, the wry despair of Thomas, recognising the absurdity of producing second-hand imitations of natural experience for readers lacking the means or the desire to gain first-hand experiences for themselves – these situations are avoided by Williamson's return to the realities of the soil. Gradually the sicknesses of civilisation are shed, and, despite all the worry and heartache, the basic feeling is a sense of triumph. He writes movingly about the ploughing of his first furrow: 'I felt a warmth of satisfaction coming over me; I was a ploughman, I had found freedom' (*SNF*, p. 182).

The Story of a Norfolk Farm is a noble book by virtue of its subject; there can be no more satisfying and appropriate theme in rural literature than the co-operation of man and nature to produce fertility.

Throughout it there runs a strong vein of rural patriotism. The whole project is undertaken 'not for my sake, not for profit, directly: but for its own sake, for England's sake' (*SNF*, p. 222). When this necessitates a battle against prejudice, irresponsibility, and vested interest, it takes on the qualities of saga. Williamson has some difficulty, however, in adapting himself to the tone of his subject. The earlier pages share many of the faults of the books of the 1930s – in particular, his initial presentation of himself is unsatisfactory. Surely, one feels, he cannot have been as naive and ignorant as he appears, and the series of accidents and misfortunes suggest a contrived comedy of errors. At times, indeed, we seem to be close to the world of *Three Men in a Boat*, and against such a background it is hard to take the writer's passionately held convictions as seriously as they deserve. As the book progresses, however, and the farm begins to take shape, the inherent dignity of the theme comes to the fore. Perhaps Williamson intended to show himself, as it were, growing up with his subject. At all events, when at the end of the second year he has broken even and what had recently been neglected and run-down is neat and productive, we rejoice in Williamson's achievement.

It is hardly necessary to add, of course, that neither Williamson's sense of achievement nor the achievement itself was long-lasting. Although the 'epigraph' to the book is dated June 1940, Williamson can bring his story to a close on a note of personal optimism. When the Second World War broke out, he comments: 'I knew the end of the final phase of a period of industrialism, with its misery and anguish for so many millions of our people, was come; and I took my eldest son away from the public school which was educating him for a mode of life which was dead. He spent his fourteenth birthday ploughing his fourteenth acre' (*SNF*, p. 343). If such a statement appears naive from the viewpoint of the 1970s, it at least rounds off the narrative with a typical and suitable challenge. Once again, however, Williamson's hopes were to be disappointed, and in *The Phasian Bird* (1948), a book which, despite its title, is better interpreted as a modern parable than as an animal story, he extended the narrative through the early war years and was thus forced to read the signs of the times in a new way. The story of the golden pheasant – symbol, like Lawrence's phoenix, of hope in a new world to be born out of the ashes of the past and to recreate the best features of that past – is counterpointed by the story of Wilbo, another of Williamson's masks, upon whose land the Phasian bird finds shelter. But Wilbo is detained under 18-B like his creator, loses his farm, and finally, in an ambitious but unconvincing climax, is shot by the local war-profiteers on the same day as the pheasant. The allegory, though more complex than it may first appear, revives the tendency towards self-pity which one hoped Williamson had outgrown. It immediately recalls the death of Willie Maddison in *The Pathway*, and the 'Father-forgive-them' death-scene is embarrassingly contrived. But the death of the symbolic bird, apparently without issue, represents a darker ending, and one which is emphasised by the impressive descriptions of a ruined countryside against which the closing events take place. As a whole, then, the book is annoyingly uneven. The earlier chapters represent Williamson at his finest; these are, of course, the most objective chapters, where he is furthest removed from his own personal experience. Yet, however we respond to the 'moral' of the parable, we cannot help admiring Williamson's brilliant presentation of the changing countryside in the years between 1937 and 1944.

* * * * *

It would be possible to trace the development of Williamson's prose style in much the same way that we traced that of Edward Thomas. A suitable starting-point would be the opening essay of *The Lone Swallows*, with all its sentimental clichés and falsities of rhythm, or the notorious sentence from the first draft of *Dandelion Days* to which J.D. Beresford objected: 'Sometimes a swallow rag-tailed and gracile passes through the fine spray upflung by the champèd waters, descanting on the silver plash and spilth of gold' (*SS*, p. 145). The temptation to write bad rural prose seems to have been irresistible in the early years of this century, but it passes, and Williamson refers later to 'the early and very precious Henry Williamson and Edward Thomas' (*LD*, p. 249). It is interesting to note that both writers follow a line of development opposite to that of their declared hero, Jefferies. Whereas Jefferies moved from straightforward directness to impassioned complexity (without ever perpetrating the bejewelled prose of the later period), Thomas and Williamson, beginning with a liking for lush sentences, end by seeking the greatest accuracy and simplicity. (Both, incidentally, admired Sturt's crisp and untrammelled prose, and were clearly influenced by his example.)

Williamson survived a bad stylistic start to become, if we judge solely by the quality of the prose, one of the purest writers of his time. Certainly of all the contributors to the rural tradition he is the most skilled in treading the middle course between the extremes of inharmonious crudeness and inappropriate elegance. Most remarkable, perhaps, is the sheer effort he puts into his work. *Tarka the Otter*, for example, went through no less than seventeen versions 'not for style but for truth' (*GWC*, p. 19), and Williamson speaks interestingly of 'rewriting as I saw more clearly, less untruly – the prose arising out of experience, spring, summer, autumn, winter' (*GWC*, p. 287). 'The prose arising out of experience' seems commonplace enough, but Williamson means it literally and absolutely. For him style is inextricably linked with vision in all the connotations of that word, and both depend upon honesty; by the same token ignorance and stupidity (which Williamson sees as identical) will necessarily be communicated in a muddled prose lacking the all important 'clarity.' Williamson makes the point most forcefully in the introduction to his 'pemmican anthology' of Jefferies:

> *Here is my belief:*
> *The base or foundation of a first-class talent is eyesight. The man who sees more, who perceives quicker than his fellows, is of larger intelligence only by reason of that superior sight. Some people, educated unnaturally, seldom see for themselves . . . Wisdom is the essence of observation.* (*RJ*, p. 21)

Whatever one may think of this as a general theory, its application to his own work is obvious. He makes reference elsewhere to his 'nervous, multi-detailed prose' (*CS*, p. 234). His continual effort is to suppress the nervousness (a concomitant of weakness) but maintain the multiplicity of detail which is the result of clear vision. For Williamson, then, style is intimately connected with the observing self, and the problem is to omit the unnecessary, whether in the objects seen or in the character of the subject. 'When in doubt, leave out' (*SS*, p. 146) became his motto. This can be documented by comparing the earlier and later versions of *The Children of Shallowford* (1939 and 1959). It is impossible to decide whether any specific alteration was dictated by considerations of material or of style, since the two are inseparable; in shedding the expendable stylistic excesses he is inevitably altering 'the portrait of the artist' that emerges in the course of the book.

This process has developed considerably in the course of Williamson's long writing life. The irritating aspects of his earlier personae (all the more annoying since they were never integral) have lessened noticeably over the years. None the less, however familiar we may become with his work, Williamson remains a paradox. This results from his being the only full-fledged idealist in the rural tradition – and it leads to all sorts of complexities. Most obvious, perhaps, is the oddity that a romantic artist with high-flown theories concerning his art should present himself as the fervent disciple of Jefferies, for whom such matters were at most peripheral. One finds a similar dichotomy in his attitude to the villagers about whom he writes. At one moment he can complain that 'the entire village life, thought and standard was based on resignation and prejudice' (*SNF*, p. 191); at another we find him asserting that 'for some time now my criterion of what is true or false, good or bad, has been based on what the ordinary working man, the sociable working man, would think of it, if he could formulate his thought. This is the nearest to the natural norm or truth I know' (*GWC*, p. 283). Williamson is aware of this dichotomy in himself; as he notes in the first version of *The Children of Shallowford*, 'the two worlds, of imagination and reality, were irreconcilable, almost hostile, within one human body' (*CS*, p. 48).

A similar division may be discerned in his writing between the intensely personal, drawing generously on autobiographical experience, and the scrupulously objective, in which the writer's own character is effaced. These might be described as the only-sometimes-overlapping worlds of Willie Maddison and Tarka. The former needs no further exemplification here; the latter is less conspicuous but equally important. When Williamson concentrates on the non-human world, his own individual concerns are necessarily excluded. As he remarks of the writing of *Tarka the Otter*: 'My part as writer seemed a small, entirely impersonal part: it was the English Countryside that mattered, the trees, the rivers, the birds, the animals, the people. Indeed, I wanted the book to be without the author's name on the title-page' (*CS*, p. 52). Certainly the emphasis in these animal stories is on the processes of nature, on the ever-recurring change that lies at the heart of life. Later, in 1943, Williamson can even write: 'The person, as I have long thought, does not matter; it is the use of talent that is important, the inner, impersonal urge to reveal the truth and glory of the visible world: the colour of corn in wind; the ant hurrying over the hot stone; the startling flame-like translucency of the kestrel's wings against the eastern arc of a cloudless sky . . .'[29] The trouble is that Williamson finds a difficulty in practising what he preaches. He can write, as if from his own experience: 'Let one take all things easily and lightly, and not curse the wheels or the fumes or the crowds of people or their ideas; otherwise one rivets bands on one's brow' (*OFD*, p. 32) – but he never learns his own lesson. Similarly, while recognising in theory the strength of writing that conforms to T.S. Eliot's ideal of 'an escape from personality,' he is continually returning to a nervous, obsessive account of his own quirks and problems.

More than any other rural writer with the exception of Borrow, Williamson is blessed with what John Middleton Murry has called 'the power of retrospective imagination.'[30] Unfortunately, although gifted with a subtler intellect and an infinitely greater stylistic sense, Williamson (and again I am limiting my generalisation to his rural writings) has never been able to manipulate this power with any of Borrow's success. He can rarely leave well enough alone. 'The Badger Dig' in *The Village Book* is a case in point. The description is brilliantly realistic, since the viewpoint is at once personal (Williamson is very much 'there'), and at the same time objective (in that the events are chronicled with the minimum of interpretation). The piece centres upon Williamson's own mixed feelings in watching the ritual: 'I felt I had been false to myself, and yet another thought told be that such feelings flourished only in nervous weakness' (*VB*, p. 32). Similarly, after the kill, his frank acknowledgement of his own involvement – 'With the dried blood stiff on my temples I climbed the hill, cursing the satanic ways of men, yet knowing myself vile' – is excellent, but he spoils it by adding that 'all the tears . . . would not wash from my brow the blood of a little brother' (*VB*, pp. 32-3). The last phrase seems so absurdly inadequate – and patronising – for the badger who had been presented as so much more than that. Williamson makes an unbelievable St Francis, and his lack of verbal tact betrays him into a cheap sentiment that lowers the tone of the whole essay.

It may well be that Williamson is a potentially great writer born too late, into an industrial world which he can never understand (hence his political excesses) and which can never understand him. The man who wanted to become a second Jefferies finds this virtually impossible in his own age, not merely because of the loneliness of such a role (which Williamson is only too ready to equate with the loneliness of the dedicated artist), but because he is himself attracted to the new world (via his motorcycle and gramophone) and finds himself unable to reconcile the two positions. As it is, though his rural writing constitutes an important and substantial part of his total output, Williamson sees his life-work as residing elsewhere – in his novel series, *A Chronicle of Ancient Sunlight*, which focuses on the experience of Phillip Maddison, Willie's urban cousin. The split remains, of course. However, as in the case of Borrow or, more cogently perhaps, of Thomas's poetry, instead of remaining an irritant continually threatening to disrupt the material, the split becomes in itself the subject of attention. It appears no longer as an awkward digression, since it is central. The creative 'wound,' in other words, strengthens rather than destroys the delicately balanced work of art. But, despite the fact that Williamson's development ultimately leads him outside the boundaries of this study, his ideal, no less in *A Chronicle of Ancient Sunlight* than in his earlier writings, remains the same – 'natural man on his natural earth' (*GWC*, p. 283).

NOTES

1 Henry Williamson, *The Pathway* (1928) (London: Faber, 1969), p.110.
2 See Henry Williamson, *The Linhay on the Downs* (1934) (London: Cape, 1938), p.129. Hereafter cited in text as *LD*.
3 See, for example, Henry Williamson, *The Story of a Norfolk Farm* (1941) (London: Readers' Union, by arrangement with Faber, 1942), pp. 186-9. Hereafter cited in text as *SNF*.
4 Henry Williamson, *The Dream of Fair Women* (1924) (London: Faber, 1968), p. 440. Hereafter cited in text as *DFW*.
5 *Richard Jefferies: Selections of His Work, with details of his Life and Circumstances, his death and Immortality*, ed. Henry Williamson (London: Faber, 1937), p. 417. Hereafter cited in text as *RJ*.
6 Henry Williamson, *Dandelion Days* (1922) (London: Faber, 1966), p. 151. Hereafter cited in text as *DD*.
7 Henry Williamson, *A Clear Water Stream* (London: Faber, 1958), pp. 20-1. Hereafter cited in text as *CWS*.
8 Henry Williamson, *The Children of Shallowford* (London: Faber, 1939), p. 265. Hereafter cited in text as *CS*.
9 Henry Williamson, *Goodbye West Country* (1937) (Boston: Little, Brown, 1938), p. 107. Hereafter cited in text as *GWC*.
10 Henry Williamson, *The Sun in the Sands* (London: Faber, 1945), p. 27. Hereafter cited in text as *SS*.
11 Henry Williamson, *The Village Book* (London: Cape, 1930), p. 150. Hereafter cited in text as *VB*.
12 See H.F. West, *The Dreamer of Devon: An Essay on Henry Williamson* (London: Ulysses Press, 1932), p. 9. (Reprinted in current *Journal*, q.v.).
13 Henry Williamson, *The Lone Swallows* (London: Collins, 1922), p.51.
14 See West, p. 19, and compare *SS*, p. 19.
15 Henry Williamson, *The Labouring Life* (London: Cape, 1932), p. 294. Hereafter cited in text as *LL*.
16 I am referring here to the revised text of the book. The whole question of the revisions of *The Flax of Dream*

tetralogy is a complex one, and outside the scope of this book. All critical statements on the novel cycle are based on later versions.

17 James Joyce, *A Portrait of the Artist as a Young Man* (1916) (New York: Viking, 1962), p. 216.
18 See H. Stevenson Balfour, *The History of Georgeham and Croyde* (Privately printed for the author, n.d.), p. 33.
19 West, p. 29.
20 Balfour, p. 26n.
21 West, p. 33.
22 Denys Thompson, 'A Cure for Amnesia,' in F.R. Leavis, ed., *A Selection from 'Scrutiny'*, 2 vols. (Cambridge: University Press, 1968), II, 219.
23 Ibid.
24 The vexed question of Williamson's admiration for Hitler during the 1930s though apparently outside concern of this study, is so conspicuous a feature within his whole career that it would be critically irresponsible to ignore it. From the perspective of the 1970s, of course, it neither requires any formal condemnation nor merits any defence. None the less, it is worth noting here that Williamson's enthusiasm was derived from Hitler's plan 'based on every man owning, in a trustee-to-nation sense, his own bit of land, and fulfilling himself in living a natural life' (*GWC*, p. 229). While deploring the catastrophic misreading of Hitler's intentions that is involved, we may at least acknowledge that Williamson's motives, however naive, had more respectable origins than most of the literary-intellectual flirtations with fascism and communism at that time.
25 Henry Williamson, *On Foot in Devon* (London: Maclehose, 1933), p. 32. Hereafter cited in text as *OFD*.
26 Henry Williamson, *Devon Holiday* (London: Cape, 1935), p. 7.
27 Henry Williamson, *The Wild Red Deer of Exmoor* (London: Faber, 1931), p. 54.
28 H.J. Massingham, *The Wisdom of the Fields* (London: Collins, 1945), p. 35.
29 Lilias Rider Haggard and Henry Williamson, *Norfolk Life* (London: Faber, 1943), pp. 11-12.
30 John Middleton Murry, 'The Novels of Henry Williamson,' in *Katherine Mansfield, and Other Literary Studies* (London: Constable, 1959), p. 161.

We are grateful to Professor Keith for permission to reproduce this chapter from his book *The Rural Tradition* (University Toronto Press, 1975, and Harvester Press, Brighton, England). Other writers considered in this book include Gilbert White, George Borrow, W.H. Hudson, Edward Thomas, Richard Jefferies, and H.J. Massingham.

Sketch of Henry Williamson's Writing Hut by Doris Walker.

The Maddison and Turney Family Trees

Will Harris

Henry Williamson's novel-sequence *A Chronicle of Ancient Sunlight* is based on his own life and the lives of the various family members. The following sketches of principal characters in the *Chronicle* are intended to highlight some of their chief characteristics, and to provide links between them, so that the reader can compare the fictional characters with their real-life counterparts. Characters are presented in chronological order, the Turneys, fictional versions of the maternal side of Williamson's family tree, appearing first, followed by the Maddisons, Williamson's paternal side. References are to be found in the first editions, published by MacDonalds: *The Dark Lantern* (TDL); *Donkey Boy* (DB); *How Dear Is Life* (HDIL); *A Fox Under My Cloak* (AFUMC); *The Golden Virgin* (TGV); *The Innocent Moon* (TIM). I am indebted to Peter Lewis for providing the fictional family trees and for researching dates of births, marriages and deaths so assiduously.

THE TURNEYS

THOMAS TURNEY, 1840-1920, married to SARAH, father of Charles, Dorothy, HUGH, HENRIETTA (HETTY), Joseph. Resembles Prince of Wales. Travelling partner in Mallard, Carter and Turney Ltd, 'printers, account-book makers, lithographers and stationers' (DBP p. 230). Well-to-do, very much the master of his house, Maybury Lodge in Cross Aulton. Strongly prejudiced against Maddisons in general because of Captain Maddison's 'racketing ways' (TDL p. 34) of which he has some direct knowledge as a result of renting a house in Brighton adjoining Captain Maddison's. His dislike of RICHARD MADDISON in particular and his disapproval of him as suitor for his daughter HETTY, are inevitable; and he is so enraged when he discovers they have married in secret, he strikes HETTY, inducing in her a fit. Following his and SARAH's removal next door to their daughter and son-in-law, he eventually comes round to tolerating RICHARD, particularly after his grandson PHILLIP is born. Knows and loves his Shakespeare, likes cigars, chuckles a lot: 'he-he-he'. A thoroughly typical Victorian middle-class gent.

SARAH TURNEY, 1841-1910, sweet-tempered, uncomplicated, disliked by no-one. Very much the Victorian wife, whose simple sense of duty and subservience to her husband runs parallel to her support for HETTY in her secret romance with and marriage to RICHARD MADDISON. Her remark to THOMAS following his entry to the maid's bedroom – 'We must all love one another, as the Good Book tells us' (TDL p. 327) – is typical.

HENRIETTA (HETTY) TURNEY, 1870-1936, second daughter of THOMAS and SARAH TURNEY, wife of RICHARD MADDISON. Possesses 'a capacity for happiness and unhappiness beyond the ordinary' (TDL p. 49). The antithesis of her husband, HETTY lives entirely and heroically for her family, but signally fails in her attempts to bring accord among its various members. Continually the butt of RICHARD's exasperation, she can never do anything right, ultimately because he regards Turneys as 'bad stock'. She, on the other hand, 'felt for RICHARD MADDISON, but not with him' (TDL p. 61). Frequently says, 'Of course, dear, naturally' (an expression she gets from her mother), irritating Richard in her efforts to agree with him and keep the peace. 'The more she did for others, the more they expected; the more they demanded' (HDIL p. 37). Saintly herself, she draws great comfort from the Church. It is distressing to think of her natural gaiety and ready laughter steadily being stifled.

HUGH (HUGHIE) TURNEY, 1874-1912, second son, third child of THOMAS and SARAH, favourite brother of HETTY. Bright, witty, and given to making 'humorous and slightly pedantic little speeches' (DB p. 242), he is sent down from university for putting a chamber pot on a statue. While at University he explores books about heraldry, and is thus responsible for his father acquiring a family crest. Following his lack of success in THOMAS's firm, he becomes a music-hall performer, playing under such names as 'Chittybucktoo, the Japanese Gipsy with his Violin' (DB p. 230), with underwhelming success. Joins up to serve in the South African War. Dies of syphilis as the result of consorting unsuitably because of the unattainability of THEODORA MADDISON.

PERCY PICKERING, 1895*-1916, son of James (Jim) Pickering and Eliza (Liz) Thacker, who is the daughter of THOMAS TURNEY's sister. Slightly deaf as a result of pneumonia in early childhood. PHILLIP sees him as 'a simple person . . . who liked his Dad, and was always happy and smiling' (AFUMC p. 123). In later years, THEODORA observes him to be 'an honest, rosy-faced country boy, a little slow perhaps, and with an ordinary mind, but that was all to the good; there was enough nervous tautness already in the family' (TGV p. 358). Percy is PHILLIP's 'country cousin', with whom he stays at the Pickering family home in Beau Brickhill from time to time. 'Beau Brickhill had always been a lovely place. It was so free and easy, never any cross words in Uncle Jim's house' (HDIL p. 86), in complete contrast to the Maddison household, to which he and his sister make return visits. Becomes attached to DORIS. Killed in Battle of Flers, 1916.

* In *Donkey Boy* we are told PHILLIP and PERCY are the same age (p. 273), but when PHILLIP visits Beau Brickhill in 1915, PERCY is stated to be 18.

POLLY PICKERING, b. 1900, PERCY's sister, 'had the Irish colouring of her great-grandmother, who had been THOMAS TURNEY's mother: red cheeks, dark curly hair, grey eyes. Polly had a definite will of her own, where her parents were concerned. Polly would do only what Polly would do' (DB p. 273). Provides PHILLIP with his first opportunities to explore the mysteries of the opposite sex. The two cousins are fond of one another, and, though they are never really in love, POLLY is able to give PHILLIP the warmth and security he so lacks in his family. Their physical and social liaisons tend to be rather unsatisfactory and tense, however.

THE MADDISONS

JOHN MADDISON, 1864?-1928, elder brother of RICHARD. Bearded. Barrister. Father of WILLIE. Well-off and successful, and happily married to Jenny (a situation contrasting sharply to RICHARD's), until her untimely death, following which he is a broken man. 'He lived in his library, while the house was run by an odd little housekeeper-cook, with the help of daily women coming in from the village'(DB p. 217).

RICHARD MADDISON (Dickie), 1867-1946, second son of Captain William Maddison, of whom he is ashamed for much the same reason that his father-in-law is disgusted by him, and Adele von Föhre. Bearded. Born and bred in the countryside, RICHARD is sensitive to and knowledgeable about natural history. Episodes illustrating this provide a welcome counterpoint to his otherwise difficult and exasperating personality. Rejected by the Navy because of defective sight in one eye. Becomes acquainted with the Turney household through playing his cello in chamber music sessions with his sister THEODORA and her great friend HETTY TURNEY and her brother HUGHIE. Marries HETTY in 1893, rather on the rebound following the death of his beloved mother; and attracted to HETTY because of her physical resemblance to Jenny, his brother JOHN's wife, who 'was highest in his secret thoughts' (TDL p. 342). Father of PHILLIP, MAVIS and DORIS. Works at Doggett's Bank, moves to the Moon Fire Insurance Office, commutes daily to London by train. Special Constable in First World War. Thoroughly disliked by HETTY's father, THOMAS TURNEY, who thinks he is a 'niminipiminy fellow' (TDL p. 198), 'a proper Dickie-bird' (TDL p. 34). No love lost between the two, and Richard's intolerance of Turney characteristics sours relations with HETTY, who is weighed down by RICHARD's humourless heavy-handedness. A stickler for detail, maddeningly predictable in his habits, and unable to show tenderness to his wife and children because they fail to conform to his ideals. Dependable, solid, honest, believes everything he reads in right-wing *Daily Trident*. Strongly opposed to Free Trade. Gets on particularly well with family cat, Zippy.

HILARY MADDISON, born 1869, sixth child of William and Adela, younger brother of RICHARD. Married first to Beatrice Lemon, second, Irene Lushington, mother of PHILLIP'S first wife, Barley. Officer in Merchant Navy, then farmer in New South Wales, Australia. 'Easily conscious that he was armigerous, that he was the son of a gentleman, a landed proprietor' (DB p. 289), and thus a complete contrast to RICHARD. An extrovert; engaging, plausible, affable. A pioneer car-driver: gives RICHARD a spin in his Panhard et Lavassor. Knighted.

THEODORA MADDISON (Dora), 1874-1947, seventh and last child of William and Adela, youngest sister of RICHARD, aunt and godmother of PHILLIP. Spinster, at one time in love with Sidney Cakebread, who became HETTY'S sister Dorothy's husband. She, in turn, is doted on by HUGHIE, who 'admires her slender fingers, the curling of the fair hair behind the ears, the tall neck, the long straight nose, and the deep blue of her eyes' (TDL p. 54). Keen educationalist, disciple of Pestalozzi, runs school with associate Rechenda until it has to close through lack of funds. Vegetarian. Associated with various charitable organisations. A keen advocate of women's suffrage, much to the consternation of RICHARD; imprisoned and force-fed. A sympathetic, warm, straightforward, deeply sensitive lady, a great friend and confidante of HETTY. Years ahead of her time.

PHILLIP MADDISON, born 1895, the chief protagonist of the *Chronicle*, and Henry Williamson's fictional alter ego. From the outset PHILLIP is torn between the deep maternal love afforded by HETTY, and his father's chronic lack of understanding of a young child's needs. He exhibits his father's love of nature from an early age, but his normal boyish behaviour is seen by RICHARD as exemplifying the Turney character, and unreasonable expectations are made of him. The normal behaviour – such as borrowing his father's precious dark lantern and accidentally breaking it – moves inexorably into more abnormal behaviour, perhaps the most spectacular example of which is burning the grass behind the family home. PHILLIP experiences all the usual joys and pangs of growing up, but the family instability does not allow him to learn from them successfully, and he develops into a young man by turns sensitive, loyal, foolish and intensely irritating. His profound experiences of the Great War add hugely to his emotional turmoil, and his post-war life is driven by his need to write, which he settles down to do in Devon. He marries Teresa Lushington (Barley), but she dies giving birth to Billy. His second wife is Lucy Copleston, by whom he fathers Peter, Rosamurid, David and Jonathan, and he fathers another son, Edward, by a lover, Felicity Ancroft. Takes up farming on land owned by his Uncle HILARY. He is a stickler for tidiness and order, and the inability of the employees on the farm in Norfolk, which he buys and runs during the Second World War, to accede to his demands, is strongly reminiscent of his father's behaviour towards him in boyhood.

WILLIAM (WILLIE) MADDISON, 1896-1923, son and only child of JOHN MADDISON, RICHARD's brother, and his wife Jenny, who dies giving birth. Comes to London to work at the Moon Fire Office, stays chez RICHARD, who sees in Willie's face 'the lineaments of his adored Jenny, who had died when the little chap was born' (HDIL p. 125). Liked by all. Joins the army at the same time as PHILLIP, and, like his cousin, becomes a writer, tending to polemic rather than fiction. After the war he works in France 'at the German Concentration Graveyard (where) the dark spirit of revenge is made manifest'. (TIM p. 66). Drowns in Devon, 'swept off the mid-river gravel ridge by tide flowing at 6-7 knots' (TIM p. 400).

MAVIS MADDISON, born 1897, second child of RICHARD and HETTY. As a little girl, her father's favourite; but the mutual adoration is spoiled as a result of RICHARD's heavy-handed treatment of Mavis believing – wrongly – that she has been up to no good with a young man. During childhood she and PHILLIP bicker constantly, like most brothers and sisters. Adept at wheedling money from HETTY to buy the latest fashion. Decides she is to be known as Elizabeth. Suffers fits. Has a great friend, Nina, with whom she shares a flat after the war. Forbidden to enter RICHARD's house because he considers her ill-mannered toward him as head of the family.

DORIS MADDISON, born 1900. Notorious for telling her father RICHARD, in one of his particularly tiresome moods, 'If you make my Mummy cry, I will kill you. I have been meaning to kill you for a long time. I have a long knife hidden to kill you with' (DB p. 365). Which says it all about *that* particular relationship. Unloved by her father, and grieving over the memory of her cousin Percy Pickering, killed in the Great War, she fails to love her husband, Bob Willoughby. Having eloped with 'Mr Willoughby' (as RICHARD calls him) she is forbidden her father's house. Is eventually referred to by her father as 'Mrs Willoughby'. One son.

A Chronicle of Ancient Sunlight — FAMILY TREES

THE TURNEY LINE

Thomas William TURNEY 1840 - 1920 = Sarah 1841 - 1910

- Charles TURNEY = ?
  - Thomas TURNEY 1899-1914
  - Peral TURNEY
  - Charles TURNEY
- Dorothy TURNEY d. 1919 = Sidney CAKEBREAD d. 1900
  - Hubert CAKEBREAD
  - Ralph CAKEBREAD
  - Gerry CAKEBREAD
  - Maude CAKEBREAD
- Henrietta TURNEY 1870 - 1936 = Richard MADDISON 1867 - 1946
  - Phillip MADDISON 1895 -
  - Mavis Elizabeth 1897 -
  - Doris MADDISON 1900 -
- Hugh TURNEY 1874 - 1912
- Joseph TURNEY = Ruth
  - Percy PICKERING d. 1916
  - Polly PICKERING

THE MADDISON LINE

CAPTAIN William MADDISON 1840 - 1895 = Adela von Führe d. 1892

- Isabelle MADDISON 1861 - 1942 Spinster
- John MADDISON d. 1928 = Jennie d. 1896
  - William (Willie) MADDISON 1896 - 1923
- Richard MADDISON 1867 - 1946 = Henrietta TURNEY 1870 - 1936
  - Phillip MADDISON 1895 - = (i) Teresa Jane (Barley) LUSHINGTON 1906 - 1925 (ii) Lucy COPLESTON (iii) ~ Felicity ANCROFT
    - Billy MADDISON 1925 - 1945
    - Peter MADDISON 1927 -
    - Rosamund MADDISON 1929 -
    - David MADDISON 1933 -
    - Jonathon MADDISON 1935 -
    - Edward ANCROFT 1929 -
  - Mavis Elizabeth MADDISON 1897 - Spinster
  - Doris MADDISON 1900 - = Bob WILLOUGHBY
    - a son
- Augusta MADDISON = ?
- Hilary MADDISON 1869 - = (i) Beatrice LEMON (ii) Irene LUSHINGTON
- Victoria MADDISON 1872 - = George Lemon
- Theodora MADDISON 1874 - 1947 Spinster

Reviews

GREEN FIELDS AND PAVEMENTS: A Norfolk Farmer in Wartime, Henry Williamson, ed. John Gregory. Illustrated by Michael Loates. Henry Williamson Society, 1995. Hardback. 174pp. £11.50.

Henry wrote these words when in his late forties, and they saw the brief light of day in the columns of the *Eastern Daily Press* during wartime England as weekly articles about the state of the countryside, farming, politics, and his personal family life. Now they are collected into a very well presented hardback book with brand new illustrations by one of Britain's foremost artists, Michael Loates. As Henry's 61st book (give or take one or two, depending how you count them) it is a fine volume with which to celebrate his centenary.

Although he died nearly twenty years ago, this curiously keeps Dad alive. His name on a new book, his photograph looking confident and happy inside, and drawings of him on his tractor with pictures scattered through the text of all his favourite things: salmon leaping, peregrine falcons diving, tawny owls staring out of trees, and even a Spitfire diving on him as he worked the fields in 1943. All this brings him back as if he were still alive. His thoughts about that time of turmoil are as piercing as anything he wrote. Nobody knew then the outcome of the war. VE Day was still a year away when he wrote the last chapter of this book.

I had not read any of these thoughts until now, or if I did do not remember doing so. I was only a boy of nine at the time. But all the pictures of my childhood have been recorded, and highly recognisable everything is. It is like walking into a time-warp.

The story of Cheepy, for example. It was unbelievable, but it happened. A ten-day-old chick fostered newly hatched guinea fowls covering them with wing stubs, the maternal instinct already developed. This 'family' in turn lived with a cat and her kittens who in turn lived with another cat and her kittens. Sixteen creatures nursed or being nursed, more or less in the same box. With army lorries and bren gun carriers charging past all the time down the village street the inevitable happened, and it was a double tragedy. Cheepy and the youngest mother cat were run over. I can still remember the choking tears as I saw my brother carrying the lovely tortoiseshell cat and the tiny 'mother' hen to be buried. What happened to the eight kittens and five guinea fowls? All came into the old cat's bed, the kittens to suckle as if nothing had happened, the chicks to cuddle up for warmth to her benign body. Her name was Eric, so Dad christened her: Eric, or litter by litter.

Then the story of trying to change the habits of the set-in-their-backward-ways village people whose drains were gradually killing the lovely River Stiffkey, one of a very few chalk streams in East Anglia, which flowed through the farm and the village. I well remember one irate councillor raking flat the stone shillets Dad had made to tumble and aerate the water so that trout could breathe. It was a time of continuous battles with a backward culture, and although much has been chronicled in the novels, here for the first time are the original accounts which are useful in comparison.

Another adventure was with the Burrel traction engine, used to reclaim one of the overgrown meadows on the farm. Turning an enormous drum beneath its boiler, the engine heaved trees from the ground with the use of a steel hawser. Nineteen times it broke, wrapping itself around the machine with a hiss and a roar.

Herein is the story of the pheasant shoot which made the cover of *Picture Post*, written by Macdonald Hastings, father of the present editor of the *Daily Telegraph*. Readers of the novels will recognise characters, places, events and animals which have been redrawn elsewhere. The romantic townspeople, for example, who wrote to the beleaguered author/farmer suggesting that they were ready to change jobs and 'tickle the good earth with a pitch-fork' at double the normal farm wage, a cottage, and some rough shooting. I remember these people. They came, they departed; one hid in the outside lavatory; another had her newspaper set on fire by us horrid little boys to persuade her to depart.

Father's memory of Edwardian Norfolk in 'Along the Coast Road' is an idyllic interlude: the memory of his holiday there in 1912, the memory of a boy who had not yet suffered the terrors of the trenches or the difficulties of doing his bit in the second Germanic war: growing food for his country. Of course the farm was eventually a success, being turned from a derelict waste (in agricultural terms) into a Category A. However, much of the work was actually carried out by my elder brother Windles, who started work at the age of 13½. You will find his Foreword of great interest, not only because of what he says but because of how he says it. That relaxed, easy style, full of worthwhile observations which is the hallmark of all of his father's better books, makes us all wish that he would do us a book, perhaps about his memories of farming in England and Canada.

Richard Williamson

FIRST WORLD WAR, Martin Gilbert. Weidenfeld & Nicholson, 1994. 616pp., inc. 80 photographs and 32 maps. £20.00.

This book was drawn to my attention by one of our members, Mick Howard, who sent me a copy of Alan Clark's review of it from the *Guardian*, 13 September 1994. Alan Clark recommended it and as he is a man well qualified to give his opinion of a book of this genre, I felt it was worth obtaining a copy for review in our *Journal*.

Having had to struggle to come to some sort of an understanding of the First World War in order to give a reasonably lucid presentation of Henry's part in it for the biography, it is a book I wished I could have had to hand before so doing; and I think those of you like myself who find war itself difficult to come to terms with and the ramifications of the various troop movements and battles even more difficult to comprehend, would find it a useful reference volume for your bookshelves.

Dr Martin Gilbert (stated to be one of the foremost historians of the twentieth century) has previously written an impressive list of books about the history of the Second World War and associated subjects, including several volumes of Churchill biography, and has made an equally impressive job of guiding his readers through the complicated labyrinth that the minotaur of the First World War created. Alan Clark points out that Dr Gilbert does not explain the war, that it is 'recorded deadpan, without comment'. For me, that is the book's strength. I need to understand the actual 'facts' of the war – what happened, when and where. There is certainly a place and a need for 'why' but that is surely for a second volume and is a separate subject which must, by its nature, overlay a cloak of subjectiveness which would obscure the essential facts if presented at one and the same time.

The book is very readable, which is perhaps an awful thing to say about a book dealing with death and destruction, but it does mean that one can get through to the last page without floundering in the mud of technical language, as those doomed men floundered in the mud of the trench system.

The parameters set out in the publisher's blurb define not just the book but the war itself: '. . . the European Empires [the 'entente', Britain, France and Russia versus the 'Central Powers', Germany and Austria-Hungary] hurled against each other everything military science could devise, including poison gas. Other nations joined the conflict and the war spread beyond Europe . . . These European Empires each began the war with high hopes of victory, [both] were ravaged by the human and economic cost of four years' relentless fighting. Four Empires were destroyed. . . . Nine million soldiers were killed during the conflict. Astounding heroism marked every battle-front. . . . When the war ended, monuments to the war dead were a feature of tens of thousands of towns and villages in every land.'

This factual account provides an excellent background to the content of war, but as Alan Clark stated: 'In the field of fiction there is no contest – Henry Williamson's [A] *Chronicle of Ancient Sunlight* (a volume for each year of the war) is without peer.' Thankyou, Alan Clark, for endorsing our collective opinion.

I have no reservations about Martin Gilbert's book, but I do have one very small quibble with Alan Clark's review. He wonders why the publishers 'funked' using the term 'The Great War' as the title. How can any war be called 'Great'? Especially one that in the next breath is called 'unnecessary'. And does not the use of such a term by definition then belittle the Second World War as being of lesser degree? *First World War* is a more exact definition; and the title reflects the matter of fact approach of its author.

AW

THE SECRET OF THE SANGRAAL, A collection of writing by Arthur Machen. Limited ed., The Tartarus Press, 1995. £22.50.

This book is rather outside the scope of what we would normally expect to review in our *Journal*, but it is drawn to your attention as presenting fugitive items previously only published in newspapers by Arthur Machen with whom HW had a connection in his early writing days.

We have been reminded about Arthur Machen by the recent reprinting of HW's 'Machen in Fleet Street' (referred to very aptly by John Gregory as 'a fragment of memory') from the book of tributes to Machen edited by Father Brocard Sewell in 1960. (See *Threnos for T.E. Lawrence and Other Writings*, HWS, 1994, pp. 72-3.)

The selection of items in this present book provides a deep insight into this man, born (as related by Wesley Sweetser in 'A Biographical Study' in the Brocard volume) of a line of Welsh clergymen at Caerleon, the seat of the mythical court of King Arthur. A lonely child, this beginning steeped in legend and wild Welsh scenery gave Machen a massive sense of the impenetrable mystery lurking behind reality. Throughout his life (1863-1947) he had a deep interest, virtually amounting to an obsession, with the search for the Holy Grail – the 'Sangraal', and it is his essays on this subject that form the core of the book. But the total subject matter is wide-ranging and all the essays have an elegance of style that mark Machen as a man of letters. Particularly recommended, with the Williamson family background in mind, is 'Rediscovery of London'.

AW

Notes on Contributors

JOHN BAILEY is a wildlife and angling writer, photographer and broadcaster, with over twenty books to his credit, including one on rivers around the world, *Rivers of Joy* (Creel Publications 1992). John Bailey has always enjoyed HW's writing and was particularly influenced by *Tarka* and *Salar* into his chosen path.

BRIAN FULLAGAR, stalwart member of the Committee and the Editorial team, has a particular interest in HW's 'London' era. This spring he led Society members on the memorable Centenary walks around HW's childhood haunts at Bromley, Keston Ponds and Holwood Park, and in Brockley itself.

I. WAVENEY GIRVAN first wrote to Henry Williamson when he was Secretary of the Liverpool First Edition Society. Henry was impressed by an article Girvan wrote about his books, which resulted in the *Bibliography* in due course. Later Waveney Girvan established the *West Country Magazine* which in turn led to the West Country Writers' Association.

WILL HARRIS, a founder member of the Henry Williamson Society, and Chairman since 1989, lives just off the Croydon Road along which Hughie drives his mother and sister to Greenwich in *The Dark Lantern* and has recently become Head Teacher at a primary school in Henry's Cross Aulton, not far from where Maybury Lodge once stood. Will regards the South London Trilogy that opens the *Chronicle* as Henry Williamson's finest achievement.

W.J. KEITH, Emeritus Professor of English, University College of Toronto, was born and brought up in England. Author of several books on English rural literature: *Richard Jefferies: A Critical Study* (1965), *The Rural Tradition* (1974), *The Poetry of Nature* (1980), *Regions of the Imagination* (1988). Keith succeeded HW as President of the Richard Jefferies Society in 1974, a position held until 1991. Fellow of the Royal Society of Canada since 1979.

PETER LEWIS is a regular contributor and staunch member of the Society, for whom he acts as auditor, and a member of the editorial panel. Peter particularly enjoys unravelling the mysteries of 'place' in HW's writings.

MICHAEL LOATES, eminent wild-life artist, and illustrator of a fine edition of *Salar the Salmon* (Webb & Bower), grew up in the Bromley area and as a boy paddled in Caesar's Well, the source of the River Ravensbourne.

JOHN ONIONS is an English teacher in Staffordshire. He took first-class honours in history at London University and then a doctorate in English. He has long had an interest in First World War literature and edited, with Dominic Hibberd, *Poetry of the Great War: An anthology* (Macmillan).

EDWARD SEAGO, distinguished Second World War artist, painted this portrait of HW in 1942. Details of the friendship between these two men can be found in the new biography *Henry Williamson, Dreamer of Devon* (Alan Sutton, 1995).

CHARLES F. TUNNICLIFFE, the eminent wild-life artist, first became famous when he illustrated HW's books, including *Tarka, Salar,* and *The Star-born* in the 1930s. Again, see biography for further details.

J. QUIDDINGTON-WEST, the pen name of HW's Aunt, Mary Leopoldina Williamson, portrayed in the *Chronicle* as Theodora Maddison. Mary Leopoldina was a great influence on HW; apart from this essay which gave him the source of his tetralogy *The Flax of Dream*, she sent him a volume of Francis Thompson's essays whilst he was in the trenches.

HERBERT FAULKNER WEST was Professor of Comparative Literature at Dartmouth College in Hanover, USA. He and HW met when HW visited the USA in early 1931. The following year West went to stay with HW at Shallowford in March, after which he wrote this essay. For further details see the new biography, op. cit.

ANNE WILLIAMSON is married to Richard Williamson, Editor of the HWSJ, manager of the Henry Williamson Literary Estate, and author of the new biography *Henry Williamson, Dreamer of Devon* (Alan Sutton, 1995). Skills learned in her professional training as a librarian have proved useful.

RICHARD WILLIAMSON, President of the Henry Williamson Society. Naturalist and author, Richard has had three books published, and written innumerable articles, including a weekly column in his local series of newspapers for over thirty years, and has written and appeared in many TV programmes. He has just retired after thirty-two years as warden of the Kingley Vale National Nature Reserve in West Sussex, and how hopes to have more time and energy to devote to writing.